P9-BBV-359

Praise for
The Trader's Guide to Key Economic Indicators
BY RICHARD YAMARONE

"This book breaks down the often complex world of economics into an easy-to-understand guidebook for investors.** Yamarone goes beyond the numbers, providing insight into what's important to financial markets and offering 'tricks from the trenches' you won't find anywhere else."

—RHONDA SCHAFFLER

Senior Correspondent/Anchor, CNNfn

"Every stock and bond trader should keep this invaluable description of relevant economic indicators within easy reach."

—DAVID M. JONES, PhD

Chairman of the Board, Investors' Security Trust Company

Former Chief Economist, Aubrey G. Langston

"Wall Street pros rely upon key economic indicators in their analysis and you should, too, if you wish to significantly increase your prospects of successful investing. **Richard Yamarone has done a masterful job of describing technical economic concepts in plain English.** This book will enable you to emulate the methods and successes of the pros by instructing you as to which indicators are the most relevant and how to use them to make money in the financial markets."

—STAN RICHELSON

Coauthor, *The Money-Making Guide to Bonds*

The Trader's Guide to Key Economic Indicators

Also available from
Bloomberg Press

New Thinking in Technical Analysis: Trading Models from the Masters
Edited by Rick Bensignor

Tom Dorsey's Trading Tips: A Playbook for Stock Market Success
by Thomas J. Dorsey and the DWA Analysts

Profit in the Futures Markets!:
Insights and Strategies for Futures and Futures Options Trading
by Jake Bernstein

Wall Street Secrets for Tax-Efficient Investing:
From Tax Pain to Investment Gain
by Robert N. Gordon with Jan M. Rosen

Investing in Hedge Funds: Strategies for the New Marketplace
by Joseph G. Nicholas

Investing Under Fire: Winning Strategies from the Masters
for Bulls, Bears, and the Bewildered
Edited by Alan R. Ackerman

The Economist Guide to Economic Indicators (5th Edition):
Making Sense of Economics

A complete list of our titles is available at
www.bloomberg.com/books

Attention Corporations

This book is available for bulk purchase at special discount. Special editions or chapter reprints can also be customized to specifications. For information, please e-mail Bloomberg Press, **press@bloomberg.com**, Attention: Director of Special Sales, or phone 609-750-5070.

BLOOMBERG PROFESSIONAL LIBRARY

The Trader's Guide to Key Economic Indicators

RICHARD YAMARONE

Bloomberg PRESS

PRINCETON

© 2004 by Richard Yamarone. All rights reserved. Protected under the Berne Convention. Printed in the United States of America. No part of this book may be reproduced, stored in a retrieval system, or transmitted, in any form or by any means, electronic, mechanical, photocopying, recording, or otherwise, without the prior written permission of the publisher except in the case of brief quotations embodied in critical articles and reviews. For information, please write: Permissions Department, Bloomberg Press, 100 Business Park Drive, P.O. Box 888, Princeton, NJ 08542-0888 U.S.A.

BLOOMBERG, BLOOMBERG NEWS, BLOOMBERG FINANCIAL MARKETS, OPEN BLOOMBERG, THE BLOOMBERG FORUM, COMPANY CONNEC-TION, COMPANY CONNEX, BLOOMBERG PRESS, BLOOMBERG PROFES-SIONAL LIBRARY, BLOOMBERG PERSONAL BOOKSHELF, and BLOOMBERG SMALL BUSINESS are trademarks and service marks of Bloomberg L.P. All rights reserved.

This publication contains the author's opinions and is designed to provide accurate and authoritative information. It is sold with the understanding that the author, publisher, and Bloomberg L.P. are not engaged in rendering legal, accounting, investment planning, business management, or other professional advice. The reader should seek the services of a qualified professional for such advice; the author, publisher, and Bloomberg L.P. cannot be held responsible for any loss incurred as a result of specific investments or planning decisions made by the reader.

First edition published 2004

1 3 5 7 9 10 8 6 4 2

Library of Congress Cataloging-in-Publication Data

Yamarone, Richard.
    The trader's guide to key economic indicators / Richard Yamarone.
        p. cm.
    Includes bibliographical references and index.
    ISBN 1-57660-139-0 (alk. paper)
1. Economic indicators--United States. 2. Investments--United States. I. Title.

    HC106.83.Y35 2004
    330'.01'5195--dc22   2003027990

Acquired by Kathleen A. Peterson
Edited by Elizabeth Ungar

To Suzie,
Milton, Oskar, and Nash—felinus economicus

Contents

Acknowledgments   xiii

Introduction   1
The Business Cycle   3
Indicators and the Markets   5
How to Use This Book   6
Who Can Benefit from This Book?   8

1 Gross Domestic Product   11
Evolution of an Indicator   13
Digging for the Data   14
    Some Definitions   16
    GDP Versus GNP   17
    Calculating GDP: The Aggregate Expenditure Approach   18
    Nominal and Real Numbers   22
    Deflators   25
    National Income   26
    Employee Compensation   27
    Other Income Categories   28
    GNP, GDP, and National Income   30
What Does It All Mean?   32
    GDP Growth   32
    Deflators   34
    Consumption Expenditures   35
    Investment Spending   36
    Government Spending   39
    Net Exports   40
    Final Sales   41
    Corporate Profits   43
How to Use What You See   46
Tricks From the Trenches   46

2 Indices of Leading, Lagging, and Coincident Indicators 51

Evolution of an Indicator 53

Digging for the Data 53

    Coincident Index 54

    Leading Economic Index 55

    Lagging Index 61

What Does It All Mean? 64

    Coincident Index 64

    Leading Economic Index 65

    Lagging Index 66

How to Use What You See 66

Tricks From the Trenches 67

3 The Employment Situation 69

Evolution of an Indicator 71

Digging for the Data 72

    Household Survey (A Tables) 73

    Establishment Survey (B Tables) 74

What Does It All Mean? 77

    Employment, Unemployment, and the Business Cycle 78

    Inflation Indicators 80

    Sentiment and Unemployment 81

    Average Hours Worked and Temporary Workers 83

How to Use What You See 85

Tricks From the Trenches 86

4 Industrial Production and Capacity Utilization 89

Evolution of an Indicator 90

Digging for the Data 91

    Industrial Production 92

    Capacity Utilization 94

What Does It All Mean? 95

    Industrial Production 95

    Capacity Utilization 100

How to Use What You See 104

Trick From the Trenches 104

5 Institute for Supply Management Indices 107

Evolution of an Indicator 108
Digging for the Data 109
What Does It All Mean? 113
    PMI 114
    ISM Employment Index 117
    ISM Price Index 119
    ISM Supplier Deliveries Index 121
    ISM Non-Manufacturing Indices 123
How to Use What You See 125
Tricks From the Trenches 126

6 Manufacturers' Shipments, Inventories, and Orders 131

Evolution of an Indicator 132
Digging for the Data 134
    Durable Goods Report 134
    Factory Orders Report 138
What Does It All Mean? 139
    Durable Goods Report 139
    Factory Orders Report 142
How to Use What You See 143
Tricks From the Trenches 144

7 Manufacturing and Trade Inventories and Sales 147

Evolution of an Indicator 149
Digging for the Data 149
What Does It All Mean? 151
    Inventories and the Business Cycle 153
    Inventories-to-Sales Ratios 154
How to Use What You See 155
Trick From the Trenches 156

8 New Residential Construction — 159

Evolution of an Indicator	160
Digging for the Data	161
What Does It All Mean?	163
Influences on Residential Construction	164
Regional Differences	166
Housing and the Business Cycle	167
Single-Family Housing Starts	169
How to Use What You See	171
Tricks From the Trenches	172

9 Conference Board Consumer Confidence and University of Michigan Consumer Sentiment Indices — 175

Evolution of an Indicator	177
Digging for the Data	177
What Does It All Mean?	179
The Expectation Indices	182
Confidence and Durables Spending	184
How to Use What You See	185
Employment and Sentiment	186
Noneconomic Influences on Sentiment	186
Tricks From the Trenches	189

10 Advance Monthly Sales for Retail Trade and Food Services — 193

Evolution of an Indicator	194
Digging for the Data	195
Surging Subcategories: Superstores and E-Commerce	198
What Does It All Mean?	200
Total Retail and Food Service Sales, Nominal and Real Figures	200
Total Sales Excluding Motor Vehicles and Parts	201
GAFO	202
How to Use What You See	204
Same-Store Sales	205
Seasonality	206
Tricks From the Trenches	207

11 Personal Income and Outlays — 209

Evolution of an Indicator — 210
Digging for the Data — 211
  Personal Income — 213
  Personal Consumption Expenditures — 213
  Personal Savings — 215
What Does It All Mean? — 215
  Personal Income — 216
  Consumer Spending — 219
  Personal Savings Rate — 220
How to Use What You See — 222
Tricks From the Trenches — 223

12 Consumer and Producer Price Indices — 229

Evolution of an Indicator — 231
  Producer Price Index — 231
  Consumer Price Index — 232
Digging for the Data — 233
  Consumer Price Index Data Sources — 233
  Producer Price Index Data Sources — 235
  Calculating the Inflation Rate — 237
What Does It All Mean? — 238
  Price Trends — 238
  Price Indices and the Markets — 240
  Price Indices and the Business Cycle — 241
How to Use What You See — 242
Tricks From the Trenches — 243

References — 245

Index — 259

Acknowledgments

THIS PROJECT COULD NEVER have been completed without the support and assistance of my wife, Suzie. She has helped in countless and immeasurable ways. Families play an integral role in dreams, aspirations, and accomplishments. My family has paved a clear path for any and every ambition that I could possibly have. They are indubitably responsible for all of my successes. My mother and father have always instilled the importance of education, hard work, free thinking, and discipline. For that I could never thank them enough. A special thanks to my brother Robert and to my in-laws, Richard and Nancy McCabe.

Educators can have a profound influence on one's life. My life, as well as this project, was no exception in the way of encouragement and wisdom disseminated by those in academia. Professors and mentors have helped, not only in the understanding of some of the roles that economic indicators and statistics assume, but as counselors to a not-so-quick-to-learn student. They include, and are not limited to, David W. Ring, William O'Dea, Robert Carson, and Thomas Gergel of the State University of New York at Oneonta. Prof. Ring taught me to work hard, Prof. Carson to look at each situation from alternative perspectives, and Prof. Gergel to have a passion about whatever task I might take on. I practice these three lessons every day of my life.

The list of professional associates who have helped me with this project could easily take up the entire book, but some individual recognition is essential. In my eighteen-plus years of work experience on Wall Street I have never been associated with a more professional outfit than Bloomberg News. To the scores of friends and acquaintances at the Bloomberg offices all around the world, thanks for all your help and input into this project. You are unaware of how helpful you have been. I especially wish to thank Vinny Del Giudice, Vince Golle, Yvette Fernandez, Monee Fields-White, Jackie Jozefek, and Al Yoon.

Undoubtedly the greatest gratitude with respect to the creation of this work has to go to my editors at Bloomberg Press, namely Kathleen Peterson, Chris Miles, Tracy Tait, and mostly, Betsy Ungar. Betsy's extraordinary talents have transformed my muddled manuscript into a more readable and effective publication.

Many thanks to the analysts at Argus Research Corp., which help me each day with insight into their respective industries, particularly, Wendy Abramowitz, Robert Becker, Kevin Calabrese, Marie Driscoll, Jeffrey Gildersleeve, Gary F. Hovis, Jim Kelleher, David Kerans, and David Ritter. I must tip my hat in appreciation to John Eade, Argus Research's CEO and Director of Research, as well as the Dorsey family for the opportunity to work at the most prestigious research institution on Wall Street.

Acknowledgment wouldn't be complete without special thanks to Charles Gilbert and Michele Johnson (Board of Governors of the Federal Reserve System); Lynn Franco (The Conference Board); Richard Deitz (Federal Reserve Bank of New York); Guhan Venkatu (Federal Reserve Bank of Cleveland); Scott Scheleur (Service Sector Statistics Division, U.S. Census Bureau); Kristen Kioa (Institute for Supply Management); Jeannine Aversa and Marty Crutsinger (Associated Press); Garrett Bekker (Kim & Co.); Steve Berman (U.S. Department of Commerce, Bureau of Census); George Hager, Barbara Hagenbaugh, Sue Kirchhoff (*USA Today*); Jason Hecht (Ramapo College); Robert Bricken (Prebon, Yamane (USA) Inc.); David Jozefek (Morgan Stanley); Thomas Feeney (Shippensburg University); Jeffrey J. Junior (Aries Appraisal Group, Inc.); and Joe Pregiato (Arbor & Ivy).

Any errors or oversights that may exist in this book were not intentional and are not the fault of any of those individuals named above.

Introduction

INVESTING WITHOUT UNDERSTANDING the economy is like taking a trip without knowing anything about the climate of your destination. Inclement weather can wreak havoc with a vacation, especially if it involves outdoor activities. Just so, putting hard-earned money into the stock or bond market when economic conditions are unfavorable can destroy financial plans for a comfortable retirement, a new house, or a child's college education.

No one understands this better than Wall Street investment banks, brokers, and research institutions. All of these have adopted a top-down approach to securities analysis that begins with a forecast of the general economic climate, including interest rate projections, currency forecasts, and estimates of domestic and foreign economic growth. In this, they are following one of the precepts laid down by Benjamin Graham and David Dodd in their 1940 investors' bible, *Security Analysis:* "Economic forecasts provide essential underpinning for stock and bond market, industry, and company projections."

You don't need to manage millions or billions of dollars, however, to study economic conditions and plan your investment strategy accordingly. You can get much of the same information that Wall Street professionals use in their analyses from the business sections of the nation's newspapers, magazines, and evening news programs. Furthermore, you don't need a degree in economics or mathematics to interpret this information. In fact, many graduates of such programs at the nation's top universities find themselves entirely unprepared for the real world of finance. This book attempts to bridge the wide gap between the sometimes mind-numbing theories of textbook economics—the principles that are taught on college campuses across the country—and the everyday world of

Wall Street. It does so by focusing on a dozen economic indicators that are among the most important of any analyst's or economist's tools. Understanding these indicators will make the study of economics more palatable and exciting.

Over the past century, thousands of economic indicators have emerged, predicting everything from the demand for gasoline to the size of harvests. Some are more fun than functional, such as those claiming links between stock performance for the year and which conference, the NFC or the AFC, wins the Super Bowl, or whether women's hemlines rise to midthigh or fall to midcalf. Others indicators are more serious, solidly based in economic observations. These range from the arcane—such as the indicator connecting the production level of titanium dioxide, an ingredient of pigments used in paints and plastics, with the demand for building materials—to the commonsensical. The price of copper, used in wiring and many other construction elements, for instance, has a clear relationship with the pace of housing activity. The same could be said of economic growth and railroad car loadings, shipping container production, wooden pallet shipments, and the manufacture of corrugated boxboard and packaging, all of which are connected with transporting freight or manufactured goods.

Over time, economists have weeded out the least successful indicators, based on the most dubious relationships, to arrive at a core of about fifty consistently reliable ones. This book presents the dozen that are must-haves in any analytical toolbox. Virtually all Wall Street economists use these indicators in the analyses and their writings. Federal Reserve officials conduct monetary policy with respect to the trends that these indicators project. They are also considered "must haves" in the sense that they are among the most accurate at depicting economic relationships as well as attendant market-movability. That is, each of these indicators at one time or another typically figures among the top-tier factors to engender big swings in the financial markets.

Some of the dozen indicators discussed are constructed by U.S. government agencies such as the U.S. Department of Commerce's Census Bureau, the U.S. Department of Labor, and the Board of

Governors of the Federal Reserve. Others are the products of private organizations such as the Institute for Supply Management, the Conference Board, and the University of Michigan. Some have excellent predictive powers. Others reflect principally the current state of the economy, and still others highlight industries that might outperform and so help identify the likely path of economic activity. All have one thing in common, however: In one way or another, they all relate to the business cycle.

THE BUSINESS CYCLE

The business cycle is one of the central concepts in modern economics. It was defined by celebrated economists Arthur Burns and Wesley Mitchell in their pioneering 1946 study, *Measuring Business Cycles*, written for the National Bureau of Economic Research (NBER), which today is the official arbiter of the U.S. business cycle. According to Burns and Mitchell, the business cycle is "a type of fluctuation found in the aggregate economic activity of nations that organize their work mainly in business enterprises: a cycle consists of expansions occurring at about the same time in many economic activities, followed by similarly general recessions, contractions, and revivals, which merge into the expansion phase of the next cycle."

No two business cycles are the same. As illustrated in FIGURE I-1, during the relatively short time that people have been measuring the U.S. economy, the length of expansions, from economic trough to peak, and of contractions, from peak to trough, have varied widely— although the former, especially recently, have generally been longer and steadier than the latter. Expansions have ranged from 120 months (April 1991 to April 2001) to 10 (March 1919 to January 1920), and downturns from 43 months (September 1929 to March 1933) to 6 (February 1980 to July 1980). The amplitude of the peaks and troughs has also differed significantly from cycle to cycle.

One way to think of the business cycle is as a graphical representation of the total economic activity of a country. Because the accepted benchmark for economic activity in the United States

Figure I-1   U.S. Business Cycle Durations

| Business Cycle Reference Dates | | Duration in Months | | | |
Peak Quarterly dates are in parentheses	Trough	Contraction Peak to trough	Expansion Previous trough to this peak	Cycle Trough from previous trough	 Peak from previous peak
	December 1854 (IV)	—	—	—	—
June 1857 (II)	December 1858 (IV)	18	30	48	—
October 1860 (III)	June 1861 (III)	8	22	30	40
April 1865 (I)	December 1867 (I)	*32*	*46*	*78*	*54*
June 1869 (II)	December 1870 (IV)	18	18	36	50
October 1873 (III)	March 1879 (I)	65	34	99	52
March 1882 (I)	May 1885 (II)	38	36	74	101
March 1887 (II)	April 1888 (I)	13	22	35	60
July 1890 (III)	May 1891 (II)	10	27	37	40
January 1893 (I)	June 1894 (II)	17	20	37	30
December 1895 (IV)	June 1897 (II)	18	18	36	35
June 1899 (III)	December 1900 (IV)	18	24	42	42
September 1902 (IV)	August 1904 (III)	23	21	44	39
May 1907 (II)	June 1908 (II)	13	33	46	56
January 1910 (I)	January 1912 (IV)	24	19	43	32
January 1913 (I)	December 1914 (IV)	23	12	35	36
August 1918 (III)	March 1919 (I)	*7*	*44*	*51*	*67*
January 1920 (I)	July 1921 (III)	18	10	28	17
May 1923 (II)	July 1924 (III)	14	22	36	40
October 1926 (III)	November 1927 (IV)	13	27	40	41
August 1929 (III)	March 1933 (I)	43	21	64	34
May 1937 (II)	June 1938 (II)	13	50	63	93
February 1945 (I)	October 1945 (IV)	*8*	*80*	*88*	*93*
November 1948 (IV)	October 1949 (IV)	11	37	48	45
July 1953 (II)	May 1954 (II)	*10*	*45*	*55*	*56*
August 1957 (III)	April 1958 (II)	8	39	47	49
April 1960 (II)	February 1961 (I)	10	24	34	32
December 1969 (IV)	November 1970 (IV)	*11*	*106*	*117*	*116*
November 1973 (IV)	March 1975 (I)	16	36	52	47
January 1980 (I)	July 1980 (III)	6	58	64	74
July 1981 (III)	November 1982 (IV)	16	12	28	18
July 1990 (III)	March 1991 (I)	8	92	100	108
March 2001 (I)	November 2001 (IV)	8	120	128	128
Average, all cycles: 1854–1991 (32 cycles) 1854–1919 (16 cycles) 1919–1945 (6 cycles) 1945–1991 (10 cycles)		17 22 18 10	38 27 35 57	55 48 53 67	56* 49† 53 67
Average, peacetime cycles: 1854–1991 (27 cycles) 1854–1919 (14 cycles) 1919–1945 (5 cycles) 1945–1991 (8 cycles)		18 22 20 10	33 24 26 52	51 46 46 63	52‡ 47§ 45 63

*31 cycles, †5 cycles, ‡26 cycles, §13 cycles

Figures printed in **bold italic** are the wartime expansions (Civil War, World Wars I and II, Korean War, and Vietnam War), the wartime contractions, and the full cycles that include the wartime expansions.

Source: NBER

Figure I-2 GDP and Highlighted Recessions

Sources: U.S. Department of Commerce, Bureau of Economic Analysis; NBER

YOY %

Shaded areas = Recession

is currently gross domestic product (GDP), economists generally identify the business cycle with the alternating increases and declines in GDP. Rising GDP marks economic expansion; falling GDP, a contraction (see **FIGURE I-2**). That said, the business cycle, as defined by Burns and Mitchell, can't be fully captured by one indicator, even the GDP. Rather, it is a compendium of indicators that reflects various aspects of the economy.

Economic indicators are classified according to how they relate to the business cycle. Those that reflect the current state of the economy are *coincident;* those that predict future conditions are *leading;* and those that confirm that a turning occurred are *lagging.*

INDICATORS AND THE MARKETS

The organization responsible for an indicator generally distributes its report about an hour before the official release time to financial news outlets such as Bloomberg News, Dow Jones Newswires, Reuters, CNBC, and CNNfN. The reporters, who are literally locked in a room and not permitted to have contact with anyone outside, ask questions of agency officials and prepare headlines and analyses of the report contents. These stories are embargoed until the official release, at which time they are transmitted over the newswires to be dissected by the Wall Street community. Most Wall Street firms employ economists to provide live broadcasts of the numbers as they run across the newswires, together with interpretation and commentary regarding the likely market reaction. This task, known as the "hoot-and-holler" or tape reading, is among the most stressful performed by an economist. One slip-up can cost a trader or entire trading floor millions of dollars.

The more an indicator deviates from Street expectations, the greater its effect on the financial markets. A 0.1 percent decline in retail sales, for example, might not move the markets much if economists were looking for a flat reading or a 0.1 percent rise. But if the consensus were for an increase of 0.7 percent, and instead the 0.1 percent decline hit the tape, the markets might well be rocked. That said, it is always prudent for traders and other market participants to keep apprised of what the Street expectations are for key economic indicators such as those covered here.

HOW TO USE THIS BOOK

You've no doubt read in a paper or heard on TV or the radio forecasts of economic expansion or recession. You also probably realize that the one is desirable and the other is not. But you may not know how the economists quoted came up with their predictions. Without this knowledge, how can you judge how well considered or rash they are—and whether to trust them in creating your investment strategy? This book seeks to help you form your own opinions about the possible direction of the economy and the markets and to decide how to act based on those opinions.

Each chapter corresponds to an indicator, beginning with the most comprehensive—the GDP and indices of leading, lagging, and coincident indicators—and continuing with those tied to particular aspects or segments of the overall economy, such as consumer prices, manufacturing, housing, and retail sales. Every chapter contains four principal sections: an introduction sketching out the major attributes of the indicator and its effect on the markets; a discussion of its origins and development; a description of how the relevant data are obtained, analyzed, and presented; and an explanation of how to incorporate these data into your investment process. The last section also contains at least one "trick"—involving either a little-known subcomponent of the indicator or a combination of subcomponents—that Wall Street economists use to get a clearer or more timely picture of business activity. At the end of the book is a listing of additional reading and resources, organized by chapter, pointing those interested to references that discuss the relevant indicator in greater detail.

In putting what you learn from this book into practice, you might take some pointers from Wall Street. Just about every investment firm has a pre-market-opening meeting in which the day's events and potential trading strategies are presented. This always includes a discussion of the economic indicators scheduled for release that day. No trader wants to be caught off guard by an unexpected market-moving release. For the same reason, many traders have on their desks calendars showing which economic release is scheduled for a particular day and indicating both the value or percentage change of the previous report and the Street's estimates—highest, lowest, and consensus—for the upcoming one. That way, when the actual figure is released, they will know how it compares with expectations and can react accordingly.

Of course, no single economic indicator will tell you all you need to know about the current or future economic climate. Each has drawbacks and may send false signals because of unforeseen shocks, faulty measurements, or suspect collection processes. Piecing together the information from all twelve indicators discussed in this book like tiles in a mosaic will give you a dynamic representation of the economy. But if you are truly serious about understanding the macroeconomic climate and individual industry conditions, you should also take advantage of the Securities and Exchange Commission's Regulation Fair Disclosure of 2000, which mandates for individual investors the same access to companies' quarterly earnings conference calls that professional analysts have.

These calls provide a great deal of insight into corporate spending plans, manufacturing and production activity, international conditions, pricing, and the general business climate. Especially informative are the announcements of industrial behemoths such as Alcoa, Boeing, Caterpillar, Cummins, Emerson Electric, Ford Motor Company, General Electric, Illinois Tool Works, Johnson Controls, and United Technologies. Many companies also offer slide presentations, handouts, and supplemental data with these quarterly presentations, which often provide even greater detail on their buying intentions, prospective employment changes, and any threats to performance that they foresee. There's no cheaper and easier way to gather anecdotal evidence about business conditions. If you can't listen in, the presentations are almost always archived on company websites, from which they may be readily retrieved 24/7.

WHO CAN BENEFIT FROM THIS BOOK?

This book was written primarily for those traders and investors lacking a formal introduction to the most popular economic indicators on Wall Street. Just because an individual is entrusted with investing millions of dollars does not guarantee a practical command of economic indicators and their meaning for investment. When newly minted MBAs arrive on the trading floors of financial firms, for example, few are equipped with a complete appreciation of these indicators—no matter from which institution that degree has come. My years of experience on a few of the largest trading floors in the world has suggested the need to fill what can be viewed as a surprisingly expansive void regarding indicators, statistics, the economic meaning of the associated figures, and the market's likely reaction.

Those new to the field of investing and economics, including students of the subject, also should benefit from the fundamental, application-oriented nature of this book. As most academics know, if students cannot see the results or directly test theories with practical data, the knowledge they hold tends to remain more theoretical than real-world and they eventually may lose interest in the field. It is here that many future economists are lost. As exercises within an imperfect "science," experiments conducted in the social discipline of economics are predominantly theorized or hypothesized and seldom tested with tangible data. In this sense, economists are not as fortunate as physicists or natural scientists, who conduct experiments in a controlled environment such as a laboratory, riverbed, or ocean. The economic indicators contained in these chapters serve as concrete guideposts within the discipline of economics, and as such make experimentation, testing, and study for investments not only possible but understandable.

Gross Domestic Product 1

E CONOMICS HAS RECEIVED A BAD RAP. In the mid-nineteenth century, the great Scottish historian Thomas Carlyle dubbed this discipline "the dismal science," and jokes about economists being more boring than accountants abound on the Street. But truth be told, there is nothing more exciting than watching the newswire on a trading floor of a money-center bank minutes ahead of the release of a major market-moving economic report. One of the top excitement generators is the report on gross domestic product (GDP)—an indicator that is a combination of economics and accounting.

Economists, policymakers, and politicians revere GDP above all other economic statistics because it is the broadest, most comprehensive barometer available of a country's overall economic condition. GDP is the sum of the market values of all final goods and services produced in a country (that is, domestically) during a specific period using that country's resources, regardless of the ownership of the resources. For example, all the automobiles made in the United States are included in the GDP—even those manufactured in U.S. plants owned by Germany's DaimlerChrysler and Japan's Lexus. In contrast, gross national product (GNP) is the sum of the market values of all final goods and services produced by a country's permanent residents and firms regardless of their location—that is, whether the production occurs domestically or abroad—during a given period. Baked goods produced in Canada by U.S. conglomerate Sarah Lee, for example, are included in the United States' GNP, but not its GDP.

GDP is a more relevant measure of U.S. economic conditions than GNP, because the resources that are utilized in the production process are predominantly domestic. There are strong parallels between the GDP data and other U.S. economic indicators, such as industrial production and the Conference Board's Index of Coincidental Indicators, which will be explored in later chapters.

The GDP is calculated and reported on a quarterly basis as part of the National Income and Product Accounts. The NIPAs, which were developed and are maintained today by the Commerce Department's Bureau of Economic Analysis (BEA), are the most comprehensive set of data available regarding U.S. national output, production, and the distribution of income. Each GDP report contains data on the following:

■ personal income and consumption expenditures
■ corporate profits
■ national income
■ inflation

These data tell the story of how the economy performed—whether it expanded or contracted—during a specific period, usually the preceding quarter. By looking at changes in the GDP's components and subcomponents and comparing these with changes that have occurred in the past, economists can draw inferences about the direction the economy might take in the future.

Of all the tasks market economists perform, generating a forecast for overall economic performance as measured by the GDP data is the one to which they dedicate the most time. In fact, the latest report on GDP is within arm's reach of most Wall Street economists. Because several departments in a trading institution rely on the economist's forecasts, this indicator has emerged as the foundation for all research and trading activity and usually sets the tone of all of Wall Street's financial prognostications.

EVOLUTION OF AN INDICATOR

Measuring a nation's output and performance is known formally as national income accounting. This process was largely pioneered by Simon Kuznets, an economist hired by the U.S. Department of Commerce in the 1930s—with additional funding from the National Bureau of Economic Research—to create an accurate representation of how much the U.S. economy was producing. Up to that time, there was no government agency calculating this most critical of economic statistics.

The initial national income estimates produced by Kuznets in 1934 were representations of income produced, measures of the national economy's net product, and the national income "paid out," or the total compensation for the work performed in the production of net product. At that time, no in-depth breakdown of components yet existed. In fact, Kuznets didn't even have a detailed representation of national consumption expenditures. This was the first step of several in the creation of a formal method of national income accounting, and yet was still a far cry from today's highly detailed representation of the macroeconomy.

The result was the National Income and Product Accounts. In addition to this immense task, Kuznets reconstructed the national income accounts of the United States back to 1869. (He was awarded a Nobel Prize in Economics in 1971 in part for this accomplishment.) Kuznets's first research report, presented to Congress in 1937, covered national income and output from 1929 through 1935.

In 1947, the first formal presentation of the national income accounts appeared as a supplement to the July issue of the Survey of Current Business. This supplement contained annual data from 1929 to 1946 disseminated in thirty-seven tables. These data were separated into six accounts:

1. national income and product account
2. income and product account for the business sector
3. government receipt/expenditure account
4. foreign account

5. personal income/expenditure account
6. gross savings and investment account

Before the creation of the NIPAs, households, investors, government policymakers, corporations, and economists had little or no information about the complete macroeconomic picture. There were indices regarding production of raw materials and commodities. There were statistics on prices and government spending. But a comprehensive representation of total economic activity wasn't available. In fact, the term *macroeconomy* didn't appear in print until 1939. Policymaking without knowing the past performance of the economy, how it operated under different conditions and scenarios, or which sectors were weak and which were strong was a daunting task. This may have been the reason for many of the economic-policy failures of the early twentieth century.

Many economists have laid the blame for the Great Depression of the 1930s on the Federal Reserve's failure to respond to the ebullient activity during the Roaring Twenties (sound familiar?). The Fed may bear much of the responsibility; but very few, if any, have defended the Federal Reserve's failures on the grounds of insufficient information. The Great Depression forced the government to develop some sort of national accounting method. World War II furthered the government's need to understand the nation's capacity, the composition of its output, and the general economic state of affairs. How could the government possibly plan for war without an accurate appreciation of its resources? The NIPAs permit policymakers to formulate reasonable objectives such as higher economic growth rates or lower inflation rates as well as to formulate policies to attain these objectives and steer the economy around any roadblocks that might impede the attainment of these goals.

DIGGING FOR THE DATA

Tracking the developments in an economy as large and dynamic as that of the United States is not easy. But through constant revision and upgrading, a relatively small group of dedicated economists at the BEA accomplishes this huge task every quarter. Each quarterly report of economic activity goes through three versions, all available on the BEA website, www.bea.gov. The first, the advance report, comes one month after the end of the quarter covered, hitting the newswires at 8:30 a.m. ET. So, the GDP report pertaining to the first three months of the year is released sometime during the last week of April, the second quarter's advance report during the last week of July, the third quarter's in October, and the fourth quarter's during the last week of January of the following year. Because not all the data are available during this initial release, the BEA must estimate some series, particularly those involving inventories and foreign trade.

As new data become available, the BEA makes the necessary refinements, deriving a more accurate estimate for GDP. The second release, called the preliminary report, comes two months after the quarter covered, one month after the advance report, and reflects the refinements made to date. The last revision to the data is contained in the final report, which is released three months after the relevant quarter and a month after the preliminary report. The release dates for 2003 are shown in **FIGURE 1-1**.

Annual revisions are calculated during July of every year, based on data that become available to the BEA only on an annual basis, such as state and local government consumption expenditures. The BEA estimates these data on a quarterly basis via a judgmental trend based on annual surveys of state and local governments. Judgmental trends are quarterly interpolations of source data that are only available on an annual basis. Because the surveys are available on an annual basis, estimates can only be made during the annual revision.

Figure 1-1   2003 Release Schedule for GDP Reports

	2002: QIV	2003: QI	2003: QI	2003: QIII
Advance report	January 30	April 25	July 31	October 30
Preliminary report (1st revision)	February 28	May 29	August 28	November 25
Final report (2nd revision)	March 27	June 26	September 26	December 23

Source: U.S. Department of Commerce, Bureau of Economic Analysis

As source data for the components of the accounts are continuously updated and revised, the components of the NIPAs must be updated to reflect these revisions. That's the primary function of the annual revision. Each of the three years (twelve quarters) worth of data is subject to revision during this annual updating. Every five years the BEA issues a so-called benchmark revision of all of the data in the NIPAs. This typically has resulted in considerable changes to the five years of quarterly figures.

Benchmark revisions are different from annual revisions in that they generally contain major overhauls to the structure of the report, usually definitional, re-classifications, and new presentations of data. New tables need to be created to account for products that are developed. As the economy evolves, new goods and services come to market and therefore need to be accounted for. Obviously, there were times when CDs, microwave ovens, MP3 players, and DVDs didn't exist. Because the U.S. economy develops and produces these goods, there needs to be a place for this production to be recorded. All of the data—quarterly and annual—are revised during benchmark revisions.

SOME DEFINITIONS

As noted previously, the GDP is the sum of the market values of all final goods and services produced by the resources (labor and property) of a country residing in that country. This definition contains two particularly important terms: *final* and *produced*. When economists refer to final goods, they mean those goods produced for their final intended use, that is, as end products, not as component or intermediate parts in another stage of manufacture. As an example, consider that each year, Goodyear Tire & Rubber produces some hundred million tires. Most are produced for use on new vehicles. But there are still quite a number created for distribution in retail and wholesale stores as replacements and spares. Those tires produced and delivered to automakers intended for use on new automobiles are not counted as production because we do not calculate the value of automobiles in the national accounts by summing the value of its components. In other words, we don't add the cost of the radio, the seats, the heating elements, the spark plugs, and so on. We only count the value of the final product, the automobile.

Obviously, the economists at the BEA would make a serious miscalculation if they counted all the tires sold by the manufacturer to Wal-Mart and Sears, as well as those sold by the automakers as part of their automobiles. The same holds true for the production of wool. BEA economists only count the wool purchased for final use. Because countless final uses exist for wool—sweaters, hats, blankets, and so on—the BEA would make the same double-counting error by adding the production of raw wool as well as the wool used in sweaters, blankets, and the like.

Let's consider the other important term, produced. Resales are not included in the accounts. Rightfully so, the BEA has determined that because the pace of reselling is not indicative of the current pace of production, it shouldn't be included in the output figures.

Another segment of the economy that the BEA excludes from the GDP release is the activity that goes on "off the books." This seems an obvious exclusion, but it's a big one. Believe it or not, some of the most conservative studies have set the size of the U.S. underground economy at around 10 percent of the official U.S. GDP, or what was roughly $1 trillion in the first quarter of 2003. The BEA doesn't count or make any adjustments for non-state-sanctioned gambling, prostitution, trade in illegal drugs, fraud, the production and sale of counterfeit merchandise, and the like because, officially, they don't exist—wink, wink, nudge, nudge. These activities aren't reported, so how can they be measured? Clandestine activity like this can understandably alter the estimate of several economic indicators, but none more than the GDP.

GDP VERSUS GNP

The NIPAs contain figures for both gross domestic product and gross national product. Before 1991, GNP was the benchmark for all economic activity in commentaries, reports, articles, and texts. The GDP became the official barometer when the BEA decided

Figure 1-2   GNP Derived From GDP (QIV 2002 Report)

U.S. GDP	$10.588 trillion
plus receipts from the rest of the world	+ $284.200 billion
minus payments to the rest of the world	− $293.400 billion
equals U.S. GNP	= $10.579 trillion

Source: U.S. Department of Commerce, Bureau of Economic Analysis

that the measure was a better fit with the United Nations System of National Accounts used by other nations, and so made international comparisons of economic growth easier.

GDP differs from GNP in what economists call "net factor income from foreign sources": the difference between the value of receipts from foreign sources and the payments made to foreign sources. The table in **FIGURE 1-2**, using data from the final GDP report of the fourth quarter of 2002, illustrates how the BEA quantifies this relationship in its GDP report.

The difference between the value of GDP and GNP is typically minuscule, usually less than 0.5 percent. In Figure 1-2, for example, GDP is approximately $10.588 trillion and GNP $10.579 trillion, a difference of under $10 billion, or 0.09 percent.

CALCULATING GDP: THE AGGREGATE EXPENDITURE APPROACH

Every transaction in an economy involves two parties, a buyer and a seller. To calculate total economic activity, economists can focus either on the buyers' actions, adding together all the expenditures on goods and services, or on the sellers' actions, tallying the total income received by those employed in the production process. These two approaches correspond to the two methods of calculating the GDP: the aggregate expenditure method, which is the more popular and the one used on most Wall Street trading floors, and the income approach. The totals reached by both measures should theoretically be the same. In practice, however, there are small differences.

To calculate GDP, the BEA uses the aggregate expenditure equation:

$$GDP = C + I + G + (X - M)$$

where C is personal consumption expenditures, I is gross private domestic investment, G is government consumption expenditures and gross investment, and $(X - M)$ is the net export value of goods and services (exports minus imports). The identity expressed in this equation is probably the most widely cited of all economic relationships and appears in virtually all introductory macroeconomic texts.

Because the U.S. economy is extremely dynamic and susceptible to sudden and unforeseen influences like inclement weather and war, the percentage of GDP contributed by each of the equation's components varies over time, even from quarter to quarter. For the most part, though, the proportions don't deviate significantly from those represented in **FIGURE 1-3**, which depicts the composition of first quarter 2003 GDP.

Personal consumption expenditures (also referred to as **consumer spending** or simply **spending**) are the largest component of GDP, accounting for roughly two-thirds of total economic output. During the first quarter of 2003, consumer spending climbed to approximately 70 percent of GDP ($7.503 trillion divided by $10.698 trillion).

Consumer spending is the total market value of household

Figure 1-3 Composition of GDP

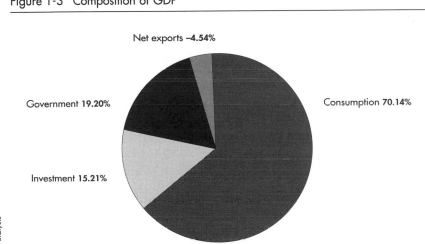

Source: U.S. Department of Commerce, Bureau of Economic Analysis

purchases during the accounting term, including items such as beer, telephone service, golf clubs, CDs, gasoline, musical instruments, and taxicab rides. As shown in the table in **FIGURE 1-4**, these items fall into three categories: durable goods, nondurable goods, and services. Durable goods are those with shelf lives of three or more years. Examples include automobiles, refrigerators, washing machines, televisions, and other big-ticket items, such as jewelry, sporting equipment, and guns. Nondurable goods are food, clothing and shoes, energy products such as gasoline and fuel oil, and other items such as tobacco, cosmetics, prescription drugs, magazines, and sundries. Services include housing, household operation, transportation, medical care, and recreation, as well as hair styling, dry cleaning, funeral services, legal services, and education.

Services constitute by far the largest category of consumer purchases. They account today for roughly 59 percent of all consumer spending, up from a mere third in 1950. No wonder the

Figure 1-4 Consumer Spending Breakdown

	2003: QI ($ in billions)	Percent of Total Spending
Consumer Spending	$7,503	100.00%
Durable Goods	$863	11.50%
Motor vehicles and parts	$366	4.88%
Furniture and household equipment	$317	4.23%
Other	$180	2.40%
Nondurable Goods	$2,197	29.28%
Food	$1,059	14.11%
Clothing and shoes	$327	4.35%
Gasoline, fuel oil, and other energy goods	$210	2.80%
Other	$601	8.01%
Services	$4,443	59.21%
Housing	$1,102	14.69%
Household operation	$419	5.58%
Transportation	$278	3.71%
Medical care	$1,193	15.89%
Recreation	$293	3.90%
Other	$1,159	15.44%

Source: U.S. Department of Commerce, Bureau of Economic Analysis

United States is said to have a service-based economy. Spending on nondurable goods is the second-largest category of expenditures, representing about 29 percent of the total. Durable goods expenditures, the most volatile component, account for the remaining 11 percent.

A more detailed summary of personal consumption expenditures is available on a monthly basis in the BEA's report on Personal Income and Outlays, which is the direct source of data for this component of the GDP report. Personal income and outlays are discussed in Chapter 11.

Gross private domestic investment encompasses spending by businesses—on equipment such as computers, on the construction of factories and production plants, and in mining operations—expenditures on residential housing and apartments; and inventories. Inventories, which consist of the goods businesses produce during a period that remain unsold, are valued by the BEA at the prevailing market price. This value fluctuates greatly from quarter to quarter, making the level of gross private domestic investment quite volatile. Accordingly, economists often look at **fixed investment**—gross private domestic investment minus inventories. This, in turn, has two major components, **residential** and **nonresidential**. The latter, which is also referred to as **capital spending**, includes expenditures on computers and peripheral equipment, industrial equipment, software, and nonresidential buildings such as plants and factories. The former comprises spending on the construction of new houses and apartment buildings and on related equipment.

Even without the volatile influence of inventories, investment spending is prone to extreme movements, because most of this activity is linked to the ever-changing interest rate environment. Gross private domestic investment usually accounts for 15 percent of GDP. During the first quarter of 2003, it represented 15.2 percent ($1.627 trillion divided by $10.698 trillion) of GDP.

Government consumption expenditures and gross investment covers all the money laid out by federal, state, and local governments for goods (both durable and nondurable) and services, for both military and nonmilitary purposes. The category includes spending on building and maintaining toll bridges, libraries, parks, highways, and federal office buildings; on compensation for government employees; on research and development, spare parts, food, clothing, ammunition; and on travel, rents, and utilities. Government expenditures and investment usually account for 20 percent of total GDP. During the first quarter of 2003, government consumption expenditures and gross investment accounted for 19.2 percent of total economic activity ($2.054 trillion divided by $10.698 trillion).

Net exports of goods and services, the last component in the equation, is simply the difference between the dollar value of the goods and services the United States sends abroad (exports) and the dollar value of those it takes in across its borders (imports). Because the country generally imports more than it exports, this figure is usually negative, thus acting as a drag on economic growth. During the first quarter of 2003, net exports subtracted 4.5 percent from total economic activity (–$485.7 billion divided by $10.698 trillion).

NOMINAL AND REAL NUMBERS

The data reported in the GDP release are presented in two forms, nominal and real. **Nominal**, also known as **current dollar**, GDP is the total value, at current prices, of all final goods and services produced during the reporting period. **Real**, or **constant dollar**, GDP is the value of these goods and services using the prices in effect in a specified base year. Economists tend to prefer the real to the nominal measure. To understand why, consider a country that produces only two goods—pencils and vodka, a very interesting economy. If during Year One, it sells two thousand pencils at $0.10 each and one thousand bottles of vodka at $5.00 a bottle (cheap vodka), its nominal GDP will be $5,200:

Pencils	2,000 x $0.10	=	$ 200
Vodka	1,000 x $5.00	=	$5,000
Nominal GDP			**$5,200**

Next year, the same country produces only a thousand pencils and five hundred bottles of vodka but doubles its selling prices, to $0.20 a pencil and $10.00 a bottle. Its nominal GDP is again $5,200:

Pencils	1,000 x $ 0.20	=	$ 200
Vodka	500 x $10.00	=	$5,000
Nominal GDP			**$5,200**

Is the economy larger during the second year? Did it produce the same amount? The difficulty in answering these questions illustrates the problem with nominal values. Economists have no way of telling whether it was the price or the quantity produced that increased, or by what magnitude. As more goods and services are considered, the problem gets bigger.

Real GDP is a more accurate indicator of changes in production. Referring to a base year eliminates the uncertainty of whether an increase in the value of the goods and services produced was the result of increased prices or of higher production. **FIGURE 1-5** shows how real GDP would be calculated in another country with two products—in this case, telescopes and hockey sticks.

To calculate Year 1 GDP, the quantities of the goods produced that year are multiplied by the prices at which they were sold and the results summed, to yield $6,000. For Year 2, instead of multiplying the quantities of goods produced by that year's prices—which would yield the nominal value—they are multiplied by their prices in the base year, Year 1. This yields a real, or inflation-adjusted, GDP of $7,650. According to this calculation, Year 2 GDP rose a real $1,650 over Year 1.

Until 1996, the BEA used 1982 as the base year for calculating

Figure 1-5 Real GDP Calculation, Using Year 1 as the Base Year

	Quantity		Price		GDP	
Product	Year 1	Year 2	Year 1	Year 2	Year 1	Year 2
Telescopes	10	14	$100	$125	$1,000	$1,400
Hockey sticks	200	250	$25	$27	$5,000	$6,250
					$6,000	**$7,650**

all real GDP estimates. Settling on one base year in this manner has the effect of imposing that year's price structure on subsequent periods and fixing the relative weights given the goods associated with these prices in the GDP calculation. The BEA found, however, that this **fixed-weight** approach introduced distortions: The farther away a period under study was from the chosen base year, the more inflated its real GDP growth rate tended to be. For example, Karl Whelan, an economist at the Federal Reserve's Board of Governors, has observed in a working paper that the growth rate of fixed-weight real GDP in 1998 was 4.5 percent when calculated using a base year of 1995, 6.5 percent using 1990 prices, 18.8 percent using 1980 prices, and an incredible 37.4 percent when 1970 is the base year.

The BEA constantly refines its measures. (That's part of the reason the economic statistics in the United States are better and more accurate than those in any other developed nation.) In the mid-1990s, the Bureau decided it was time to refine its weighting method and, in late 1995, adopted chain weighting. The chain-weighting process is far too complex for this introduction, but in essence, rather than holding constant a basket of goods and services, as in the fixed-weight system, it holds the "utility" of the basket constant, allowing substitution of cheaper for more expensive items. Moreover, the base year is moved forward as the estimate progresses through time. The result is a series of links, or a "chain" of estimates that minimizes deviations.

The primary drawback of using chain-weighted (chained) data is the loss of additivity. In the fixed-weight calculation, total real GDP measured in 1996 dollars was equal to the sum of its components valued in 1996 dollars, and the value of each component was equal to the sum of the values of its subcomponents. As illustrated in **FIGURE 1-6**, this is not the case when chain weighting is used. Note that when the real chained components are summed, they do not add up to the actual real chained dollar total consumption figure of $6,637.9 billion.

Figure 1-6   First Quarter 2003 Consumption Expenditures ($ in billions)

	Nominal (Current Dollar)	Real Chained Dollar
Nondurable goods	$2,150.0	$1,950.0
Durable goods	873.9	1,010.6
Services	4,401.5	3,707.0
Total consumption	= **$7,425.4**	**$6,637.9**

Source: U.S. Department of Commerce, Bureau of Economic Analysis

DEFLATORS

The difference between nominal GDP and real GDP is essentially inflation. It is thus possible to compute an economy's inflation rate from this difference. The result of the computation is called an implicit price deflator.

Every GDP report contains implicit price deflators for the headline GDP number and also for many of its subcomponents, such as consumption expenditures, government spending, and gross private domestic investment. Economists at the BEA calculate the GDP implicit price deflator using the formula:

(Nominal Value)/(Real Value) x 100 = Implicit deflator,

For example, using data from the 2003 first quarter GDP report, the GDP deflator for that period would be:

$$\frac{\$10.698}{\$\ 9.556} \times 100 = 111.947, \text{ or approximately } 111.95$$

An annualized inflation rate for a period can be derived using the formula:

[(current-period deflator / previous-period deflator $)^4$ – 1] x 100 = annualized inflation.

To compute the annualized inflation rate for first quarter 2003, for example, the first quarter 2003 GDP deflator computed above and the fourth quarter 2002 deflator of 111.25

would be plugged into the formula, to give

$$[(111.95 / 111.25)^4 - 1] \times 100 = [(1.00629)^4 - 1] \times 100$$
$$= (1.025398 - 1) \times 100 = 2.539\%, \text{ or approximately } 2.54\%.$$

A similar formula is used to calculate the annualized quarterly growth rate of GDP as a whole as well as each of its components and subcomponents:

$$[(\text{current quarter} / \text{previous quarter})^4 - 1] \times 100$$
$$= \text{quarterly annualized growth rate.}$$

For example, to compute the fourth quarter 2002 growth rate, the third and fourth quarter 2002 GDP figures would be plugged into the formula, giving:

$$[(\text{QIII 2002 GDP}) / (\text{QIV 2002 GDP})^4 - 1] \times 100$$
$$= [(9,518.2 / 9,485.6)^4 - 1] \times 100$$
$$= [(1.00344)4 - 1] \times 100 = [(1.013831165) - 1] \times 100$$
$$= 0.013831165 \times 100$$
$$= 1.383\%, \text{ or approximately } 1.4\%$$

NATIONAL INCOME

As noted earlier, economic activity has two sides—expenditures and income—which correspond to two different ways of calculating GDP. The discussion so far has involved expenditures. The income side of GDP calculation is less sexy than the expenditure approach because it doesn't identify the industries or products that are being created. Traders tend to pay less attention to the factors involved in national income, but it is equally important. Investors, particularly equity traders, like to see the quarterly performance of their respective investment industries. For example, those traders heavily invested in software stocks want to know how software investment fared during the particular quarter. The income-determined approach of GDP calculations does not provide this perspective.

The sum of the incomes generated in the course of production is termed **national income**. Its components fall into the following five categories:

1. compensation of employees (wages and salaries, plus supplements)
2. net interest
3. proprietors' income
4. rental income of persons
5. corporate profits

FIGURE 1-7, from the BEA's fourth quarter 2002 report on GDP, identifies these components together with the percentage each contributes to total national income. Unlike expenditure-based GDP and its components, the income data are reported only in nominal terms—that is, they are valued only in current prices. They are also subjected to valuation adjustments.

EMPLOYEE COMPENSATION

Employee compensation accounts for roughly 70 percent of national income. It comprises two parts. The largest is composed of wages and salaries, including commissions, tips, bonuses, and employee contributions to deferred compensation plans such as

Figure 1-7 National Income ($ in billions)

	2002: QIV	Percent of Total Income
Compensation of employees	$6,048.8	71.62%
Wage and salary accruals	*$5,052.4*	*59.82%*
Supplements to wages and salaries	*$996.4*	*11.80%*
Proprietors' income with inventory valuation and capital consumption adjustments	$771.6	9.14%
Rental income of persons with capital consumption adjustment	$130.6	1.55%
Corporate profits with inventory valuation and capital consumption adjustments	$796.1	9.43%
Net interest	$698.3	8.27%
National Income	**$8,445.4**	**100.00%**

Source: U.S. Department of Commerce, Bureau of Economic Analysis

401(k)s. For the most part, the BEA estimates this component by multiplying employment in the Bureau of Labor Statistics' monthly Employment Situation report (described in Chapter 3) by earnings and the number of hours worked. The second component of compensation, accounting for approximately 16 percent of the total, is composed of "supplements," such as employer contributions for social and unemployment insurance.

Net interest is the interest that businesses, foreign corporations operating in the United States, life insurance companies, and several other related interest-disseminating sources pay out as part of the expense of operating, less the interest they receive. Interest payments on mortgages and on home improvement and equity loans are considered business costs because the NIPAs treat home ownership as a business. The BEA gathers most of the data for the net interest calculation from Internal Revenue Service (IRS) tax returns, the Federal Reserve Board, regulatory agency annual reports, and the Department of Agriculture.

OTHER INCOME CATEGORIES

The last three categories—proprietors' income, rental income, and corporate profits—are usually tweaked, through the application of an inventory valuation adjustment (IVA) and a capital consumption adjustment (CCAdj). The IVA adjusts for the data discrepancies that occur because some businesses value their inventories at initial-acquisition, or historical, cost rather than at current-replacement cost, which is the BEA's method. The CCAdj deals with the fact that businesses account differently from national income accountants (i.e., the BEA) for depreciation (referred to by economists as capital consumption)—that is, the reduction in value throughout the measurement period of income, profits, inventories, and goods. Because businesses have several methods of inventory accounting, including the BEA's CCAdj, the BEA has adopted the CCAdj as a more consistent and uniform inventory and capital consumption adjustment system. The IVA and CCAdj are two reasons that the income and the expenditure computations of GDP aren't the same.

Proprietors' income comprises the earnings of nonincorporated businesses (sole proprietorships and partnerships). The dollar amount of this income is calculated using IRS business tax returns, with inventory valuation and capital consumption adjustments. The category accounts for about 9 percent of total income.

Rental income is composed of the rents earned from residential and nonresidential property by people not primarily engaged in the real estate business, plus royalties received from copyrights and patents.

The GDP report refers to several types of corporate profits. **Pretax profits**, also known as book profits, are what companies earn before paying taxes and distributing dividends to shareholders. Applying the IVA and CCAdj to this total results in **profits from current production**, termed **operating profits** in the business community. This is the corporate profits figure used in computing national income. Subtracting companies' tax liabilities from book profit gives **after-tax profits**. **FIGURE 1-8**, taken from the final GDP report of fourth quarter 2002, illustrates how the various corporate profit measures are related.

The corporate profits data are obtained from IRS tabulations, as well as from the Census Bureau's quarterly survey of corporate profits and publicly available corporate financial statements. Corporate profits account for approximately 10 percent of total national income.

Figure 1-8   Corporate Profits ($ in billions)

	2002-I	2002-II	2002-III	2002-IV
Corporate profits with inventory valuation and capital consumption adjustments	$797.6	$785	$771	$796.1
Corporate profits with inventory valuation adjustment	641.3	652.2	653.4	686.4
Profits before tax	639.4	657.9	668.5	694.9
Profits tax liability	202.4	213.7	214.7	222.4
Profits after tax	437	444.3	453.8	472.5
Dividends	424.2	430.8	437.7	444.3
Undistributed profits	12.8	13.5	16.1	28.2
Inventory valuation adjustment	1.9	-5.7	-15.1	-8.5
Capital consumption adjustment	156.3	132.8	117.6	109.7
Net interest	672.8	678.1	687.6	698.3

Source: U.S. Department of Commerce, Bureau of Economic Analysis

Not every GDP report depicts corporate profits in the same detail as the table shown in Figure 1-8. Because corporate earnings reports are scattered throughout the quarter and IRS processing of corporate tax returns is rather lengthy, accurate tallies are only possible months after the end of the quarter. The most complete presentation of corporate profits is usually provided in a year's final report of GDP.

GNP, GDP, AND NATIONAL INCOME

National income, as noted above, is the sum of all the incomes generated by the factors involved in production. This total does not equal the expenditure-determined GDP. To reach equality, several adjustments must be made. These adjustments are shown in **FIGURE 1-9**, which reproduces Table 8 of the fourth quarter 2002 GDP report.

The largest adjustment concerns the consumption of fixed capital. This is essentially the depreciation charge taken by private and government owners of fixed capital located in the United States to account for the assets used up in the course of production. The amount of the charge is estimated by the BEA from IRS business tax returns and studies of resale prices of used equipment and structures.

The next category of adjustments involves indirect business taxes (such as sales, excise, and property taxes, and customs duties) and nontax liabilities, which include fines. The BEA estimates most of these using a so-called judgmental trend based on the Census Bureau's quinquennial censuses and annual and quarterly surveys. Again, because data are not always available on a quarterly basis, the BEA must extrapolate quarterly data from annual surveys. This process of extrapolation and interpolation is referred to by the BEA as a judgment trend.

The third category consists of transfer payments—distributions that private (i.e., nongovernmental) businesses make to individuals without any product changing hands or services being rendered. Two examples are charitable donations and liability payments made

Figure 1-9 Relation of GDP, GNP, and National Income ($ in billions)

	QIV: 2002
Gross Domestic Product	**$10,588.8**
Plus: Income receipts from the rest of the world	$284.2
Less: Income payments to the rest of the world	$293.4
Equals: Gross National Product	**$10,579.6**
Less: Consumption of fixed capital	$1,415.4
Less: Indirect business tax and nontax liability	$813.3
Less: Business transfer payments	$44.3
Less: Statistical discrepancy	$109.6
Plus: Subsidies less current surplus of government enterprises	$29.0
Equals: National Income	**$8,445.2**

Source: U.S. Department of Commerce, Bureau of Economic Analysis

for personal injury. The BEA gets these data from IRS business tax refunds, government agency reports, and other trade sources.

All these figures—for depreciation, taxes, and transfers—are added to national income. In contrast, the fourth category of adjustments, subsidies less the current surplus of government enterprises, is subtracted. The subsidies referred to are the distributions that government agencies make to private businesses as well as to other levels of government, such as to the U.S. Post Office.

After all these adjustments are made, gross domestic income should equal the gross domestic product. However, a difference, termed the **statistical discrepancy**, still remains—fourth quarter 2002 GDP, for instance, was $10.579.6 billion and gross domestic income $10,689.2 billion by the income-based calculation, a difference of $109.6 billion. This discrepancy reflects differences in the sources for data used in the two calculations. Those used in deriving national income are less directly observable, and so less reliable. As mentioned earlier, moreover, illicit expenditures are not reported or estimated.

This section of the chapter has described the multitude of figures included in the GDP report, how they are related to one another, and how they are derived. Next comes the nuts and bolts:

how economists and traders use the report numbers in determining both big-picture issues, such as the future course of the business cycle, and smaller ones, such as when to put their money where.

WHAT DOES IT ALL MEAN?

The GDP report is a mother lode of information about the nation's economy. Each of its components tells a different story about a particular group, sector, industry, or activity. Not surprisingly, then, different market participants look at different sections and draw different inferences. Retail analysts, for instance, focus mostly on consumer spending. Those covering housing, construction, or real estate investment trusts (REITs) concentrate on the residential activity in investment spending. Military and defense industry analysts focus on the national defense spending component of government consumption expenditures and gross investment. Fixed-income analysts and investors, ever wary of the eroding effects of inflation, concern themselves with the GDP deflators and GDP growth rate. Traders, who are always on the lookout for possible market movers, watch for numbers that contradict expectations, which they track carefully, often jotting them down in notebooks kept at their desks, for quick reference when the real figures are announced.

GDP GROWTH

The quarterly annualized growth rate of real GDP is the headline number of the GDP report. As with most economic figures, strong positive postings are generally good news for the economy, corporate profits, and stock valuations. Not so for bonds, however. Inflation erodes the value of fixed-income securities, and more torrid economic growth is usually associated with higher rates of inflation.

Market reactions—both positive and negative—are more pronounced when the announced numbers differ from the expected ones. The larger the difference, the greater the market move. Say the Street consensus for the third quarter was for an annualized GDP growth rate of 4.2 percent. On the one hand, a weak posting of between 1.0 and 2.0 percent would probably spark a sell-off in the stock market and boost the price of fixed-income securities, lowering yields. Stronger-than-expected growth of 5.5 to 6.5 percent, on the other hand, would be well received by equity traders and frowned upon by fixed-income dealers.

Although the quarterly annualized figure is important, many economists prefer to look at the year-over-year change in GDP. The longer perspective makes it is easier to spot turning points in the economy, such as an approaching recession or an acceleration of activity. **FIGURE 1-10** illustrates this predictive effect.

As the chart shows, in the past twenty years the U.S. economy has experienced two recessions—in 1990–91 and 2001—both of which were preceded by significant declines in the growth rates of real and nominal GDP. Note that although the real GDP growth rate falls below zero, the nominal rate declines but stays out of negative territory. This is because the nominal figure incorporates the effects of inflation, which is almost always rising. For the growth rate of nominal GDP to become negative, the inflation rate would have to be falling— a condition known as deflation—at the same time that the economy was contracting. Deflation is extremely rare in the United States and indeed has been recorded only a couple of times anywhere.

Figure 1-10   Year-Over-Year Percent Change in Real and Nominal GDP

Sources: U.S. Department of Commerce, Bureau of Economic Analysis; NBER

On average, the year-over-year growth rate in GDP starts declining four to five quarters before a recession. Not all slowdowns, however, result in recession. By the time the warning signals appear, government policymakers have usually put in place measures to avert an economic downturn. Still, watching changes in year-over-year GDP growth can be useful for short-term forecasts: Very rarely do trends reverse immediately. It takes a great deal to knock a $10 trillion economy like that of the United States off kilter. Luckily for those in the financial markets, several "leading" indicators usually send alerts when the behemoth is running out of energy.

In order to form a clearer picture, economists like to look at several indicators at once. This helps reduce the transmission of false signals. There are times when some individual indicators trend lower, suggesting a potential decline in activity. If several indicators are observed, and a majority point to positive activity, then it is possible to dismiss the weaker performing indicators as outliers, and draw the conclusion that the economy isn't on course to fall off track.

DEFLATORS

If GDP growth is the most important number in the release, the GDP deflators run a close second. As indicators of inflation, these deflators are preferred to the Consumer Price Index (CPI), the Producer Price Index (PPI), and other commodity price gauges by many traders and economists, including those at the Federal Reserve. Special favorites are the deflators for government consumption expenditures and gross investment, for personal consumption expenditures, and for personal consumption expenditures less food and energy, also known as PCEDXF&E. The Street has adopted the last deflator as an unofficial benchmark for the core rate of inflation. Bond traders in particular watch the deflators, knowing that greater-than-expected increases in these numbers usually depress fixed-income prices.

Why have the deflators superseded the other inflation measures? For starters, policymakers, traders, and investors in general, want to see overarching economic trends, not smaller, more targeted ones.

GDP deflators reflect price activity in the broader economy. The CPI, in contrast, is merely a "basket" of a few hundred goods and services, chosen by the Bureau of Labor Statistics. (For a fuller explanation of price activity and the core rate of inflation, see Chapter 12, Consumer and Producer Price Indices.)

Traders focus on movements in the personal consumption expenditure deflator excluding food and energy, commonly referred to as the Core PCED. This inflation measure is preferred to most of the others as it measures the core, ex-food and energy, rate of inflation that consumers face. Because prices of food and energy can fluctuate greatly during the month, economists like to view price trends without these noisy readings. Also, because private individuals are doing the overwhelming majority of the economy's consumption, and this indicator contains all of the goods and services consumed, as opposed to a couple of hundred as in the case with the CPI, the Core PCED has risen to the top of the list of most watched inflation gauges.

CONSUMPTION EXPENDITURES

As the consumer goes, so goes the U.S. economy. And this old saw may be more truthful than ever before. It is believed that the consumer's utter resilience to recent disruptions such as war, attacks against the United States on U.S. soil, widespread corporate malfeasance, eight of the top ten corporate bankruptcies in U.S. history, and presidential impeachment proceedings is the reason for the underlying strength of the economy. In previous decades, any single one of these disruptions likely would have upended the U.S. economy. Now it seems as though the consumer is capable of keeping the economy humming. It is the consumer that has prolonged expansion, and made recessions shorter and milder.

Generally, a drop in the growth rate of consumer spending is a surefire sign that the economy is on the verge of petering out. When people are feeling uneasy about the economic climate—perhaps unemployment is on the rise, or inflation is eroding the dollar's purchasing power, or individuals are just feeling tapped out—

it shows in their spending habits. As the chart in **FIGURE 1-11** shows, pronounced declines in the year-over-year growth in consumer expenditures have preceded each of the six recessions in the United States since 1963. Traditionally, the first retrenchment occurs in purchases of big-ticket items, such as durable goods. So it is in that portion of consumer spending where you'll find early warnings of economic downturns.

(For a more detailed discussion of consumer spending and its trends, see Chapter 11, Personal Income and Outlays.)

INVESTMENT SPENDING

Capital equipment comprises all the industrial and technological items used to produce other goods and services for sale. The amount of money companies invest in this equipment is thus a good predictor of future economic activity. It indicates whether corporate profitability is accelerating or decelerating, how managers view future economic conditions, and how strong or weak the economy is.

As explained earlier, the Street tends to focus on fixed investment—gross domestic investment minus inventories. Of the two categories of fixed investment, residential and nonresidential (or

Figure 1-11   Personal Consumption Expenditures

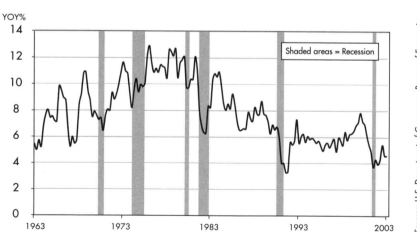

Sources: U.S. Department of Commerce, Bureau of Economic Analysis; NBER

capital spending), the former is by far the smaller, accounting for just 25 to 30 percent of the total. One shouldn't underestimate the influence of residential business investment, however. It represents roughly 4.5 percent of total economic output, and housing construction has a tremendous multiplier effect on the economy: Once a house or apartment building has been erected, personal consumption expenditures usually receive a big boost as owners head out to paint, decorate, and furnish their homes.

That said, analysts and economists tend to pay more attention to nonresidential investment. In part, this is because of the component's size—it accounts for almost three quarters of total fixed investment. It also provides a great deal of insight into how the corporate sector views economic conditions. Finally, many equity traders, especially those active in the Nasdaq and on the lookout for the next Microsoft or Intel, are particularly interested in technology investment, which falls into the nonresidential category.

A certain amount of nonresidential fixed investment always needs to be performed through the year regardless of the overall state of the economy. Equipment and machinery, for example, constantly need to be refurbished, updated, and repaired. Every year the auto industry shuts down its plants for about two weeks to allow engineers to retool machinery for upcoming new car models. Weather, overuse, and just plain wear and tear cause capital equipment to break down. During booming periods of technological advances, some capital equipment becomes obsolete. Upgrades often help a business raise its level of productivity, which in turn helps the company's bottom line.

Rising capital spending is generally associated with periods of solid corporate profitability and economic prosperity. For businesses to invest in new capital equipment, they need sufficient profit growth. After all, they can't spend what they don't have. (Actually businesses can spend or invest by borrowing via issuance of bonds. But if the company doesn't have respected profit growth, then the ability to obtain the financing is hampered. With a poor financial history, companies are saddled with low credit ratings and are forced to pay higher returns for borrowing those needed funds.)

Management also needs to be positive about the economic outlook. If conditions are soft and consumer demand unpromising, they will be less inclined to purchase new machinery and equipment. If, however, the economy is expanding at a respectable pace, economic fundamentals are conducive to continuing growth (low interest rates, low inflation, firm labor market growth), and consumers are spending, then businesses will be more likely to pick up the pace of their investment.

Capital equipment is generally very costly—think of the specialized machinery on automakers' assembly lines, the ovens and packaging systems in food-processing plants, the industrial-size kilns of cement manufacturers. Companies thus usually need to borrow to purchase it. So the amount of business investment is closely related to the level of interest rates: Lower rates ease spending; higher rates make it more difficult. Accordingly, the Federal Reserve can influence capital spending by altering its target for the Federal funds rate, the rate banks charge each other for overnight loans used to meet reserve requirements. If the Fed wants to spark capital spending, it lowers the overnight rate. Over time, yields on the entire maturity spectrum, from three-month Treasury bills to the ten-year Treasury note, decline as well, making it less expensive for businesses to finance costly investments such as new plants, factories, and equipment.

When investors realize that interest rates may be headed lower, whether as a result of slower inflation rates or by the Federal Reserve's influence, they know that businesses are likely to pick up the pace of investment, because the financing of those products and services is going to be cheaper. In order to capitalize on such developments, traders might bid-up the prices of those stocks that have their primary business in investment-related concerns like technology, machinery, tools, or capital equipment. Some of the more common companies that are involved in capital equipment include: Cummins Inc., Deere & Co., Paccar Inc., Briggs & Stratton, Danaher Corp., Dover Corp., Eaton Corp., Illinois Tool Works, Ingersoll-Rand, Parker-Hannifin Corp., Timken Co., and Wolverine Tube Inc.

GOVERNMENT SPENDING

Wall Street doesn't generally pay much attention to government consumption expenditures and gross investment. One reason is that number's stability. Since 1947, government spending and investment has accounted for about 15 percent of total economic output. Only during periods of profound economic weakness or military conflict does the percentage rise, as the government picks up the pace of spending to boost economic growth or to support the war effort. In the post–World War II era, a peak of 24 percent was registered in 1953, at the end of the Korean War.

Within the government data, however, is one item to which some economists do pay attention, especially in recent times. That item is national defense spending. The long-term trend in national defense as a percentage of total government spending since the end of World War II has been consistently downward. Still, increases (in some instances, slight) have occurred when the government has ramped up purchases for military conflicts such as the Korean War, in the early 1950s; Vietnam, in the mid-1960s to early 1970s; Desert Storm, in 1990; and, most recently, the war against terrorism in Afghanistan and Iraq. Keep in mind that government spending on national defense isn't limited to the increased output of aircraft, electronic tracking devices, and missiles. Greater defense spending raises the level of employment—everything from engineers to manufacturing positions. And due to security reasons, those jobs tend to stay here in the United States and are not shipped abroad as so many of the manufacturing positions have been in recent years.

Stock analysts responsible for the defense contractors and aerospace companies, such as Northrop Grumman, Raytheon, Lockheed Martin, General Dynamics, Curtiss-Wright, and Boeing, find the detail on national defense expenditures in the report a treasure trove. The category is broken down into spending on aircraft, missiles, ships, vehicles, electronics and software, ammunition, petroleum, and compensation. If the government bought it, it'll be recorded here.

NET EXPORTS

When the United States imports more than it exports—as has been the case for the better part of the past three decades—the net export balance is said to be in deficit. This reduces the level of GDP produced in a given period. Conversely, when exports outweigh imports, the trade balance is said to be in surplus. This results in an addition to economic activity. Such an outcome stands to reason, as U.S. export goods are produced by plants located in the United States whereas imports have been produced by foreigners and sent to the United States. **FIGURE 1-12** represents the value of net exports as a percent of GDP. This percentage has been negative for a majority of the last thirty years, implying that the pace of imports is greater than that of exports, which reduces the level of domestic economic activity.

Imports needn't have a negative connotation, however. A number of resources are not as abundant in the United States as they are outside its borders. One obvious example is crude oil. The United States has domestic sources of oil but not enough to fuel its consumption. For that reason, it has to import about half its crude oil from foreign countries. Should we consider these imports disapprovingly? Absolutely not. The mere fact that the United States consumes so much crude is testament to its economic vitality. Its plants and factories need a great deal of oil to produce what is the largest output in the world, employing millions of people and creating an economic climate that permits its citizens to prosper like no others on Earth. Spending on imports to heat our homes, run our transportation system, and conduct business should not be considered a drag on prosperity but an enhancement.

As with government expenditures, the trading community has little reason to get excited about the net export balance. It's true that the business community frowns on widening trade deficits, because increasing imports slow U.S. GDP growth. But rising imports also mean that U.S. businesses and households are consuming more goods and services that they deem attractive. Nobody forces consumers to purchase Italian wine, Japanese cars, or Canadian lumber.

Figure 1-12   Net Exports as a Percentage of GDP

Source: U.S. Department of Commerce, Bureau of Economic Analysis

U.S. businesses and households purchase foreign-made goods for any number of reasons including, price, quality, size, and taste. The primary force behind demand for foreign-produced goods is simply desirability.

Furthermore, several foreign produced goods tend to be cheaper. Because many countries in the world, particularly China, India, and several Asian-Pacific nations, have practically free labor, they are capable of producing goods at little cost. These low-priced products are usually sent to the United States, which influences the prices of similar U.S.-produced good. This globalization has led to a lower in-flation rate here in the United States—especially since the mid 1990s.

Perhaps the major reason investors ignore the trade data is the data's minor influence on total economic activity. Over the past fifty-five years, the net export position has averaged a mere half a percentage point of total economic output.

FINAL SALES

Included in the addenda to Table 1 in the GDP report are three measures little noted by the financial media but closely scrutinized by the trading community because of the insights they provide into the underlying spending patterns in the GDP numbers. These three indicators are the final sales of domestic product, gross domestic purchases, and final sales to domestic purchasers.

Final sales of domestic product is a measure of the dollar value of goods produced in the United States in a particular period that are actually sold, rather than put into inventory. To calculate this figure, the BEA first computes "the change in private inventories," or CPI, by comparing the current level of inventories with that of the previous period. This indicates how many goods have been added to businesses storage and thus how much of current production has remained unsold. CPI is then subtracted from GDP to give final sales. This is an important number, because it paints a more accurate picture than GDP of the current pace of spending in the economy. Economists say current pace because the quarterly figure excludes inventories that have been produced in previous quarters. Many times economists will compare the growth rates of GDP with those of final sales to determine whether economic growth is being driven by new production or by the consumption of goods that were previously produced and stored as inventories.

Gross domestic purchases measures all the goods U.S. residents have bought, no matter where the goods were produced. This figure is obtained by subtracting net exports from GDP. There is indeed a difference between GDP and gross domestic purchases. GDP is a measure of domestically-produced goods and services, while gross domestic purchases is a measure of all the goods domestically purchased. Strong quarterly increases in gross domestic purchases generally imply solid demand by U.S. consumers as only those purchases of domestic goods are calculated.

Final sales to domestic purchasers is the level of gross domestic purchases less the change in private inventories. It depicts the desire of Americans, both households and businesses, to spend, no matter where the goods or services are produced. Some economists consider it a good indicator of overall economic well-being. Slumping final sales to domestic purchasers suggests that U.S. consumers are tapped out.

Economists keep track of the year-over-year percentage change in final sales to domestic purchasers because of this measure's excellent record of foretelling periods of softer economic growth. As the chart in **FIGURE 1-13** illustrates, each of the four recessions since 1980 was preceded by about a three quarter long decline in the year-over-year growth rate of final sales to domestic purchasers.

CORPORATE PROFITS

Market participants don't generally pay as much attention to the income side as to the expenditure side of GDP. That isn't to say the trends in wages and salaries aren't important to economists or to analysts who cover retail issues. What could be more telling about the future pace of spending, after all, than the amount of income earned by would-be consumers? It's just that the trends of the expenditure side are accepted as being more accurate, because they aren't subject to inventory and capital-consumption value adjustments, as the income-determined data are. Still, some income-side components can give valuable insights into economic trends. Among the most important of these are the measures of corporate profits.

Figure 1-13   Final Sales to Domestic Purchasers

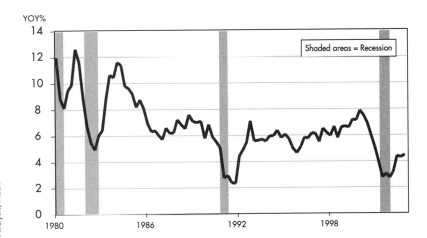

Sources: U.S. Department of Commerce, Bureau of Economic Analysis; NBER

As with most of the other measures discussed, a rise in corporate profits indicates a healthy business climate. The economy's growth cycle really starts with a lift in corporate profits. When businesses are successful, their incomes exceed costs, and they make profits. This permits them to invest in new capital equipment or employees.

Even more significant than pretax earnings are after-tax profits. From this figure, economists and analysts can judge how much money companies actually have to spend on new equipment or additional staff. As the chart in **FIGURE 1-14** shows, businesses generally shed workers when corporate profit growth contracted (below zero in the chart). The same holds true for business investment. After-tax corporate profits decline approximately three quarters prior to periods of slowing economic growth or recessions.

The best measure of the funds that companies have available for spending and hiring, however, is the level of undistributed profits. These are a company's earnings after tax payments and dividend distributions. One striking feature of the chart in **FIGURE 1-15**, which shows the amount of undistributed profits in the last third of the twentieth century, is the paltry level of undistributed profits during the early 1970s, 1987, and 2002. All three periods were associated

Figure 1-14   After-Tax Corporate Profits and Payroll Growth

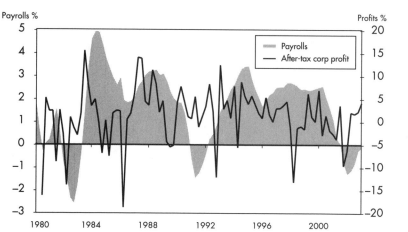

Sources: U.S. Department of Commerce, Bureau of Economic Analysis; U.S. Department of Labor, Bureau of Labor Statistics

with tumbling stock prices, high unemployment rates, and lackluster business investment.

The economic signals associated with corporate profits might not be as telling as they once were. As was noted earlier, in recent years the U.S. economy has become practically impervious to a whole host of negative influences that, if they had occurred in previous periods, would have resulted in recession and, in some instances, quite possibly depression. Beginning in early 2001, the stock market bubble of the late 1990s burst, wiping out trillions of dollars in personal wealth. Widespread accounting scandals and egregious corporate impropriety also hammered investors' confidence, stalling the financial markets. For the first time in more than fifty years, the United States was attacked on its own soil, virtually paralyzing the economy. Hundreds of thousands of businesses closed for weeks, and the borders were sealed. Fear of anthrax attacks was widespread. As if all of this weren't enough, U.S. armed forces engaged in military conflicts in Afghanistan and Iraq. Yet despite all these profoundly negative influences in a relatively short period, the economy managed to avoid a deep or prolonged recession. Perhaps the ultimate sign of resiliency is that consumer spending never fell.

Figure 1-15   Undistributed Profits

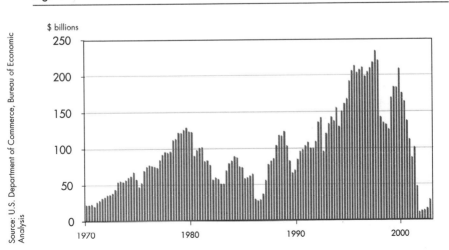

Source: U.S. Department of Commerce, Bureau of Economic Analysis

How to Use What You See

There aren't as many tricks associated with the National Income and Product Accounts as with other economic series. One reason may be that these accounts are the benchmark of economic activity, and traders use other indicators to anticipate movements in GDP. In other words, the level of GDP is usually the variable that other indicators attempt to forecast or emulate. GDP is also released on a quarterly basis, and the economic associations and relationships it points to aren't as predictive as those expressed on a monthly or weekly basis. That said, Wall Street economists and policymakers do have one particularly useful strategy that employs data from the GDP report: calculating the output gap.

Tricks From the Trenches

The output gap is the difference between the economy's actual and potential levels of production. This difference yields insight into important economic conditions, such as employment and inflation.

The economy's potential output is the amount of goods and services it would produce if it utilized all its resources. To determine this figure—the trend level—economists estimate the rate at which the economy can expand without sparking a rise in inflation. It is not an easy calculation, and it yields as many different answers as there are economists with different definitions for the maximum level of output, productivity, hours worked, and so on. Luckily, a widely accepted estimate of potential output is reported relatively frequently, about once a quarter, by the Congressional Budget Office. The CBO's website, www.cbo.gov, contains information about its methodology and underlying assumptions in computing the trend level, as well as a detailed historical data set.

A negative output gap exists when actual GDP growth is below its estimated potential. This suggests that the economy isn't utilizing all its labor and capital resources. Such periods of "undercapacitization" are usually characterized by high unemployment and low inflation, with plants and factories closing down, workers furloughed, and machinery idled. The chart in **FIGURE 1-16** shows that in 1990–91 and 2001–02, periods of profound economic weakness, the actual growth rate of real GDP was considerably below its potential.

When GDP growth exceeds its calculated potential, creating a positive gap, the economy is pushed to its limit. All plants and factories are running at capacity, the labor force is fully employed, and economic output is sky-rocketing. The chart in **FIGURE 1-17** illustrates the relationship between a positive gap and falling unemployment. In periods of overcapacitization, such as 1997–2001, strains on the system develop, usually sparking inflation.

Economists sometimes express the output gap in the form of a ratio, derived by dividing actual output by potential output. When this ratio falls below zero, conditions are recessional; when it rises above zero, conditions are expansionary.

Because the output gap provides such telling economic insight into a whole host of economic relationships, it is a favorite of policymakers. The Federal Reserve, for example, considers it in determining where to set the Fed funds rate. If the gap is negative, indicating that the economy is growing below its

Figure 1-16   GDP Versus Potential GDP

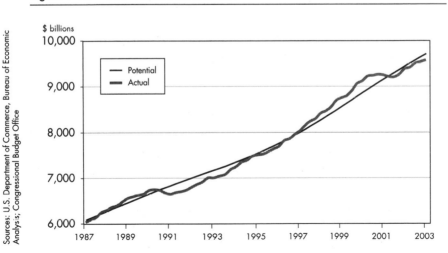

Sources: U.S. Department of Commerce, Bureau of Economic Analysis; Congressional Budget Office

Figure 1-17   Output Gap and Unemployment (inverted scale)

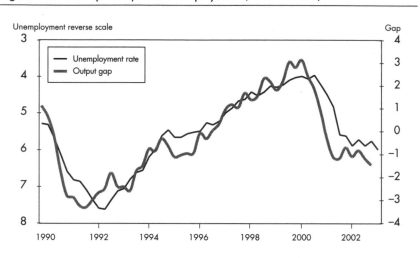

Sources: U.S. Department of Commerce, Bureau of Economic Analysis; Congressional Budget
Office; U.S. Department of Labor, Bureau of Labor Statistics

Figure 1-18   Output Gap and Fed Funds Rate

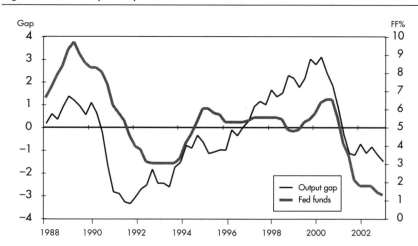

Sources: U.S. Department of Commerce, Bureau of Economic Analysis; Congressional Budget
Office; Board of Governors of the Federal Reserve System

potential, the Fed may try to spark activity by lowering the overnight rate. This results in a decline all along the maturity spectrum, making it easier for companies to fund capital projects. It also spurs individuals' spending by rendering loans to purchase items such as automobiles and homes more affordable. Conversely, when the gap is positive, indicating that the economic party is getting a bit out of hand, the Fed may take away the punch bowl by increasing its overnight target rate, thus discouraging consumers and businesses from spending and investing. The chart in **FIGURE 1-18** illustrates the tendency of the Fed funds rate to follow the output gap.

Indices of Leading, Lagging, and Coincident Indicators 2

I F A MARKET ECONOMIST were given one wish, it might be for a single indicator that would consistently predict both the direction and the pace of the economy. Unfortunately, none has so far been discovered that fits the entire bill. Some indicators are wonderful at pinpointing levels of activity but fail to depict trends. Others excel at identifying particular areas of economic strength and weakness but can't measure broad-based performance.

Unable to find a single omnipotent indicator, economists have taken an assortment of those showing the most predictive accuracy and combined them into the index of leading economic indicators (LEI). The LEI is one of three composite indices—along with the indices of lagging and coincident indicators—that the Conference Board compiles and publishes in its monthly Business Cycle Indicators report. This report is usually released to the public at 10:00 a.m. ET four to five weeks after the end of the record month. It is available, together with historical data and explanations of the methodology behind the indices, on the Conference Board's website, www.conference-board.org or www.globalindicators.org, and by subscription for a small annual fee.

Wall Streeters often refer to the entire Business Cycle Indicators report as the index of leading indicators, because that's the part to which they pay the most attention. In actuality, the charts, commentary, and data provided on all three indices are extremely useful in identifying and explaining the different phases of the business cycle. Whereas the leading economic index points to future trends and turning points, the coincident index identifies those that are in

Figure 2-1 Timing of the Composite Indices Relative to Cyclical Turning Points

	Composite Leading Index		Composite Coincident Index		Composite Lagging Index	
Leads (-) or lags (+) at business cycle peaks (months)						
Apr 1960	-11		0	-3*	+3	
Dec 1969	-8	-11*	-2		+3	
Nov 1973	-9		0		+13	
Jan 1980	-15		0		+3	
Jul 1981	-3	-8*	+1		+2	+3*
Jul 1990	-6**	-18*	-1		-9	-8*
Leads (-) or lags (+) at business cycle troughs (months)						
Feb 1961	-3	-2*	0		+9	+6*
Nov 1970	-7	-1*	0		+15	
Mar 1975	-1		0		+18	+21*
Jul 1980	-3	-2*	0		+3	
Nov 1982	-8	-10*	+1		+6	+7*
Mar 1991	-2		0		+21	+36*

*Timing of current (1997) version when different from the Department of Commerce peak/tough designations
**-25 for absolute peak in cycle

Source: The Conference Board

the process of developing, and the lagging index confirms that these events have indeed occurred. The table in **FIGURE 2-1** shows the number of months by which the three composite indicators led or lagged behind business cycle peaks or troughs, as defined by the National Bureau of Economic Research (NBER), from 1960 through 1991.

Because the indices' components are all released earlier than the indices themselves, the markets generally don't react strongly to the indicator report. Market participants, however, can still glean a great deal of information from the movements of the indices and their components, not to mention the commentary and interpretation that the Conference Board's staff economists supply each month.

EVOLUTION OF AN INDICATOR

The concept of composite economic indicators is not new, nor did it originate with the Conference Board. In the early 1930s, economists Arthur Burns and Wesley Mitchell at the NBER were already combining economic data series to identify trends and turning points in the economy. NBER first published the results of these efforts in 1938. By the 1960s, the U.S. Department of Commerce was releasing monthly reports containing the NBER's leading, lagging, and coincident indicators. The Commerce Department–NBER collaboration lasted until 1995, when the Conference Board—a private, nonprofit, nonadvocacy research and business-membership group—assumed the responsibilities of calculating, reporting, and maintaining the composite indices.

The leading, lagging, and coincident indices have all undergone considerable revision in the course of their history. As the structure of the U.S. economy has changed, newer indicators have periodically replaced older ones that no longer accurately reflected the business cycle or simply weren't calculated any more. As recently as November 1996, the Conference Board dropped two indicators—the price of sensitive materials and the volume of unfilled orders for manufactured durable goods—from the leading index and added a new one: the yield spread. This fine-tuning has kept the report an accurate tool for Wall Street economists and market participants.

DIGGING FOR THE DATA

The three indices in the Conference Board's report are composed from series of cyclical indicators, most of which are seasonally adjusted. When the indices are constructed, some of the components must be estimated; all are subject to later revision. The indices themselves thus also need to be revised. The monthly release contains both initial values for the record month and revisions for the previous six months.

In constructing an index, each component's month-over-month percentage change is calculated and then "standardized"—that is, it is adjusted for volatility so that indicators with more dramatic month-to-month movements won't dominate the index. The standardized percentage changes for all the index's components are then added together. The sums derived for the leading and lagging indices are adjusted again, so that their standard deviations equal that of the coincident index. Finally, the results for all three indices are translated into levels representing changes from a base date, currently 1996, whose level is set at 100.

Because the composition of the three indices is modified as the structure of the economy evolves, to remain in or be added to one of the indices, a component must demonstrate consistency as a leading, coincident, or lagging indicator. It must also be the end product of a reliable data-collection process; adhere to a timely publication schedule; and be subject to only minor, or no, revisions.

COINCIDENT INDEX

The four components of the Conference Board's coincident index are the number of employees on nonagricultural (i.e., nonfarm) payrolls (thousands), personal income less transfer payments (nominal rate in billions 1996$), industrial production index (1997=100), and manufacturing and retail trade sales (in millions of 1996$).

The **number of employees on nonagricultural payrolls,** is obtained from a survey of about 160,000 businesses, conducted by the Bureau of Labor Statistics. The change in this number is one of the headline figures in the BLS's monthly Employment Situation report (see Chapter 3). The path followed by nonfarm payrolls has, in the main, paralleled that of growth in gross domestic product (GDP).

Personal income less transfer payments is derived from the Personal Income and Outlays report, produced by the Bureau of Economic Analysis (BEA) (see Chapter 11). The largest income source is wages and salaries, which account for about 55 percent of the total; transfer payments—government disbursements such as Social Security payments, veteran's benefits, and food stamps—usually constitute about 15 percent. Transfer payments are generally spent immediately on basic necessities, such as food or rent, not on durable goods and services. They thus have relatively little influence on macroeconomic activity. So income less transfer payments is generally considered a stronger, more representative economic indicator.

The total industrial production index is the headliner of the monthly Industrial Production and Capacity Utilization report published by the Federal Reserve (see Chapter 4). It is constructed of 295 components—representing the manufacturing, mining, and utilities industries—that are weighted according to the value they add during the production process. The index mirrors the general economy so closely that it is often used as a more timely proxy for the quarterly GDP report.

Manufacturing and retail trade sales data are collected as part of the National Income and Product Accounts calculations. These data may be found in the Manufacturing and Trade Inventories and Sales (MTIS) report published by the Department of Commerce. (For additional information, see the discussion of the sales portion of the MTIS report examined in Chapter 7.)

LEADING ECONOMIC INDEX

The ten components of the leading index are the following:
1. Average weekly hours worked in manufacturing
2. Average weekly initial claims for unemployment insurance
3. Manufacturers' new orders for consumer goods and materials
4. The slower deliveries diffusion index of vendor performance
5. Manufacturers' new orders for nondefense capital goods
6. Monthly building permits for new private housing
7. Stock prices, 500 common stocks
8. The M2 money supply (in 1996 dollars)
9. The interest rate spread between the 10-year Treasury bond and the federal funds rate
10. The Index of Consumer Expectations

The rationale behind including some of these indicators is clear from their names: new "orders" and "expectations," for instance, are obviously forward looking. The inclusion of others is less self-evident. All the components, however, were chosen because of their potency as *predictors* of economic activity.

The number of **average weekly hours worked in manufacturing** is derived from the same survey as the nonagricultural payroll figure described above and is also published in the BLS's Employment Situation report. Average weekly manufacturing hours constitute a good measure of future production levels and economic strength. Assuming workers maintain the same level of productivity, the more hours they put in on the job, the greater their output. When manufacturers foresee a softening in demand for their products, they tend to reduce the number of workers' hours before cutting staff, which is more time-consuming and expensive to implement. It is also easier and cheaper to extend hours, should business seem poised to pick up, than to hire new employees. Substantial changes in the average hours worked thus reflect companies' pessimism or optimism about future economic conditions.

The **average number of weekly initial claims for unemployment** reflects the condition of the labor market (see Chapter 3). A rise in claims, as businesses lay off more and more employees, usually occurs in the early stages of economic downturns and can thus point to a coming recession. The correlation between jobless claims and the economy is not precise, however, in part because unemployment statistics are distorted by the differing eligibility requirements imposed by different states.

Manufacturers' new orders for consumer goods and materials and for nondefense capital goods are excellent signs of how businesses regard the coming economic climate (see Chapter 6). Given the expenses involved in financing large purchases and in carrying inventory, wholesalers and retailers don't place orders for consumer goods unless they foresee a demand for these products. Similarly, companies don't invest in costly capital goods unless they believe they'll need the additional production capacity or efficiency created by such investments. Capital goods orders constitute a particularly powerful leading indicator, because business investment makes up approximately 15 percent of total GDP.

The **vendor performance diffusion index** is one of the five seasonally adjusted diffusion indices that the Institute for Supply Management uses to construct the Purchasing Managers' Index (PMI), the headline index of its monthly Manufacturing ISM Report on Business (see Chapter 5). The vendor index—which the ISM creates from responses to its survey of approximately 400 purchasing managers across the United States—measures how long it takes suppliers to deliver parts and materials that are integral to the production process. Readings above 50 percent indicate slowing deliveries, usually a sign of increased demand and robust economic activity; readings below 50 percent indicate faster deliveries and economic stagnation.

Statistics concerning **building permits for new private housing** are contained in the New Residential Construction report, released jointly by the U.S. Department of Housing and Urban Development and the U.S. Department of Commerce's Census Bureau (see Chapter 8). These data present insights into an element of the U.S. economy that both is crucial to its growth and signals its general well-being. Although new housing construction accounts directly for only a small percentage of GDP, it drives other activity, such as purchases of paint, home furnishings, and countless other consumer durables. Moreover, because buying a house is a huge undertaking for most individuals, it implies confidence in the stability of employment and earnings, as well as sound economic fundamentals.

The **stock price** component of the LEI is the monthly average for the S&P 500 Index, published in the S&P publication *The Outlook*. Inclusion of this has been questioned by some economists, who argue that stock prices are determined by speculation rather than by economic fundamentals and so should not be considered accurate gauges of future economic activity. The rationale for including stock prices is that they reflect the informed expectations of sophisticated traders and investors. To get ahead of the curve, these knowledgeable market participants make their trades before earnings are actually announced. Rising equity prices thus indicate expectations of greater corporate profitability, which in turn implies an expanding economy: When businesses are more profitable, they are better able to invest in new projects, plants, and factories, and to hire additional workers. Falling prices, conversely, indicate that investors expect lower profitability, which in turn means a slower economy.

Money supply is simply the amount of money in the economy. The Federal Reserve recognizes three types of monetary aggregates, which it labels M1, M2, and M3. The leading economic index uses M2, which in addition to currency in circulation and deposits in savings and checking accounts includes money market fund shares and other liquid assets, such as overnight repurchase agreements issued by commercial banks.

Economists commonly refer to money as the oil in the engine of economic activity. So it makes sense that the growth rate of the money supply is related to the growth rate of the economy. The relationship that associates money with economic activity is called the quantity theory of money, which may be summed in the following expression: $M \times V = GDP$, where M is the money supply; V is the velocity of money—how often a dollar changes hands in a given period—and GDP is the nominal gross domestic product (see Chapter 1).

Economists have assumed that velocity changes slowly, if at all, over time. Given this assumption, any increase in the money supply would be mirrored by an increase in nominal GDP. Conversely, a contraction in money supply would be reflected in a contracting economy. This relationship is illustrated in the chart in **FIGURE 2-2**.

Economists have discovered, however, that the velocity of money has not been constant. Without V as a constant, the equation of exchange breaks down. Historically, velocity levels have varied for a number of reasons, including new regulations and innovations in banking such as the advent of ATM machines, direct-deposit banking, and e-banking. Still, the relationship between money and economic activity enjoys a long, successful association, as evidenced in the associated chart, and is therefore included in the index of leading economic indicators.

Figure 2-2　Changes in Money Supply and in GDP

Sources: Board of Governors of the Federal Reserve System; The Conference Board

The **interest rate spread** component of the leading index is the difference between the 10-year Treasury note yield and the Federal funds rate—the rate banks charge one another on overnight loans needed to meet reserve requirements set by the Federal Reserve. For instance, if the Fed funds rate is 3.25 percent and the 10-year Treasury is yielding 5.35 percent, the spread is 2.10 percent, or 210 basis points (a basis point is one-hundredth of a percent). The interest rate spread is included among the leading indicators because the shape of the yield curve embodies fixed-income traders' expectations about the economy, and interest rate spreads determine the shape of the yield curve.

The yield curve plots yields of U.S. Treasury securities against their maturities. Longer-term rates are usually higher than shorter-term ones, because more things can affect the value of the bond in ten years than in two, and lenders require greater rewards for undertaking these greater risks. Thus, under "normal," economically favorable conditions, interest rate spreads are positive, and the shape of the yield curve is gently convex—rising somewhat more steeply at the short end and leveling off a bit at the longer maturities.

Steep curves—large spreads—may temporarily be the result of current economic weakness. The Federal Reserve seeks to counter such weakness by pushing down the overnight rate, thus lowering borrowing costs and encouraging business investment and consumer spending on interest rate–sensitive goods and services like housing and automobiles. This move stimulates the economy but can spark inflationary fears among the fixed-income community. Inflation erodes the value of future interest and principal payments. In anticipation, fixed-income investors sell off longer-term (more inflation-sensitive) bonds, depressing their prices and raising their yields. This, combined with the Fed's lowering of the short-term rate, steepens the yield curve. Conversely, when the economy seems to be running too hot, the Fed may seek to forestall a rise in inflation by raising its overnight target rate, discouraging spending and so slowing growth. The result is a flatter curve (smaller spreads).

The curve may also invert, with short-term rates rising above long-term ones and spreads falling below zero. This situation is generally associated with economic downturns, even recessions, as illustrated in **FIGURE 2-3**: The coincident index—which, because it reflects current economic conditions, may serve as a proxy for the business cycle—declines every time the spread between the Fed funds rate and the 10-year Treasury becomes negative. This close correlation is one reason the Conference Board decided to

Figure 2-3   The Interest Rate Spread and the Coincident Index

Sources: Board of Governors of the Federal Reserve System; The Conference Board

include this gauge in its index of leading economic indicators.

Why does an inverted yield curve predict recessions? There is no definitive answer. Actually, one answer sometimes put forward is that an inverted curve may result from the Fed overdoing it—raising rates so high they not only cool but stifle growth (as well as any fears of inflation). What is clear is that expectations of weak economic conditions may encourage expectations of lower interest rates. This in turn leads to more purchases of longer-term bonds, pushing up their prices and lowering their yields. The result is an inverted curve.

The **Index of Consumer Expectations** is compiled monthly, along with the indices of Consumer Sentiment and Current Economic Conditions, by the University of Michigan's Survey Research Center, using responses to the university's Survey of Consumers. The survey asks consumers about their personal financial situations, overall economic conditions, and their buying attitudes, as well as various current issues and concerns. The Index of Consumer Expectations summarizes the economic trends the respondents foresee.

Including this index among the leading indicators is a no-brainer. Consumer expectations about the economy are mainly shaped by their experiences in the workplace. High confidence springs from expanding employment, increased production schedules, and rising wages and thus points to a positive economic climate. It also helps foster that climate by encouraging spending, one of the major contributors to GDP. On the other hand, consumers are among the first to sense worsening economic conditions, reflected in slowdowns at their workplaces, and to retrench. This generally depresses the economy further. Not surprisingly, then, the Index of Consumer Expectations has a good record of predicting turning points in both consumer spending and total economic activity.

LAGGING INDEX

The lagging index has the following seven components:
1. Average duration of unemployment
2. Ratio of manufacturing and trade inventories to sales

3. Manufacturing labor cost per unit of output
4. Average prime rate
5. Commercial and industrial loans outstanding
6. Ratio of consumer installment credit to personal income
7. Change in the Consumer Price Index for services

The average duration of unemployment is the average number of weeks that people are out of work (see also Chapter 3). As this number rises, so does consumer frustration, which depresses spending and holds back economic growth. Decreases in the length of unemployment traditionally occur after a recovery is already under way. This is generally a function of business's reluctance to take on new workers until they are absolutely assured of recovery. Similarly, the steepest rises generally take place after a downturn has begun. That is why this is a lagging indicator.

The ratio of manufacturing and trade inventories to sales is calculated by the U.S. Department of Commerce's Census Bureau, using data from its Manufacturers' Shipments, Inventories, and Orders, or M3, survey (see Chapter 6) and its Wholesale Trade Survey. The results are published in the Commerce Department's monthly Manufacturing and Trade Inventories and Sales (MTIS) report (see Chapter 7). The ratio indicates how many months, given the current pace of sales, it will take for inventories to be entirely liquidated. A rising ratio means that businesses are unable to effect a steady reduction in their back stock, either because sales are too weak or their inventories are accumulating too fast. In either case, this is a sign of economic weakness. A falling ratio, conversely, indicates that companies' shelves are emptying and that manufacturers may soon have to ramp up production to replenish their disappearing stocks—a bullish economic signal. Although economists watch the ratio for insight into future production activity, it is a lagging economic indicator. That's because, historically, inventories rise long after sales growth has halted. So the ratio reaches its peak in the middle of a recession.

The percentage change in **manufacturing labor cost per unit of output** is measured by an index constructed by the Conference

Board from sources including the BEA's seasonally adjusted data on manufacturing employees' compensation and by the Federal Reserve Board's data on manufacturing production. The index rises when manufacturers' labor costs increase faster than their output. Because monthly index movements are erratic, the percentage change used is measured over a six-month period. Peaks in the six-month rate of change are typically reached during recessions.

Data on the average monthly **prime rate** are compiled by the Fed. As the interest rate that banks charge their most creditworthy customers, such as blue-chip companies, the prime rate serves as a benchmark for loans to lesser credits. For instance, a smaller, younger company might have to pay two percentage points over prime. Because the prime rate moves with respect to changes in the federal funds overnight rate, periods of rising prime rates are usually the result of rate hikes instituted by the Federal Reserve, foreseeing a potential overheating in the economy and possible mounting inflationary pressures. Falling prime rates are usually the result of Fed rate reductions in their overnight target rate, which are engendered to stimulate economic activity. Banks tend to change the prime rate only after movements occur in the general economy.

The value of **outstanding commercial and industrial loans** is computed by the Fed and adjusted for inflation by the Conference Board. High commercial and industrial loan levels are an indication that businesses have a favorable economic outlook, and are willing to build and expand their operations, and finance these plans via loaned monies. Conversely, when the outlook is less encouraging, and businesses skeptical, loan growth is weaker. It tends to reach a peak after an expansion reaches its high-water mark and to bottom out more than a year after the end of a recession.

The **ratio of consumer installment credit to personal income** is computed using data from the Fed's monthly release detailing the amount of currently outstanding consumer credit as well as from the BEA's monthly Personal Income and Outlays report (see Chapter 11). Consumer credit is not included in the BEA income figure, but for many Americans it is a critical income supplement. In times of financial insecurity, such as those that occur during downturns and recessions, people tend to reduce their personal borrowing and don't pick up the pace again until a trend of increasing income is firmly established. Accordingly, this ratio generally reaches its nadir a year or more after the end of a recession.

Change in the Consumer Price Index for services measures the movement in the services component of the CPI, which is composed monthly by the BLS (see Chapter 12). The month-to-month change in the CPI is the most popular measure of inflation. Service-sector inflation tends to increase after a recession has already begun and decrease even after it has ended. These tendencies result from what has been termed recognition lags and other such rigidities in the market.

WHAT DOES IT ALL MEAN?

The Conference Board's function in creating, refining, and maintaining the leading, lagging, and coincident indices, presented monthly in its Business Cycle Indicators report, shouldn't be confused with what the National Bureau of Economic Research does. The NBER is the official arbiter of peaks and troughs in the business cycle. In pinpointing the dates of these crucial turning points, the bureau's economists consider many factors and consult several indicators, including, but not limited to, components of the coincident index. The Conference Board's Business Cycle Indicators report does not determine the official peaks and troughs of the U.S. economy. However, the turning points these indicators signal are remarkably similar to those the NBER designates.

COINCIDENT INDEX

The coincident index is rarely mentioned in the business press. Still, it is very useful for assessing the current pace of economic activity. As the table in Figure 2-1 demonstrates, the coincident index tracks closely the turning points in the business cycles. It can thus serve as a benchmark in assessing the relationship of any economic statistic to the business cycle. One of the most commonly used representatives of this cycle is the GDP. A simple linear regression between

Figure 2-4 Index of Coincident Economic Indicators and GDP

Sources: The Conference Board; U.S. Department of Commerce, Bureau of Economic Analysis

the growth rates of real GDP and the coincident index yields an impressive correlation of 86 percent. This close correlation, illustrated in **FIGURE 2-4**, makes the coincident index a useful, more timely proxy for the quarterly GDP.

LEADING ECONOMIC INDEX

The individual indicators composing the LEI differ considerably in their abilities to predict economic turning points. Some are very far-seeing, others relatively nearsighted. The composite index combines these components in such away that the whole outperforms any of its parts. The predictive accuracy of the composite is illustrated in **FIGURE 2-5**, which charts the quarterly year-over-year percent change in the LEI against real GDP.

The chart clearly shows that hikes and dips in the LEI precede those in the economy by significant periods. According to the latest research, the index's average lead time is nine months. The individual periods composing this average, however, vary considerable. This is in part because of the revisions that the index's components undergo, necessitating commensurate revisions in the composite. It also reflects the fact that every recession and every

Figure 2-5   Index of Leading Economic Indicators and GDP

Sources: The Conference Board; U.S. Department of Commerce, Bureau of Economic Analysis; NBER

recovery is caused by different sets of circumstances. The LEI's ability to foresee these turning points therefore also varies.

LAGGING INDEX

The lagging index follows downturns in the business cycle (as represented by the coincident index) by about three months and expansions by about fifteen. At first blush, this may seem to be pretty useless information—like driving a car by looking through the rearview mirror. Economists, however, argue that you can't know where you're going if you don't know where you've been. The index of lagging economic indicators confirms that turning points in economic activity that were identified by the leading and coincident indices actually have occurred. It thus helps prevent the transmission of false signals.

HOW TO USE WHAT YOU SEE

Market participants don't generally pay a great deal of attention to the Conference Board's Business Cycle Indicators report because they've already had a chance to view and process for themselves the underlying data. Nevertheless, economists and businesses have traditionally looked for longer-term trends in the leading index to predict turning points in the economy.

The old rule of thumb was that three consecutive monthly declines in the index signaled a recession within a year, whereas three consecutive increases signaled a recovery. This rule was roughly accurate. It did predict several recessions that failed to materialize, however, and in the case of some correct calls, the lead times were negative—that is, the predictions came after the recession was already established. A reason for false recession predictions could be that although the index contains components representing the manufacturing, consumer, financial, employment, and business investment sectors, it has none that reflect demand for or investment and employment in the services industries that now dominate the economy. Moreover, the financial sectors that are represented often move in ways that don't parallel movement in the broader economy, generating both volatility and some of the false signals mentioned.

The LEI's record of calling, as a popular quip has it, "seven of the last five recessions" has led some cynics to term it the index of *mis*leading indicators. That's not really fair. Still, to improve its predictive accuracy, economists often consider the LEI's moves in three dimensions—duration, depth, and diffusion—instead of just one, duration, as the three-month rule did. That is, in addition to requiring that changes extend over three months, the refined method looks at how large changes are and how many components are involved. For example, if nine of the index's ten components show increases, but one—say the level of average weekly hours worked in manufacturing—falls, an expansion is more certain than if only four components increase, three decrease, and three are unchanged.

TRICKS FROM THE TRENCHES

Wall Streeters, being innovators, have sought ways to improve even on the three-dimensional analysis. Their trick, with respect to the Business Cycle Indicators report, is to compute the ratio of the co-

Figure 2-6   Coincident-to-Lagging Ratio and Recessions*

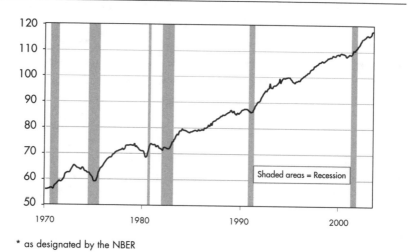

Shaded areas = Recession

Sources: The Conference Board; NBER

* as designated by the NBER

incident index to the lagging index. The theory behind this ratio, informally referred to as the coincident-to-lagging index, is this: In the early stages of a recovery, coincident indicators are rising while lagging ones, reflecting the conditions of earlier months, remain unchanged, resulting in a rising ratio. When an expansion is peaking, both sets of indicators will be rising, but the rate of increase for the coincident ones will be slower, so the ratio will fall. Similarly, near the nadir of a recession, all the component indicators will again be moving in the same direction—this time, down—but the coincident ones will fall more slowly, so the ratio will rise.

As you can see from the chart in **FIGURE 2-6**, the coincident-to-lagging ratio, like the LEI, has declined before every recession since 1959. But it has transmitted fewer false signals. One explanation for this relative success is that the coincident and lagging indices do a better job of representing, respectively, current and past economic performance than the leading index does of assessing future activity.

The Employment Situation 3

THE MOST IMPORTANT economic indicator by far is the monthly Employment Situation, published by the Bureau of Labor Statistics (BLS). No economic release can move stocks and bonds like employment, and no indicator is more revealing of general economic conditions than labor market data. This is why the first Friday of every month, when the Employment Situation is released, is the most important trading session of the month.

The fixed-income market often moves violently, in a matter of seconds, after the employment report is released. The Dow Jones Industrial Average, which begins trading an hour after the report's release, has on occasion opened up or down from the previous day's close by a couple hundred points. The employment report is so crucial to financial market participants that dealers, brokers, and economists plan their vacations around its release. Many traders can "make their month" (i.e., earn a month's salary in a single trading session) on the day the report is released. People have actually been fired for missing the 8:30 a.m. EST release.

Employment data are important because they reveal how firms, corporations, and others responsible for hiring decisions view the current and upcoming economic environment. Companies will not shoulder the expenses involved in adding to their payrolls if they believe they won't need the extra workers in the near future. Similarly, they will be reluctant to dismiss workers if they foresee increasing demand for their wares. From the household perspective, nothing is more important than employment status. It is said that consumers can be expected to cut spending when faced with higher prices or declining wealth. Truth be told, consumers will indeed continue to spend despite higher prices and lower portfolio values. But nothing erodes consumer attitudes and subsequently stops a consumer from spending like the loss of a job. Because consumer expenditures account for about 70 percent of economic activity, every economist, trader, and investor should know the current condition of the labor market.

The monthly employment report is based on two separate surveys: the Current Population Survey (CPS), known as the household survey, and the Current Employment Statistics survey (CES), referred to as the establishment, or payrolls, survey. The household data are aggregated and disseminated in the "A" tables found in the first half of the report; the establishment survey information is presented in the "B" tables. The Street tends to pay more attention to the B than to the A tables.

Supplemental to each release, the commissioner of the Bureau of Labor Statistics provides a statement to the Joint Economic Committee of the U.S. Congress. The statement, generally three pages long, highlights significant strengths and weaknesses in the month's employment statistics.

The employment report contains several headliners, but top billing is generally shared by two figures: the unemployment rate and the monthly change in nonfarm payrolls. Average hourly earnings, hours worked, overtime hours worked, and the monthly change in manufacturing jobs also command a great deal of Wall Street's attention. Unlike many other economic releases, the Employment Situation takes a great deal of time to digest.

When unexpected increases in the unemployment rate occur, the equity markets generally sell off. The same occurs when nonfarm payrolls decline by a particularly large amount—usually in the vicinity of 150,000 or more. Because employment determines income and spending, and consumer spending accounts for the largest portion of economic activity, traders like to see solid employment growth. When the unemployment rate declines and jobs are being created, stock prices tend to rise.

Things are different in the fixed-income market, which is sensitive to inflation threats. Increasing nonfarm payrolls and a falling unemployment rate spark inflation fears, which can cause a sell-off in bonds, depressing prices and raising yields.

EVOLUTION OF AN INDICATOR

Like many of the most respected economic indicators, the Employment Situation report was born in the 1930s, during the Great Depression. The BLS had conducted the first monthly studies of employment and payrolls in 1915, but these covered only four manufacturing industries. By 1932, ninety-one manufacturing and fifteen nonmanufacturing industries were participating in the surveys. The deepening economic crisis of the early 1930s led the Hoover administration to expand the BLS program to include working hours and earnings series. Statistics on average weekly hours and hourly earnings were published for the first time in 1933. At the same time that this program was proceeding nationally, another was being rolled out on the state level. In 1915, New York and Wisconsin entered into agreements with the BLS to provide the agency with state employment data. This pact grew to embrace all the states in the union plus the District of Columbia and, today, Puerto Rico and the Virgin Islands. The state and national efforts evolved into the Current Employment Statistics survey, the source for Table B data in the employment report.

The Current Population Survey, the source for Table A, started as a program of the Work Projects Administration, or WPA, which in 1940 initiated a national survey of households called the Monthly Report of Unemployment. Responsibility for the survey was transferred to the Census Bureau in late 1942, and a few years later its name was changed to the Current Population Survey. In 1959, the Bureau of Labor Statistics, within the Census Bureau, took over the job.

Both surveys have undergone refinements in sampling and reporting techniques, incorporating advances in computer-aided data-gathering and voice-recognition technologies. The result is that today we have a timely, accurate, and comprehensive indicator of labor market conditions, reported from both the employees' and the employers' perspective.

DIGGING FOR THE DATA

In its employment surveys, the BLS includes only persons older than sixteen. That seems logical, because most U.S. states have compulsory education for youths through sixteen years of age, and several states prohibit the employment of minors in many jobs. Also excluded from surveys are people in mental or penal institutions and members of the armed forces.

The monthly employment report includes figures for one-month, three-month, six-month, and twelve-month periods. To understand the significance of these figures, you need to know what is denoted by terms such as *employed* and *unemployed*. The meanings may seem obvious, but BLS uses these and related words in quite precise senses, developed through years of debate and experience.

People qualify as employed in two ways. First are those who, during a given period, have worked as paid employees in someone else's company or in their own businesses or on their own farms or have done fifteen hours or more of unpaid labor in a family-operated enterprise. Second are those with jobs or in businesses from which they have taken temporary leave, paid or unpaid, because of illness, bad weather, vacation, child-care problems, labor disputes, maternity or paternity leave, or other family or personal obligations.

Unemployed people are those not working during the period in question, whether because they voluntarily terminated their employment, in which case they are classified as *job leavers*, or because they were involuntarily laid off, making them *job losers*. Although the report doesn't make this distinction, economists identify several types of unemployment: *Seasonal unemployment* results from short-term cyclical changes in the labor market; examples include the January layoffs of retail staff who were added to take care of the Christmas shopping push, and the winter furloughs of construction and landscaping workers in regions where harsh weather make such activity virtually impossible. *Frictional unemployment* refers to the situation of workers in the process of changing occupations who are temporarily between jobs. *Structural unemployment* is the result of economic restructuring caused by new technologies or other innovations, as when the invention of the automobile put buggy-whip makers out of a job. Finally, *cyclical unemployment*, the most relevant type for Wall Street economists, occurs when jobs are eliminated as part of the business cycle, because of declining demand and the consequent drop in production.

To be included among the unemployed, a person must have made an effort to find work. Those who have given up looking, believing their skills, qualifications, or geographic area preclude finding a job, are regarded as *discouraged workers*. Increasing numbers of discouraged workers usually signal a weak economy.

Discouraged workers and others who don't fit into either the employed or unemployed groups are classified as "not in the labor force." The percentage of the employable population that *is* in the labor force is known as the **labor force participation rate**. This rate is generally in the mid-60 percent range. The **employment-population ratio** is the percentage of employed persons in the total population. It is usually lower than the participation rate.

HOUSEHOLD SURVEY (A TABLES)

Officially called the Current Population Survey, the household survey contains the responses of a sample of about 60,000 households to questions about work and job searches. It is generally conducted during the week containing the nineteenth day of the month. This is known as the **survey week**. It addresses employment conditions during the week containing the twelfth of the month, which is known as the **reference week**. The statistics gathered are compiled and presented in the following tables:

- **Table A.** Major indicators of labor market activity, seasonally adjusted
- **Table A-1.** Employment status of the civilian population by sex and age

- **Table A-2.** Employment status of the civilian population by race, sex, and age
- **Table A-3.** Employment status of the Hispanic or Latino population by sex and age
- **Table A-4.** Employment status of the civilian population 25 years and over by educational attainment
- **Table A-5.** Employed persons by class of worker and part-time status
- **Table A-6.** Selected employment indicators
- **Table A-7.** Selected unemployment indicators, seasonally adjusted
- **Table A-8.** Unemployed persons by reason for unemployment
- **Table A-9.** Unemployed persons by duration of unemployment
- **Table A-10.** Employed and unemployed persons by occupation, not seasonally adjusted
- **Table A-11.** Unemployed persons by industry, not seasonally adjusted
- **Table A-12.** Alternative measures of labor underutilization
- **Table A-13.** Persons not in the labor force and multiple jobholders by sex, not seasonally adjusted

The nation's civilian unemployment rate is calculated by dividing the number of unemployed workers by the civilian labor force, the figures of which are listed in the household survey. In June 2003, for example, the unemployment rate was computed to be 6.4 percent: 9.358 million unemployed divided by the 147.096 million person labor force.

ESTABLISHMENT SURVEY (B TABLES)

The establishment survey is based on a sample of about 160,000 businesses comprising some 400,000 individual work sites. Like the household survey, it is conducted with respect to a reference week, in this case the pay period containing the twelfth day of the month. The data are organized in the following tables:

- **Table B-1.** Employees on nonfarm payrolls by industry sector and selected industry detail
- **Table B-2.** Average weekly hours of production or nonsupervisory workers on nonfarm payrolls by industry sector and selected industry detail
- **Table B-3.** Average hourly and weekly earnings of production or nonsupervisory workers on nonfarm payrolls by industry sector and selected industry detail
- **Table B-4.** Average hourly earnings of production or nonsupervisory workers on nonfarm payrolls by industry sector and selected industry detail, seasonally adjusted
- **Table B-5.** Indices of aggregate weekly hours of production or nonsupervisory workers on nonfarm payrolls by industry sector and selected industry detail
- **Table B-6.** Indices of aggregate weekly payrolls of production or nonsupervisory workers on nonfarm payrolls by industry sector and selected industry detail
- **Table B-7.** Diffusion indices of employment change, seasonally adjusted

Nonfarm payrolls fall into two categories: goods-producing and goods-providing. The goods-producing category includes manufacturing jobs, which account for 66 percent of the category total; construction jobs, accounting for 30 percent; and jobs in natural resources and mining, 4 percent. The majority of manufacturing positions are in the production of transportation equipment, mostly motor vehicles. Other big manufacturing sectors are food manufacturing, fabricated metal products, computer and electronic products, machinery, and chemicals. The majority of construction jobs are with specialty trade contractors, such as tradesmen engaged in practices such as drywall and insulation, framing, roofing, siding, electrical, masonry, and painting.

Over the past six decades, the U.S. economy has changed from one based on manufacturing, with a heavily unionized labor force, to one dominated by service industries. Service jobs, which fall in the goods-providing category, currently make up about 81 percent of total nonfarm payrolls, compared with 56 percent during World War II. Service payrolls are grouped into the following categories:

- government
- education and health services
- professional and business services
- retail trade
- leisure and hospitality
- finance, insurance, and real estate (FIRE)
- transportation and warehousing
- information
- other

Economists pay particular attention to the growth rate of total private payrolls, that is, the number of employees on nonfarm and nongovernmental payrolls. During periods of sub-par economic growth, economists ideally wish to see widespread growth in payrolls across several industries. If job creation is limited to the government sector, it may be a signal that private industry is not very confident with the economic environment and may not be willing to hire new workers.

As shown by the chart in FIGURE 3-1, the level of employment deduced from the household survey is different from, and generally higher than, that gleaned from the establishment survey. This is largely because of the differences between their methodologies, pools of respondents, sample sizes, and reference periods. That said, the trends in employment revealed by the two surveys are largely the same.

The data obtained in the establishment survey are used in constructing the personal income report (aggregate earnings), industrial production and capacity utilization report (aggregate hours in manufacturing, mining, and public utilities), the Conference Board's indices of leading and coincident economic indicators (average weekly hours in manufacturing and employment, respectively), and the quarterly productivity measures (aggregate hours). This survey attracts considerable attention from the investment

Figure 3-1   Employment Levels per Household Survey Versus Establishment Survey

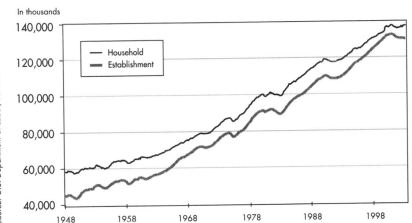

Source: U.S. Department of Labor, Bureau of Labor Statistics

community and the business media. Because the data come directly from corporations and firms, economists tend to trust these figures more than the household statistics that are gathered via subjective, and less scientific telephone interviews.

WHAT DOES IT ALL MEAN?

As has been noted, no indicator is as telling about the economic state of affairs, on as timely a basis, as the BLS's monthly Employment Situation. It is the first comprehensive report of the month that presents both business and household perspectives on the most important of all economic measures: employment.

Strong relationships exist between the employment data and virtually every other economic indicator. The growth rate of nonfarm payrolls, for instance, is strongly correlated with the growth rate of GDP, industrial production and capacity utilization, consumer confidence, spending, income—even with Federal Reserve activity. If it's relevant to economic activity, it will have links with the payrolls data.

Figure 3-2 Nonfarm Payroll Growth and GDP

Sources: U.S. Department of Labor, Bureau of Labor Statistics; U.S. Department of Commerce, Bureau of Economic Analysis

EMPLOYMENT, UNEMPLOYMENT, AND THE BUSINESS CYCLE

The ties between employment and the business cycle are extremely close. As **FIGURE 3-2** illustrates, the quarterly change in nonfarm payrolls has, in the main, hewed closely to the path of quarterly GDP growth. This association is very useful for those monitoring economic growth. The GDP report is released quarterly, with a one-month delay. The employment report is monthly. So those needing a timely read on the economy can infer its growth rate from the payrolls data.

One corollary of employment's intimate relationship with GDP growth is the coincidence of declining payrolls and recession. **FIGURE 3-3** shows that, since 1960, there has never been an instance when three consecutive monthly reductions in nonfarm payrolls haven't been accompanied by an economic downturn. Conversely, each of the last ten post–World War II recessions was characterized by at least three consecutive months—and most by three consecutive quarters—of falling nonfarm payrolls.

In recoveries, unemployment is a lagging indicator—that is, it continues to rise for several months after a definitive bottom has been reached. The lag has become more marked in recent years. A

Figure 3-3 Growth Rate in Nonfarm Payrolls and Recessions

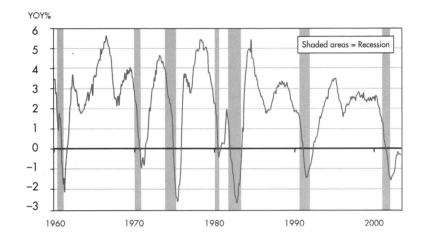

Sources: U.S. Department of Labor, Bureau of Labor Statistics; NBER

Figure 3-4 Unemployment Rate and Recessions

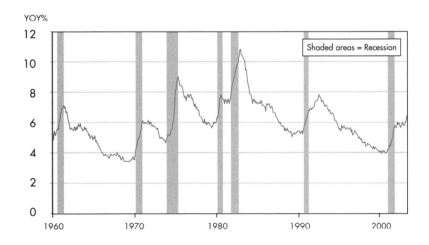

Sources: U.S. Department of Labor, Bureau of Labor Statistics; NBER

look at **FIGURES 3-3 AND 3-4** reveal that the last two U.S. recessions (1990–91 and 2001) were both followed by protracted periods of joblessness.

INFLATION INDICATORS

Average hourly earnings are considered a proxy for inflation and, as such, are closely watched by fixed-income traders. When monthly earnings are increasing at a torrential rate, the bond market usually sells off, because inflation erodes the value of fixed-income holdings.

Inflation is inversely related to unemployment. That insight grew out of a 1958 study by New Zealand–born economist A. W. Phillips. The study demonstrated that when annual wage-growth and unemployment rates were plotted against each other, the result was a shallow convex curve. Known as the Phillips Curve, it served to represent the fact that, during the period studied, years of low unemployment coincided with rapid wage increases, whereas years with high rates of unemployment saw inflation slow or even reverse. This suggested a trade-off between inflation and unemployment that could be exploited by economic policymakers: The central bank could keep inflation low by accepting higher unemployment levels or vice versa. This relationship soon became one of the most disputed in economics.

The Phillips Curve and its policy implications led to the notion of a non-accelerating inflation rate of unemployment. NAIRU, as it is called, is the lowest level to which unemployment may fall without increasing the inflation rate. For decades economists believed that NAIRU, sometimes referred to as the natural unemployment rate, was around 6.0 percent. As the chart in **FIGURE 3-5** graphically illustrates, particularly in the 1960s and 1970s, higher unemployment rates—above 6.0 percent—were soon followed by periods of falling inflation. Conversely, especially in the late 1980s, as employment fell below 6.0 percent, inflation gathered steam. The hypothesis pretty much lost its luster in the late 1990s, when the unemployment rate tumbled to 3.9 percent and inflation didn't move higher. In fact, inflation actually fell during the period, sparking fears of

Figure 3-5   Unemployment Rate and Inflation

Sources: U.S. Department of Labor, Bureau of Labor Statistics; NBER

deflation at the Federal Reserve and in the investment community.

Economists seeking another link between unemployment and inflation latched on to the notion of "available labor pool." This is the number of unemployed who are actually available for work, calculated by adding the number of unemployed (the traditional measure defined as in the labor force, unemployed, and still looking for employment) to the number of workers not in the labor force who currently want a job. The reasoning is that when the pool of available workers begins to evaporate, employers have to jack up wages to attract the employees they want, often having to outbid other employers, and that this sparks widespread inflation. The theory hasn't been borne out, however. The available labor pool shrank in the mid- to late 1990s to one of the lowest levels in history, yet harmful rates of inflation never developed.

SENTIMENT AND UNEMPLOYMENT

President Truman once remarked: "It's a recession when your neighbor loses his job. It's a depression when you lose yours." The barometer that best measures the downbeat sentiment associated with job loss is the median duration of unemployment—that is,

Figure 3-6   Median Weeks of Unemployment Versus University of Michigan's
Consumer Sentiment Index

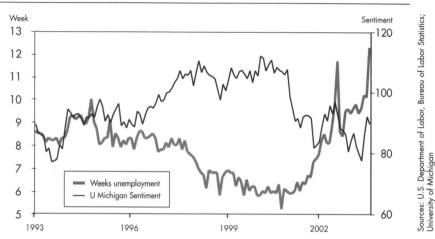

Sources: U.S. Department of Labor, Bureau of Labor Statistics; University of Michigan

the median number of weeks that people are out of work. **FIGURE 3-6** suggests that as the number of median weeks of unemployment rises, workers become more and more frustrated, evidenced by declines in the University of Michigan's Consumer Sentiment Index. Notice how the two spikes in the duration of unemployment during 2002 and 2003 were quickly followed by some of the lowest levels of consumer sentiment in the decade. Keep in mind that this measure is the median—the center point—not the average number of weeks.

During extended periods of unemployment, marriages may be strained and families disrupted. Depression is common. As underlying labor market conditions worsen, consumers become increasingly aware of how difficult it is to find a job. They hear of friends, neighbors, and immediate family members losing their jobs. Then distant relatives call asking about any available positions. Daily reminders in the newspapers and evening news only increase the gloom. These conditions aren't exactly conducive to greater consumer spending and positive economic growth.

AVERAGE HOURS WORKED AND TEMPORARY WORKERS

The BLS calculates the aggregate weekly hours worked index, formed by dividing the current month's estimates of aggregate hours by the corresponding annual average levels. This index, as well as several sub-indices, are found in Table B-5 of the monthly Employment Situation.

Because economic activity is basically a function of the number of people employed and the amount of time they are working, economists have discovered the ability to arrive at a "synthetic" forecast for economic growth, by charting the year-over-year percentage change in the quarterly average of the aggregate hours index. Clearly, there is an extremely tight correlation between these two indicators.

When economic conditions begin to sour, employers reduce the number of hours worked before they eliminate staff. That way, if economic activity recovers, they can ramp up production quickly by merely adding hours, rather than having to spend time and money finding and training new hires. This makes the aggregate hours worked index, in some instances, a leading indicator of economic growth. **FIGURE 3-7** charts the average hours worked index over the past two decades.

Figure 3-7   Average Hours Worked Index and Recessions

Sources: U.S. Department of Labor, Bureau of Labor Statistics; NBER

Figure 3-8 Temporary Employment and Recessions

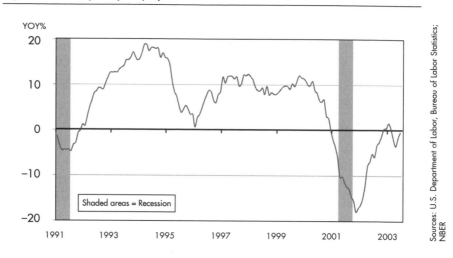

If economic conditions—and profits—continue to deteriorate, management's next step is to reduce the number of workers on the payroll. Among the first people to get pink slips are temporary, or contingent, workers. The tasks they perform are not critical to the day-to-day performance of the company—otherwise, they would be employed full time. Furthermore, temp workers usually aren't unionized, so they can be cut most easily and cheaply during downturns. Temporary workers aren't usually entitled to severance or unemployment benefit insurance. Conversely, in the initial stages of recovery, companies are not sure of future demand, so rather than go through the costly process of hiring full-time workers, they add temporary ones.

FIGURE 3-8 shows that a decline in temporary-help payrolls preceded the 2001 economic recession by a considerable degree, approximately six months. In general, increases in the growth rate of temporary workers precede the upturn in the business cycle.

Knowing that businesses operate in this fashion, traders like to keep a close eye on the trends in employment at temporary help service establishments. An alternative manner at appreciating the goings on in the temporary services sector may be identified by watching the quarterly earnings announcements of the temporary staffing and recruiting agencies. Many companies, such as Adecco, Kelly Services, Manpower, and Robert Half, provide a great deal of information regarding industry trends, statistics, and forecasts. Trade organizations such as the American Staffing Association provide timely outlooks and related publications on temporary help and flexible staffing.

HOW TO USE WHAT YOU SEE

As always, the main strategy is to find ways to predict what a potentially market-moving number will be before it is released. Because the payrolls figure is such an accurate indicator of economic activity, for instance, economists and traders try to get ahead of the curve by forecasting it. Many keep a journal by their desks, recording events they come across in their daily reading that could influence employment. Unexpected disruptions like labor strikes, mass layoffs, and natural disasters like hurricanes, tornados, floods, and blizzards can greatly alter the number of workers in a given month.

Economists also watch a number of alternative indicators for evidence to support or refute the developments suggested by data in the employment report. One of these alternative indicators is the index of monthly layoff announcements made by companies. The index, compiled by the employment consulting firm Challenger, Gray and Christmas, measures intended dismissals rather than actual firings. It is thus something of a leading indicator. It gives economists an insight into industries that may be experiencing difficulties. Movements in the index are also helpful in gauging the bigger picture contained in the BLS employment report. That is, increases in the number of layoff announcements usually portend a softer payroll picture, while a decline in the number of announced layoffs generally results in stronger payroll growth.

Another resource is the Help-Wanted Advertising Index. Created and maintained by the Conference Board, it tracks the monthly volume of help-wanted advertisements in the top fifty-one newspapers across the nation, thus identifying regional demand for labor. Since the advent of the Internet, however, businesses have had other ways to advertise available positions, so the popularity of the index has faded. Still, it can be helpful in determining general trends in demand for workers.

Probably the most helpful resource for predicting movements in monthly payrolls is the weekly claims for unemployment benefit insurance. Rising jobless claims usually portend a deteriorating labor market. Many economists argue that when the four-week moving average of claims tops 400,000, job creation is stagnant. Of course, the correlation between claims for jobless benefits and the employment data is not precise. Employment conditions can change at any time, and short-lived changes are more likely to show up in the weekly jobless-claims report than in the monthly BLS employment report. Also, although unemployment-insurance benefits generally last only thirteen weeks, bear in mind that people can be out of work for months at a time. Finally, some unemployed workers are not entitled to jobless benefits.

TRICKS FROM THE TRENCHES

This chapter's trick is simply to call your attention to a little-known, but very useful, section of the employment report: the diffusion indices. The BLS provides diffusion indices for one-, three-, six-, and twelve-month periods, both for private nonfarm payrolls, which comprise 278 industries, and for manufacturing payrolls, which represent 84 industries. Economists tend to gravitate to the one-month indices, as they are not as noisy as the others.

The diffusion indices are derived from establishments' responses to questions about whether they intend to add or eliminate workers or leave payrolls unchanged. To calculate the indices, the percent of responses indicating an intention to add workers is added to half the percentage of the unchanged responses. When the indices are above 50, indicating that a greater percentage of industries intend to add workers than to lay them off or remain stable, employment conditions are strong. High readings are usually accompanied by economic expansions. When the indices fall

Figure 3-9   Employment Diffusion Index and Recessions

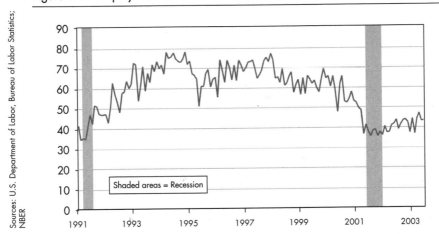

Sources: U.S. Department of Labor, Bureau of Labor Statistics; NBER

below 50, industries are leaning toward cutting their payrolls. That situation is typical of recession. As shown by **FIGURE 3-9**, most of the recessions designated by the NBER coincide with sub-50 postings in the BLS diffusion indices.

Industrial Production and Capacity Utilization

4

THE INDUSTRIAL PRODUCTION AND CAPACITY UTILIZATION report, assembled and released around the fifteenth of each month by the Board of Governors of the Federal Reserve System, presents data on the output of the nation's manufacturing, mining, and utility sectors. The Federal Reserve's G17 report, as it is also known, organizes these data into industrial production and capacity utilization indices. The former measure the physical volume of the output of various industries and markets; the latter show what portion of the nation's production capacity was involved in creating that output. The total industrial production index is usually the headline grabber. Investors may react strongly to the monthly percentage change in this index, especially when it deviates from the Street's consensus estimates. But market participants also value the report's individual-industry, aggregate-industry, and market indices.

Equity analysts scan the Industrial Production and Capacity Utilization report for telling details about the condition of the chemical, home electronics, paper, textile, fabricated metals, lumber, or industrial machinery sectors. Economists scrutinize the data for early insights into what the quarterly National Income and Product Accounts, or NIPAs (see Chapter 1), will say about the health of the economy. Policymakers search the numbers for inflationary trends. And the National Bureau of Economic Research (NBER), the official arbiter of U.S. business cycles, incorporates the industrial production index—which it finds a good marker of the start and end of recessions—in its statement on the status of the economy. The

Industrial Production and Capacity Utilization release, together with historical data, is available on the Federal Reserve's website, www.federalreserve.gov.

EVOLUTION OF AN INDICATOR

The index of industrial production is among the oldest measures of U.S. manufacturing and macroeconomic activity, predating even the venerable National Income and Product Accounts. It is as old, in fact, as the Federal Reserve Board of Governors. Soon after the central bank was created, with the passage of the Federal Reserve Act on December 23, 1913, its officials realized that they needed a pool of accurate economic data and measurements if they were to steer the nation through the widespread bank failures, frequent recessions, and bouts of joblessness that characterized the late nineteenth and early twentieth centuries. No formal measurement of economic activity existed, however, in 1913. The National Bureau of Economic Research, now the primary agency responsible for maintaining the national accounts, didn't begin estimating income until 1920. So the Fed created its own *Physical Volume of Trade* report. This consisted of unaggregated indices tracking the production of commodities such as coal, coke, crude oil, steel, textiles, metals, and paper, measured in tons, feet, barrels, and other relevant physical units. By 1919, these indices represented seven sectors of the economy: agriculture, forestry, mining, manufacturing, trade and transportation, banking and finance, and labor.

In 1922, the Fed introduced the monthly *Indexes of Domestic Business* report, which combined fifty-five gauges of commodity production into indices representing three facets of production: agriculture, mining, and manufacturing. Later that year, it created the more detailed Index of Production in Selected Basic Industries. This was composed of twenty-two commodities weighted according to the level of employment in manufacturing process of each respective commodity industry, which was obtained in the 1919 census, and the value added by each industry—that is, the portion of a good's final value that is contributed by the industry in the course of production. The two largest components in the index were pig iron and cotton, with weights of 18 and 15 percent, respectively. In structure it was similar to the industrial production index of today.

The industrial production index was used to estimate industrial capacity utilization for about two decades after World War II. In the 1960s, the Federal Reserve developed a process for estimating industry capacity and capacity utilization rates, releasing these estimates in a separate statistical report called *Capacity Utilization: Manufacturing, Mining, Utilities and Industrial Materials.* This monthly report, known as statistical release G.3, was released one business day after the industrial production report. In addition to surveys of industry businessmen, capacity indices were estimated using data obtained from McGraw-Hill and the U.S. Bureau of the Census surveys of plant capacity.

Most of the meaningful changes to the capacity utilization measures occurred in the 1970s, particularly in 1974 with the revision of the materials measures, and then again in 1976 with the augmentation of total materials data in the industrial production index.

In December 2002, the Federal Reserve conducted a revision of the industrial-production and capacity-utilization measures. This consisted primarily of switching from the Standard Industrial Classification (SIC) to the new North American Industry Classification System (NAICS). It also introduced more reliable methods of calculating manufacturing activity in the communication equipment, semiconductor, light vehicle, and newspaper industries and regrouped the major market classes according to stage of processing, very much like the system used by the producer price index (PPI).

DIGGING FOR THE DATA

The Industrial Production and Capacity Utilization report is an assemblage of fifteen tables arranged over nineteen or twenty pages. The tables display the current month's values for the various industrial-production and capacity-utilization indices, revisions to previous months' values, month-to-month percentage changes in the indices, and their quarterly and annual rates of growth. The front page of the release contains a summary of the most important indicators—the monthly percentage changes in the total industrial production index and the capacity utilization rate—as well as revisions to the three previous months. The Federal Reserve also provides a number of detailed charts—a trader's best friend—before the meat of the report is presented.

INDUSTRIAL PRODUCTION

The industrial production indices measure quantity of output (i.e., in terms of production units like tons, cubic feet, or kilowatt hours), not dollar volume, relative to a base year, currently 1997, whose value is set at 100. An index value of 109, for instance, denotes that output for that month was 9 percent higher than the average for 1997.

The Federal Reserve obtains the production data it uses to construct these indices both directly and indirectly. Direct sources include trade associations such as the American Forest and Paper Association (for pulp, wood, and paper and paperboard output), the U.S. Geological Survey (for copper, lead, zinc, gold, and silver ore numbers), the Internal Revenue Service (for beer, wine, and brandy), and the Tanner's Council of America (for leather and belting figures). Actual production data, however, are available at different times for different industries. When hard figures aren't available, the Federal Reserve estimates output based on the number of production-worker hours in the Bureau of Labor Statistics' monthly Employment Situation report or on electric power use by industry. Only a few sectors—usually motor vehicles, steel and other metals, lumber, and paper—have hard figures ready for the initial release. By the third monthly revision, actual physical production accounts for 46 percent of the data by value added, production-worker hours for 31 percent, electric power use for 19 percent, and Federal Reserve judgments based on anecdotal evidence for 4 percent.

The total industrial production index is constructed from 295 components, or individual series such as copper, instruments, computers, or lumber, each of which is weighted according to the value of the associated sector added during the production process in the

Figure 4-1 Industry Groups

	2002 Proportion
Total Industrial Production	**100.00**
Manufacturing	84.62
Durable	*43.41*
Nondurable	*35.90*
Other manufacturing (non-NAICS)	*5.30*
Mining	6.03
Utilities	9.34

Source: Board of Governors of the Federal Reserve System

base year. Each individual series is expressed in its own respective quantity (i.e., steel in tons, automobiles in units) so that month-to-month changes in production are measured without respect to price movements. The report presents these components according to two different classification schemes: by industry, representing the supplier perspective; and by market, representing the demand perspective.

The industry schema is based on the North American Industry Classification System (NAICS). The three primary industry groups are manufacturing, mining, and utilities. Manufacturing is subdivided into durable and nondurable goods. The table in **FIGURE 4-1** shows the major groupings together with the percentage each contributed to production growth in 2002.

In the classification by market groups, shown in **FIGURE 4-2**, the total index is divided into two major groups: final products/

Figure 4-2 Market Groups

	2002 Proportion
Total Industrial Production	**100.00**
Final product and nonindustrial supplies	59.81
Consumer goods	*30.46*
Durable	*7.52*
Nondurable	*22.93*
Business Equipment	*9.65*
Defense and space equipment	*2.20*
Construction supplies	*6.84*
Business supplies	*0.30*
Materials	40.19

Source: Board of Governors of the Federal Reserve System

nonindustrial supplies and materials. Final products/nonindustrial supplies is itself divided into consumer goods (further subdivided into durable and nondurable), business equipment, defense and space equipment, construction supplies, and business supplies.

CAPACITY UTILIZATION

Capacity utilization is a measure of how close the nation's manufacturing sector is to running at full capacity. Formally, it is the ratio of the index of industrial production to an index of full capacity. But what is meant by full capacity? The Fed defines it as sustainable practical capacity, or "the greatest level of output that a plant can maintain within the framework of a realistic work schedule, taking account of normal downtime and assuming sufficient availability of inputs to operate the machinery and equipment in place."

The annual full capacity number is derived through a complex process that involves both hard data, obtained from industry surveys such as the U.S. Census Bureau's Annual Survey of Plant Capacity, which all businesses (with a class D SIC code classification, manufacturing) with five employees or more must complete, and by inference, using the ratio given above. The Fed assumes that month-to-month growth is smooth and so derives the monthly capacity figure by straight-line interpolation from the annual number.

The monthly capacity utilization rate is derived by dividing the monthly industrial production number by the monthly capacity figure. For example, during July 2003 the index of industrial production was 98.6 and the capacity index was 132.7. Dividing the former by the latter (98.6 / 132.7) results in a capacity utilization rate of 74.3 percent. In layman's terms, this suggests that factories were running at 74.3 percent of full capacity.

The report contains capacity and capacity utilization rates for eighty-five industries, including the following major categories:
- semiconductors and related electronic components
- motor vehicles and parts
- apparel and leather
- paper

- chemicals
- wood products
- electric utilities

The total capacity utilization rate is compiled from these components, weighted as shown in **FIGURE 4-3**.

Figure 4-3   Capacity Utilization Percentage of Capacity, Seasonally Adjusted

Source: Board of Governors of the Federal Reserve System

	2002 Proportion
Total Industry	**100.00**
Manufacturing	86.69
Durable	47.13
Nondurable	34.66
Other manufacturing	4.89
Mining	5.20
Utilities	8.12

What Does It All Mean?

Economists, analysts, and investors look to the Industrial Production and Capacity Utilization report for timely indications of overall economic health as well as manufacturing and inflationary trends. The two main sections of the report provide different types of information and signals.

Industrial Production

The index of industrial production is *procyclical*—that is, it moves in unison with the business cycle. As the chart in **FIGURE 4-4** illustrates, the correlation between the index and economic activity is quite tight—so tight, in fact, that the monthly index is used as a more timely proxy for the quarterly GDP report.

The National Bureau of Economic Research uses the index to discern turning points in the business cycle. As the chart in **FIGURE 4-5** shows, each of the NBER-designated recessions since 1950 has coincided with a precipitous drop in the 12-month growth rate

Figure 4-4 Industrial Production and Real GDP

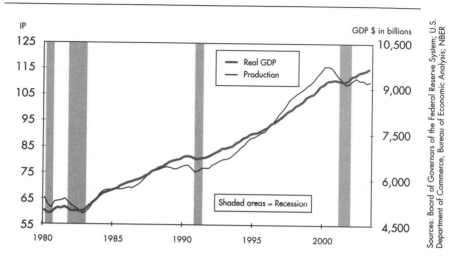

Sources: Board of Governors of the Federal Reserve System; U.S. Department of Commerce, Bureau of Economic Analysis; NBER

of industrial production. The converse, however, is not necessarily true: The manufacturing sector can be in recession while the broader economy continues to prosper.

At first blush, the close relationship between the industrial production index and the overall economy seems odd. Manufacturing, after all, accounts for only 20 percent of total economic activity. The United States has evolved from a smokestack to a services-dominant economy, and mammoth service industries, such as health care, software, telecommunications, travel and entertainment, pharmaceuticals, and banking and finance, are not directly represented in the industrial production index. Nor does the index contain any measure of construction-related activity, although it does represent industries that manufacture construction machinery such as wheel loaders and wheel tractors.

On closer examination, however, the close relationship between the index and the broad economy makes sense. For starters, one-fifth of total activity isn't altogether small. The U.S. manufacturing sector moves very much in line with aggregate demand, just as retail sales, another small and equally cyclical statistic, moves with consumer spending. Moreover, manufacturing and production activity have a large "multiplier effect." Manufactures,

Figure 4-5 Industrial Production and Recessions

especially durable goods—those with expected shelf lives of three or more years—generally come with service contracts that cover the cost of repairs, damages, and maintenance. Obviously, the value and level of such services are driven by the demand for the products themselves.

Finally, and most crucially, many service industries are large consumers of manufactures. Taxi companies require automobiles; airlines need jets and electronic security systems; bars and restaurants use refrigerators, dishwashers, ovens, and foodstuffs. Financial institutions and law firms are big customers for computers and peripherals, and the health care industry is one of the largest consumers of industrial products, including operating tables, beds, lamps, imaging machines, and surgical supplies.

The industrial production index shows another strong correlation—with the Purchasing Managers' Index (PMI), published by the Institute for Supply Management (ISM). The relationship between the two indices is illustrated in the scatter chart in **FIGURE 4-6**. The points in the upper-right quadrant represent periods of extremely strong manufacturing output, such as recoveries from recession or the 1991–2001 economic expansion, the longest in U.S. history. The points in the lower-left quadrant represent periods of severe

Sources: Board of Governors of the Federal Reserve System; NBER

Figure 4-6   Correlation of Purchasing Managers' Index and Industrial
Production Index

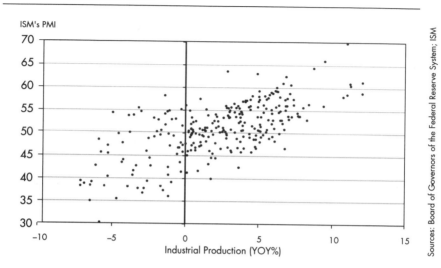

Sources: Board of Governors of the Federal Reserve System; ISM

manufacturing weakness, generally recessions. A simple econometric analysis suggests that when the PMI is at 50, a level generally consistent with an expansion in manufacturing, the industrial production index is advancing at an annual rate of approximately 2 percent.

At a more detailed level, the industrial production sub-indices can depict, and in some instances explain, what is happening in specific industries. Take the spectacular expansion and equally spectacular collapse in the technology sector that occurred during the late 1990s and early 2000s. The chart in **FIGURE 4-7** shows that while high tech was soaring, the production of nontechnology goods was plodding along, posting average annual gains of around 2 percent.

It was during this period that Federal Reserve chairman Alan Greenspan uttered his famous "irrational exuberance" comment during an American Enterprise Institute Francis Boyer Lecture. Although he was referring to asset prices, Chairman Greenspan was doubtless aware that production of high-tech goods such as computers, communications equipment, and semiconductors was

Figure 4-7 Industrial Production Index: High-Tech and Excluding High-Tech

Source: Board of Governors of the Federal Reserve System

growing at more than 40 percent annually, dwarfing the 15 percent or so registered a mere year and a half earlier.

That pace was not sustainable. Beginning in late 2000, the chart shows, there was a precipitous decline in the high-tech growth rate. Manufacturers, afraid to miss out on the hot market for their goods, had overproduced. When demand, inevitably, slackened, these companies—particularly telecommunications-equipment providers—were left with record inventories. In reaction, they slashed production and, consequently, staff until consumers could draw down existing stock. Inventory depletion took the better part of three years. This situation, exacerbated by fraudulent accounting practices, misstated earnings, and countless corporate improprieties, forced Global Crossing, World-Com, and Qwest, among other companies, into bankruptcy. Not surprisingly, the stock market plunged between 2000 and 2002. This entire story can be traced in the contrasting paths of the high-tech and ex-tech indices shown in the figure.

CAPACITY UTILIZATION

Economists, particularly central bankers, look at the total capacity utilization rate to discern trends in production, general economic activity, manufacturing conditions, and inflation. In addition, the rates for particular industries can pinpoint areas of overcapacitization (production that pushes capacity to its limit) that could become manufacturing bottlenecks, constraining production farther down the line and possibly pushing up prices. Such information is useful not only to economists but also to company managers trying to forecast costs and plan production schedules.

Low levels of capacity utilization—78 percent or below—indicate that the economy is headed to, or already in, recession. In fact, as the chart in **FIGURE 4-8** illustrates, each of the last six economic recessions was characterized by rates in that range. This relationship is logical: Subpar economic conditions simply don't warrant strong production.

When demand and commerce are booming, on the other hand, factories tend to ramp up and produce at rates closer to their capacity. The downside to this is that the higher production rates tend to stoke inflation.

Figure 4-8 Capacity Utilization and Recessions

Sources: Board of Governors of the Federal Reserve System; NBER

When factories approach their maximum production potential, machinery and other goods-producing capital are strained. As a result, electronic components may short, pumps overheat, lubricants dry up, or core parts crack. If the overworked equipment cannot be repaired in a reasonable, profitable period of time, mass lay-offs could ensue. Complicating matters is the fact that all this occurs just when demand is greatest and increased production most necessary. To understand how this cycle can spark inflation, consider the case of a company that produces about 50,000 tons of cement a week.

During normal conditions the company's plants operate at 80 percent of capacity. At that rate, market conditions dictate a price of $50 a ton for the cement. Over time, though, a housing boom develops, and demand for cement surges. To capture more of the increased market, the company begins operating its plants at 92 percent of their full capacity. At this rate, the rotating kiln breaks down because it is not accustomed to so much pressure. The damage may take weeks, even months to repair. Beyond laying off the workers that operated the broken machinery, what can the company do to offset the lost revenue?

Answer: Raise prices. Rather than charge the normal market rate of $50 a ton, the cement manufacturer tells wholesalers that it expects $55, $60, or even $65 a ton. Because demand has skyrocketed, the wholesalers will gladly fork over the additional money, knowing that they too will be able to pass along the increase, to contractors and retailers. These price hikes are transferred to new homes, driveways, sidewalks, and highways and eventually into the general economy.

As this example illustrates, during periods of high capacity utilization, inflationary pressures mount. The economic consequences can be serious. Inflation erodes the purchasing power of bonds' coupon and principal payments, depressing their prices and raising yields. Higher interest rates, in turn, impede future investment. Concerned over this vicious cycle, economists have sought to quantify the relationship between the capacity utilization rate and inflation, just as they did for the unemployment rate (see Chapter 3).

Figure 4-9 Manufacturing Capacity Utilization and PPI for Intermediate Goods

Sources: Board of Governors of the Federal Reserve System; U.S. Department of Labor, Bureau of Labor Statistics

And just as they identified a minimum level of unemployment that could be sustained without sparking inflation—the non-accelerating inflation rate of unemployment, or NAIRU—they have identified a maximum non-accelerating inflationary rate of capacity utilization, or NAICU.

The NAICU for the manufacturing sector as a whole has long been accepted to be 84 percent. Individual businesses differ, however, in their susceptibility to technical innovations, legal barriers, work stoppages, and cyclical abandonment rates, all of which can drastically affect total capacity. Each industry thus has its own NAICU. Some rates are higher than 84 percent, like the paper industry's 87 percent; some are lower, like the mining sector's 80 percent. Of course, none of these is set in stone. Changing business conditions can alter particular NAICUs. It is thus best to regard individual industry numbers as shorthands for ranges, rather than as precise rates.

Even with this looser definition, the applicability of NAICUs in today's economy has been called into question, much as the applicability of the NAIRU has been. The chart in **FIGURE 4-9** shows why. The expected relationship between the general manufacturing NAICU and inflation appears to exist through the late 1980s, but then disappears. A sustained period of capacity utilization above 84 percent that occurred in the late 1970s was indeed followed by an acceleration in the growth of the Producer Price Index for intermediate materials; likewise, depressed capacity utilization rates during the early 1980s did precede a period of disinflation—positive but slowing price growth—and even deflation, or falling prices. In the 1990s and early 2000s, however, a disconnect occurred, with capacity utilization rising to fairly high rates without spawning inflation.

Does this mean that the theory no longer holds and that high capacity utilization rates do not increase inflationary pressures? Probably not. It is more likely that the breakdown in the relationship illustrated in the chart occurred because of the heavy business investment in productivity-enhancing technologies that took place in the latter half of the 1990s, increasing manufacturing capacity. The substitution of low-priced imports for domestic products played an important role, as well, by keeping manufacturing costs low and inflation in check. That said, it is also possible that the true capacity utilization threshold may be a tick or two higher than 84 percent, say 85 or 86 percent.

One indication that the general reasoning behind NAICUs still holds is the reaction of the Federal Reserve to high capacity utilization readings. The Fed is concerned with keeping a lid on inflation and adjusts its monetary policy accordingly. At the first signs of an overheating economy, it generally raises its target for the Fed funds rate (the interest rate banks charge each other for overnight loans used to meet reserve requirements; see Chapter 1). This increase eventually extends throughout the maturity spectrum, discouraging borrowing and so slowing the pace of investment and production.

If the Fed governors are still using NAICU as an inflation indicator, you'd expect hikes in the Fed funds rate to correspond to high rates of capacity utilization. And that does seem to be the case. The chart in **FIGURE 4-10** shows that from 1989 through 2003, whenever the capacity utilization rate rose into the high 80s, the Fed funds rate rose, as well.

The conclusion: Although the relationship has loosened in recent years, the Federal Reserve clearly believes that capacity utiliza-

Figure 4-10   Capacity Utilization and Growth in Fed Funds Rate

Sources: Board of Governors of the Federal Reserve System

tion is still a powerful inflation marker and watches the reported rate carefully. That's a good enough reason for traders, especially those in the fixed-income market, to keep a close eye on capacity utilization, too.

How to Use What You See

As with most indicators, Wall Streeters want to get a preview of what's inside the Industrial Production and Capacity Utilization report: The earlier they can approximate the industrial production index readings, the earlier they can capitalize on any anomalies in the numbers. Useful tools in this project are the number of worker hours in the Department of Labor's monthly employment report. This chapter's Tricks describe how market participants use the Labor Department's data in forecasting the industrial production indexes.

Trick From the Trenches

As noted above, when the actual data are not available, the Federal Reserve may estimate industrial production based on the number of production-worker hours. Wall Street economists use the same statistics in a simple back-of-the-envelope calculation to predict the industrial production index reading up to two weeks before it is released. Here's what the computation would look like using the data in the Bureau of Labor Statistics' March 2002 Employment Situation report, released on April 5 of that year. The BLS report stated that in February, 16.869 million people were employed in manufacturing, working an average of 40.7 hours a week, whereas in March, 16.831 people worked 41.1 hours a week on average. The first step in the computation is to calculate the total number of manpower hours (m/h) worked in each month:

February: 16.869 million workers x 40.7 hours = 686.5683 m/h
March: 16.831 million workers x 41.1 hours = 691.7541 m/h

The next step is to determine how many more or fewer man hours were worked in March:

691.7541 – 686.5683 = 5.1858

The last is to derive the percent month-over-month change:

(5.1858 ÷ 691.7541) x 100 = 0.7496 percent.

So the predicted change in the March industrial production index, based on the number of manufacturing workers and the hours they worked, is 0.75 percent. The actual index reading in the report released on April 16 was 138.8, a 0.65 percent increase over the revised February reading of 137.9. Of course, the result of the calculation is not always that close to the actual reading. But the method is certainly simple, and it is helpful in determining the direction, if not always the magnitude, of change in the index—an extremely important statistic.

Institute for Supply Management Indices **5**

THE PURCHASING MANAGERS' INDEX (PMI) garners more attention than any other economic release except the monthly Employment Situation report (see Chapter 3). Markets move considerably on its readings, and rumor has it that the index is Federal Reserve chairman Alan Greenspan's Desert Island Statistic—that is, if he were stranded on an island and needed to conduct policy with respect to only one economic indicator, this would be it.

The PMI is the headline index of the Manufacturing ISM Report on Business. This report is created by the Tempe, Arizona–based Institute for Supply Management (ISM), a not-for-profit professional association, and is made available on ISM's website (at www.ism.ws) on the first business day of every month, after 10 a.m. ET. In addition to providing a comprehensive introduction of the various indices contained in the report, the website houses a complete historical data set subject to timely revisions and updates.

The ISM's Report on Business describes and discusses the current readings of ten seasonally adjusted diffusion indices constructed by the ISM from the responses to a survey of approximately 400 purchasing managers across the United States. Conducted about the middle of the previous month, it polls participants about their opinions on prices of materials paid in the production process, production level, new orders, order backlog, the speed of supplier deliveries, inventories, customer inventories, employment, new export orders, and imports. The PMI is a weighted composite of the following five of these indices:

- new orders
- production

- employment
- vendor performance
- inventories

Economists look at the PMI primarily to determine the health of the manufacturing sector, but the index provides an accurate picture of the broader economy as well. Its movements closely parallel those of the index of leading economic indicators (LEI, see Chapter 2), and it has shown an uncanny ability to predict recessions months before the National Bureau of Economic Research (NBER) declares them. This may not be so surprising: Consider, what better way is there to find out about manufacturing activity and associated spending than from those business people who are responsible for making the purchasing decisions for the nation's manufacturers?

According to research conducted by the Federal Reserve Bank of New York, the financial markets, in particular the fixed-income market, react very strongly to the monthly postings of the ISM's PMI. On several occasions, the PMI has been identified as the biggest market mover in the monthly reporting cycle of indicators.

EVOLUTION OF AN INDICATOR

The Manufacturing Report on Business has its origins in the 1920s, when the ISM's predecessor association (first called the National Association of Purchasing Agents, then, the National Association of Purchasing Management) began polling members sporadically—at first, only about commodity availability across the country, but soon about other types of information, as well. In 1930, the association was part of a committee formed by the Chamber of Commerce (CoC) under President Herbert Hoover in response to the stock market collapse and the Great Depression. The committee was charged with collecting business data from CoC members. Although the committee was disbanded in 1931, the association decided to carry on the project and, with encouragement from the government, started conducting surveys and publishing the results on a regular basis.

This project has continued ever since except for a four-year hiatus during World War II, when the spotty availability of data disrupted publication. The PMI—also known as the ISM index or, among old-timers, the NAPM index (in reference to the association's name until May 2001)—has been part of the association's monthly report since 1948.

DIGGING FOR THE DATA

As noted above, the ten diffusion indices contained in the Report on Business reflect the survey responses of purchasing managers from various regions of the United States. The participants are drawn from twenty manufacturing industries, based on the Standard Industrial Classification (SIC) system, with each industry represented according to its contribution to gross domestic product (GDP). The twenty industries include the following:

- Apparel
- Chemicals
- Electronic Components & Equipment
- Fabricated Metals
- Food
- Furniture
- Glass, Stone & Aggregate
- Industrial & Commercial Equipment & Computers
- Leather
- Miscellaneous (e.g., jewelry, toys, sporting equipment, and musical instruments)
- Paper
- Petroleum
- Photographic Equipment
- Primary Metals
- Printing & Publishing
- Rubber & Plastic Products
- Textiles
- Tobacco
- Transportation & Equipment
- Wood & Wood Products

The Institute for Supply Management™ 2003 Survey Questions

1. GENERAL REMARKS: Comment regarding any business condition (local, national, or international) that affects your purchasing operation or the outlook for your company or industry. Your opinion and comments are very important.

2. PRODUCTION:

Check the ONE box that best expresses the current month's level (units, not dollars) compared to the previous month.

❑ Better than a month ago ❑ Same as a month ago ❑ Worse than a month ago

3. NEW ORDERS:

Check the ONE box that best expresses the current month's new orders (units, not dollars) compared to the previous month.

❑ Better than a month ago ❑ Same as a month ago ❑ Worse than a month ago

4. BACKLOG OF ORDERS:

Check the ONE box that best expresses the current month's backlog of orders (unfilled sales orders) (units, not dollars) compared to the previous month.

❑ Do not measure backlog of orders ❑ Greater than a month ago
❑ Same as a month ago ❑ Less than a month ago

5. NEW EXPORT ORDERS:

Check the ONE box that best expresses the current month's new export orders (units, not dollars) compared to the previous month.

❑ Do not export ❑ Better than a month ago
❑ Same as a month ago ❑ Worse than a month ago

6. COMMODITY PRICES:

Check the ONE box that indicates the current month's level of change in approximate net weighted average prices of the commodities you buy compared to the previous month.

❑ Higher than a month ago ❑ Same as a month ago ❑ Lower than a month ago

List specific commodities (use generic terms, not proprietary) which are up or down in price since the last report.

UP IN PRICE:_____   DOWN IN PRICE:_____

7. INVENTORIES OF PURCHASED MATERIALS:

Check the OVERALL inventory level (units, not dollars) including raw, MRO

(Maintenance, Repair, Operating Supplies), intermediates, etc. (not finished goods, unless purchased) compared to the previous month.

❑ Higher than a month ago ❑ Same as a month ago ❑ Lower than a month ago

Do you perceive THIS MONTH, your customers' inventories of products they order from you, as being: ❑ Too High ❑ About Right ❑ Too Low

8. IMPORTS:
Check the ONE box that best expresses the current month's OVERALL imports (units, not dollars) including raw, MRO (Maintenance, Repair, Operating Supplies), components, intermediates, etc. (not finished goods unless purchased) compared to the previous month.

❑ Do not import   ❑ Higher than a month ago
❑ Same as a month ago   ❑ Lower than a month ago

9. EMPLOYMENT:
Check the OVERALL level of employment compared to the previous month.

❑ Greater than a month ago ❑ Same as a month ago ❑ Less than a month ago

10. SUPPLIER DELIVERIES:
Check the ONE box that best expresses the current month's OVERALL delivery performance compared to the previous month.

❑ Faster than a month ago ❑ Same as a month ago ❑ Slower than a month ago

11. ITEMS IN SHORT SUPPLY:
Report specific commodities (use generic names, not proprietary) you purchase that are in short supply, even if mentioned in previous reports.

12: BUYING POLICY:
Indicate by checking ONE appropriate box for each category of purchases and the approximate weighted number of days ahead for which you are committed. Do not report hedging or speculative purchases.

Production Materials
❑ Hand to Mouth ❑ 30 Days ❑ 60 Days ❑ 90 Days ❑ 6 Months ❑ Year

MRO Supplies
❑ Hand to Mouth ❑ 30 Days ❑ 60 Days ❑ 90 Days ❑ 6 Months ❑ Year

Capital Expenditures
❑ Hand to Mouth ❑ 30 Days ❑ 60 Days ❑ 90 Days ❑ 6 Months ❑ Year

Reprinted with permission from The Institute for Supply Management™, 2003.

Each month, the ISM asks its member companies within the above industries twelve questions (reprinted on the preceding pages with permission from The Institute for Supply Management™, 2003). The responses are then aggregated by around the 20th or 21st of the month.

In addition to direct responses, which are used in the calculation of the diffusion indices, the ISM asks for remarks after each question regarding the reasons for higher or lower commodity prices, or greater or less employment. The ISM also asks its participants to report specific commodities (using generic, not proprietary, names) they purchase that are in short supply, even if mentioned in previous reports. These remarks are used in the text prepared for the monthly report, as well as the summary provided in the beginning of the report that precedes the presentation of the individual components.

The ISM separates the responses to each question into positive, neutral, and negative groups and calculates the percentage of the whole that each represents. It then plugs the appropriate percentages for each question into the following formula:

Percentage of Positive Responses + [1/2]
(Percentage of Neutral Responses)

The result is a diffusion index. Say the question regarding the level of employment received 350 responses, of which 20 are negative, or "lower than a month ago"; 275 neutral, or "same as a month ago"; and 55 positive, or "higher than a month ago." Plugging those numbers into the formula would give a value for the ISM Employment Index as follows:

$$= [55 \div 350] + [1/2] [275 \div 350]$$
$$= 15.7 + [1/2] [78.57]$$
$$= 15.7 + 39.28$$
$$= 54.9$$

Indices calculated in this manner have values between 0 and 100. Values above 50 are interpreted as predicting expansion; those under 50, contraction. Thus, the expansion/contraction cut-off level is 50, and not 0. Historically, the individual ISM indices tend to fluctuate between 35 and 70, depending on the current phase of the business cycle and the individual index. For example, the Price Index has fluctuated between 30 and 90, whereas the Export Index has maintained a range of 40 to 70.

Five of these indices, as was noted earlier, are weighted and summed to create the PMI. The indices and their associated weightings are: new orders (30 percent), production (25 percent), employment (20 percent), supplier deliveries (15 percent), and inventories (10 percent). The September 2002 PMI, for instance, was calculated as follows:

PMI (September 2002) = new orders (0.30 x 49.7)
+ production (0.25 x 55.6)
+ employment (0.20 x 45.8)
+ supplier deliveries (0.15 x 53.4)
and inventories (0.10 x 45.2)
= 14.91 + 13.90 + 9.16 + 8.01 + 4.52
= 50.5

The heaviest weighting is given to new orders and reflects the fact that it has the greatest predictive value of the five components. This makes economic sense because orders are, by definition, a representation of intended purchases. This weighting, in turn, contributes to the accuracy of the composite PMI in forecasting turning points in the business cycle.

WHAT DOES IT ALL MEAN?

The ISM manufacturing report is valued not only for the diffusion indices but also for the accompanying discussion and comments made by the purchasing and supply executives participating in the survey. Together, the indices and executives' anecdotal insights paint a detailed picture of the state of the manufacturing sector.

The information is also timely, because the report is released on the first business day of the month, thus unofficially kicking off the monthly cycle of economic indicators.

All these features make the report a valued tool for Wall Street economists, government forecasters, and business planners. Because these professionals' concerns, actions, and pronouncements all affect the stock and bond markets, investors, too, need to pay close attention to the report.

When strong postings are registered in the PMI, production, new orders, and employment indices, it is generally a safe bet that many of the nation's manufacturers are experiencing some positive growth. Granted that countless factors and risks influence the value of a particular company and industry, but when economic fundamentals are strong (i.e., low inflation, low interest rates, solid employment growth, and increased global demand for U.S. manufactures), and the ISM's indices are on the rise, industrial companies like Caterpillar, Ingersoll-Rand, International Paper, United Technologies, Eaton Corp., and Leggett & Platt tend to prosper.

The following sections discuss the economic significance of the PMI and a few of the sub-indices contained in the Report on Business, as well as some of the associations that they possess with other economic indicators. There are countless relationships between each of the sub-indices and various other economic indicators, far too many, in fact, for inclusion in this introductory book. It is highly recommended that readers attempt to discover some of these relationships by charting the data from the ISM's website against other economic indicators. Let's examine a handful of the more popular relationships studied by Wall Streeters.

PMI

A few characteristics that set the PMI apart from most other economic indicators discussed in this book, and that contribute greatly to its appeal for analysts, economists, and investors, are its relative simplicity, its strong correlation with macroeconomic trends, and its unique perspective. The fact that it is more of an anecdotal representation of the goings-on in the economy, from the perspective of those responsible for the actual purchasing of manufactured goods, than a calculated measure of output or volume of production is indeed a distinctive quality of this index. Perhaps the most attractive feature of the PMI and its sub-indices, however, is its ease of interpretation, permitting the trader to interpret month-to-month changes almost instantly.

The PMI is not solely an indicator of manufacturing activity. **FIGURE 5-1** shows that monthly movements in the index closely mirror the year-over-year percentage change in nominal GDP. This makes the PMI extremely valuable as a predictor of total macroeconomic activity.

The chart depicts the relationship between the PMI and GDP as a concurrent or coincidental association. That's because the PMI in Figure 5-1 is charted on a quarterly basis, with the quarterly calculation of PMI derived by averaging the individual months' data for each respective quarter. But because the ISM's PMI is released on a monthly basis, and the GDP report is on a delayed, quarterly basis, the PMI in fact assumes a leading, or predictive, tenor.

As discussed previously, a level of 50 is considered the cut-off between expansion and contraction for manufacturing conditions.

Figure 5-1 GDP Compared Against ISM's Purchasing Managers Index

Sources: ISM; U.S. Department of Commerce, Bureau of Economic Analysis

But when it comes to movements in the broader macroeconomy, different levels are associated with expansion and contraction. For example, a reading of about 46.0 in the PMI serves to identify turning points in the overall business cycle.

The reason for the lower level is due to the underlying composition of the economy. From the 1940s through the 1970s, manufacturing activity was a much greater influence on the total U.S. economy than during the 1980s, when the economy became less industrialized and more services-oriented. So, in earlier times when manufacturing fell into a slump, it dragged the entire economy into recession. Today, manufacturing accounts for only 20 percent or so of total economic output. As a result, declines in manufacturing activity don't always result in macroeconomic recessions. This is the reason why, in the case of the PMI, lower index levels equate to macroeconomic recessions.

FIGURE 5-2 shows that post–World War II recessions in the United States have been associated with steep declines in the PMI, which sometimes preceded the downturn and always continued through them. Before the 1980s, virtually every time the PMI fell below 50, the economy slipped into recession. After the 1980s, however,

Figure 5-2   Recessionary Periods Compared Against ISM's Purchasing Managers Index

PMI

Shaded areas = Recession

Sources: ISM; NBER

sub-50 readings were associated with only two, very short and mild, recessions. If you were to go back and review press clippings about the sub-50 postings that occurred in 1995–96 and in late 1998, for example, you'd find many an economist predicting recession. Those recessions never developed—again, underlining the fact that manufacturing slumps no longer designate overall recession. That is, the manufacturing sector can experience a recession without the broader economy falling into recession.

ISM EMPLOYMENT INDEX

The PMI by itself depicts the general state of the manufacturing sector and of the larger economy. It does so in broad strokes, however. For a more detailed view, economists and traders look at the sub-indices, each of which possesses a considerable amount of predictive power with respect to the particular aspect of manufacturing condition and activity that it portrays.

The ISM Employment Index, which is compiled from the answers to how the current level of employment compares with last month's, shows the employment trends at U.S. manufacturers.

Figure 5-3   ISM's Employment Index Compared Against Manufacturing Payrolls

Sources: ISM; U.S. Department of Labor, Bureau of Labor Statistics

For instance, **FIGURE 5-3** charts the Employment Index against the year-over-year percentage change in manufacturing payrolls as reported by the Bureau of Labor Statistics and gives more evidence of the movement in the U.S. economy away from manufacturing and toward service industries: From 1980 through 2002, the index was below the 50 level for a staggering 190 of the 276 months. In other words, for roughly 69 percent of the last quarter century, manufacturing employment has been contracting, rather than expanding.

The relationship between manufacturing payroll growth and the ISM's Employment Index is indeed close. Figure 5-3 also shows that the Employment Index is good at predicting declines in the growth rate of manufacturing payrolls but not so good at signaling upturns. During the period covered, whenever the index fell below 50 and stayed there for at least five months, manufacturing payroll growth turned negative about six months after the first sub-50 posting. In contrast, since 1980, the Employment Index rarely, if ever, predicted positive manufacturing payroll growth. The reason behind this inability probably lies in the fact that manufacturers shed an overwhelming proportion of workers during the 1980–2003 period—with many manufacturing positions sent abroad.

Economists have recently begun to conclude that there has been a structural change in the U.S. economy, particularly in the employment of manufacturing workers. With soaring productivity rates beginning in the latter half of the 1990s—economists define productivity as the amount of output produced per hour worked—businesses could get away with employing fewer workers. What's more, multinational manufacturers had looked overseas to nations like China, India, the Czech Republic, and Mexico for lower-cost labor. It has been argued that these job eliminations are permanent and the jobs are never coming back. This trend is supported by the extended sub-50 postings in the ISM's Employment Index from the mid-1990s to today.

ISM PRICE INDEX

The ISM Price Index, which is compiled from the answers to the question about current prices paid by manufacturers of commodities used in the production process compared with last month's prices, provides an indication of possible inflationary pressures faced by manufacturers. The index receives a considerable amount of attention from the Street, especially the credit markets, because inflation erodes the value of fixed-income securities. And because the Federal Reserve is so concerned with the possibility of rising inflation, it is atop the Fed's economic indicator watch list as well.

Of course, the index *directly* indicates only how prices are moving in the manufacturing industry. How accurate a reflection it is of inflation in this sector is shown in **FIGURE 5-4**, which charts the ISM Price Index against the year-over-year rate of growth in the intermediate goods producer price index. The intermediate goods index is one of the wholesale price measures calculated by the Bureau of Labor Statistics (BLS) as the Producer Price Index (PPI). It is a representation of price activity of goods that are one stage after raw materials, in other words, intermediate goods that have received some processing, and includes products such as flooring, newsprint, rubber tires and inner tubes, steel wire, and refined sugar. These are

Figure 5-4   ISM's Price Index Compared Against Intermediate PPI

Sources: ISM; U.S. Department of Labor, Bureau of Labor Statistics

the types of materials that manufacturing companies are most likely to buy. Once again, who better to know about price developments in this area than the purchasing managers of those goods? That's why the ISM Price Index is so closely respected and watched by the financial markets, as well as the Federal Reserve.

One question that reasonably might arise is, if these two indices are so closely related, why not just watch the intermediate goods PPI? Because the ISM's Report on Business is released on the first business day of the month, it precedes the release of the BLS's PPI report by about two weeks. To a bond trader, two weeks is an eternity. Decisions regarding the purchase and sale of fixed-income securities are made in a matter of seconds. The faster a bond trader can get the skinny on developing inflation trends the more money he stands to make.

Investors and economists watch the Price Index to glean information beyond the cost of intermediate goods. The greatest concern for policymakers is that manufacturers may pass any higher costs on to the final user of the goods being produced. If any such increased prices are widespread and sustained, the general price level could increase, which by definition, signals inflation. In addition to the corrosive influences in the fixed-income securities market, inflation impedes the pace of consumer spending because workers have to earn more (i.e., by working longer) just to afford the same amount of goods and services they used to get at lower prices.

The Price Index is thus a useful indicator of the potential for inflation, in both the manufacturing sector and the broader economy. According to a recent Report on Business, a Price Index below 46.9 for a sustained period of time is generally consistent with a decline in the BLS's Index of Manufacturing Prices, which is one of the measures of price inflation on the wholesale level.

As with all sections of the ISM's Report on Business, the anecdotal commentary and remarks following each sub-index contribute greatly to this report's value. Because of the detail and insight that the monthly report provides, basic materials and commodities analysts—for example, those covering metals, chemicals, cement, lumber, paper and packaging—scurry each month to get their hands on a copy.

Investors can benefit by comments such as those in the September 2003 report, which stated that the twelve industries paying higher prices for that month were Tobacco; Wood & Wood Products; Textiles; Primary Metals; Instruments & Photographic Equipment; Food; Fabricated Metals; Furniture; Transportation & Equipment; Chemicals; Industrial & Commercial Equipment & Computers; and Rubber & Plastic Products.

If investors know which industries are paying higher prices during slower economic periods, they can tell that activity in these respective industries may be beginning to turn around. One of the most common characteristics of slower economic times is the inability—and undesirability—of businesses to raise prices. Because slower economic times mean income growth is sluggish and job creation scant, businesses rarely get away with raising prices during such periods. (The only time a company can raise prices during gloomy economic conditions is if that company is selling a necessity, like health or medical care.) So when prices are rising, it's generally a signal of better times to come.

A high correlation also exists between the ISM Price Index and the spot price of West Texas intermediate crude oil. Again, this isn't surprising because manufacturers employ a great deal of oil in the production process. Smelters, kilns, compressors, furnaces, and machinery at countless plants and factories utilize some form of crude oil or one of its derivatives. So when the price of crude oil rises, so too does the cost of manufacturer's inputs. These increases are usually reflected in the ISM's Price Index, because it is a measure of prices that manufacturers pay. Again, the concern among policymakers is that if input prices are rising, there is an increased likelihood that those prices will be transferred to the final product, which would be a higher cost to the end-user, the consumer.

ISM SUPPLIER DELIVERIES INDEX

The ISM's Price Index isn't the only inflation barometer in the ISM's monthly Report on Business. The ISM Supplier Deliveries Index, also referred to as the vendor supplier index, provides clues to the future direction of prices.

The Supplier Deliveries Index, which is compiled from the responses to the question regarding delivery performance, is a measure of how long it takes suppliers to deliver parts and materials that are integral to the production process. When the index exceeds 50, it means that delivery has slowed, indicating that greater demand is making it more difficult for suppliers (vendors) to get crucial materials to manufacturers. Sub-50 postings alternatively indicate faster deliveries.

Lengthening delivery times often result from labor disputes that lead to strikes or lockouts. Such disputes occur more frequently among companies involved in the manufacturing process—particularly those in the machinists, rail workers, dockworkers, and trucking industries—than in the services sector. When the delivery time for supplies (inputs in the production process) lengthens, bottlenecks could be developing that can, if sustained, result in higher prices because of the inability to fabricate and deliver necessary inputs.

This process is in agreement with the basic laws of supply and demand. Impeded deliveries, for whatever reason, limit the amount of production that can be performed and consequently reduce the

Figure 5-5   ISM's Supplier Deliveries Index Compared Against JOC-ECRI Industrial Materials Price Index

Sources: ISM; ECRI

availability of final goods produced. This, by definition, is a decline in supply. When the supply of a good declines, its price rises. The longer the labor dispute, the longer the delivery time, the greater the potential for inflation. Moreover, any time supplier backlogs develop, the manufacturer incurs greater costs as well as the increased potential for lost business, which may exacerbate the inflationary environment.

The *Journal of Commerce*'s Industrial Materials Price Index is an index calculated on a daily basis by the Economic Cycle Research Institute, representing eighteen industrial commodity materials, including nickel, cotton, polyester, burlap, copper, red oak, plywood, tallow, steel, crude oil, benzene, and ethylene. As previously stated, when these industrial commodity prices rise, it is often a sign that conditions are improving. This index, presented in **FIGURE 5-5**, is simply another proxy for raw material or commodity prices for comparison with the ISM Supplier Deliveries Index. As the chart illustrates, higher postings in the Supplier Deliveries Index are soon accompanied by increases in the prices of industrial commodities, as represented by the *Journal of Commerce*'s Industrial Materials Price Index. Conversely, precipitous declines and sub-50 postings in the Index result in lower industrial price levels.

ISM NON-MANUFACTURING INDICES

Because manufacturing currently accounts for only 20 percent or so of total economic output, not surprisingly, economists have wanted a measure similar to the PMI that would address the condition of the businesses constituting the other 80 percent of the economy. In response, the ISM created the Non-Manufacturing Report on Business in July 1997. The non-manufacturing survey is similar to the manufacturing survey and, like its older sibling, possesses some degree of predictive power. It is based on data from responses to questions asked of more than 370 purchasing and supply managers in approximately 62 industries, including entertainment, utilities, hotels, real estate, retail, insurance, finance and banking, accounting, communications, mining, agriculture, engineering, educational services, construction, and health services—in other words, just about anything that doesn't fall under the heading of manufacturing. Because a considerable number of service businesses are represented in this survey, the business press often refers to the non-manufacturing survey as the ISM services report.

Among the indices represented in the Non-Manufacturing Report on Business are the following:

- total business activity
- new orders
- backlog of orders
- new export orders
- imports
- prices
- employment
- supplier deliveries
- inventory sentiment
- inventory change

Parallel to the ISM manufacturing report's PMI, the non-manufacturing report has a headline index called Total Business Activity. This index is frequently referred to as the non-manufacturing, or services, PMI. Unlike the manufacturing report's PMI, however, the non-manufacturing Total Business Activity index is not a composite index or a weighted average of sub-indices.

Because the non-manufacturing report is, relatively speaking, in its infancy, the monthly report—usually released two business days after the manufacturing report, or the third business day of the month—doesn't possess the same ability to move the financial markets as its older, more esteemed manufacturing counterpart. Its predictive nature isn't exactly known, considering that the number of economic downturns since its initiation in 1997 has been rather limited.

FIGURE 5-6 shows how closely the ISM's non-manufacturing PMI tracks the Commerce Department's twelve-month rate of consumption of services in the economy. This relationship is to be expected because services dominate the non-manufacturing sectors surveyed.

Figure 5-6   ISM's Non-Manufacturing PMI and Consumption Spending on Services

Sources: ISM; U.S. Department of Commerce

Economists have found that an index reading of 50 equates to a growth rate of about 3.5 percent (year-over-year) in the consumption of services.

The indices in the non-manufacturing survey clearly possess a high degree of correlation with a considerable portion of U.S. economic activity. There's no doubt that the ISM's non-manufacturing survey will eventually become a top-tier economic indicator, especially because the United States has steadily evolved from a smokestack industrialized nation to a more services-dominated one. But before than can occur, a longer history, as well as a weighted composite index similar to the Manufacturing ISM Report on Business PMI, will be needed.

HOW TO USE WHAT YOU SEE

The stock market tends to react in sync with movements in the PMI and Production Index. This is understandable, because manufacturing activity in spite of its reduced role has proven to provide a good representation of total economic conditions. When businesses foresee stronger consumer demand—as evidenced through declining inventories and acceleration in consumer spending—they pick up the pace of production. So, upticks in the PMI or the Production Index and postings higher than 50 usually portend better things for equity issues because greater demand usually results in higher sales and, subsequently, profitability.

Normally, the fixed-income market would react adversely to large increases in the PMI. In other words, higher postings, above 50, would be regarded as inflationary, thereby eroding the value of fixed-income securities, sending prices of bonds lower (and yields higher). Bear in mind that the ISM's Report on Business contains as well the Price Index that also captures the attention of bond traders. The loftier the posting of the Price Index, the greater the inflation fear and the greater the sell-off in bonds. So, to better understand the fixed-income market reactions, Wall Streeters usually look squarely to the Price Index and its direction as the ultimate inflation barometer of this report.

TRICKS FROM THE TRENCHES

When economists get their hands on a proven set of economic indicators like those contained in the ISM's Report on Business, they tend to get creative and conjure up their own indicators, usually derivations of the more successful components in the series. One of the more popular tricks performed by Wall Streeters is to take the difference between the ISM's New Orders Index and the Inventories Index. The resulting statistic, depicted in **FIGURE 5-7**, has exhibited a relatively strong correlation with the year-over-year percentage change in real GDP.

Because gross domestic product is reported on a quarterly basis, and is prone to rather lengthy delays, some economists find this measure a timely (available monthly as opposed to quarterly) and accurate depiction of the economic growth rate.

Like the many diffusion indices examined in this chapter, the New Orders minus Inventories (NO-INV) Index doesn't project a specific magnitude for real economic growth, or GDP, but it is quite telling about the likelihood of economic contraction or expansion. During some phases of the business cycle when the identification

Figure 5-7 ISM'S New Orders Minus Inventories Versus Real GDP

Sources: U.S. Department of Commerce, Bureau of Economic Analysis; ISM

of recession isn't exactly clear, this trick becomes another helpful indicator on the state of economic affairs.

Economists look out for low or negative readings in the NO-INV Index. Anytime there is no difference between the Inventories and New Orders Indices, that is, when the NO-INV Index is zero, the economic growth rate tends to contract. Historically, negative readings have been associated with economic recessions. Readings in the NO-INV of 10 or higher historically have equated to real economic growth rates in excess of 3.5 percent—a rate generally considered to be strong.

Are these levels gospel? Absolutely not. This is nothing more than a crude model and should only be used as a guide to projecting economic activity on a monthly basis (because GDP is not readily available). However, as this indicator has, on occasion, possessed somewhat of a leading quality, some economists look for trends in the index to forecast GDP growth.

Another crude model applied by economists is formed by taking the difference between the ISM's New Orders Index and the Price Index. The resultant measure has displayed a relationship with the year-over-year percentage change in the total return of the S&P 500. The possible economic explanation behind this association

Figure 5-8   ISM's New Orders Minus Price Index Versus S&P 500 Total Return

Sources: Standard & Poor's; ISM

may be that the Price Index is in effect a proxy for costs, and New Orders for revenues. The difference between these two measures would be profits. In this case, profits are reflected in the year-over-year total return of the S&P 500 Index. As suggested in **FIGURE 5-8**, there is indeed a close association between these indicators.

Problems with this little-known index include that input prices as measured by the ISM Price Index are not a highly accurate proxy for costs. A number of costs manufacturers incur are not captured by the Price Index, the largest being labor, for example. Furthermore, new orders are hardly the best representation of revenues. Orders aren't always filled, many are delayed, and ultimately different volumes may be shipped. Still, the so-called NO-P makes for a "quick and dirty" model for predicting the total return of the S&P 500. A simple regression analysis reveals that the total return on the S&P 500 (on a year-over-year basis) will be positive as long as the difference between the ISM New Orders Index and the Price Index is greater than –20.

Bear in mind that this index doesn't always pan out as the greatest forecasting model of stock market levels. Despite the aftermath of the burst stock market bubble in early 2000, the NO-P began to register some hefty readings in early 2001, suggesting the total return of the S&P 500 would be strong. Clearly this was a false signal, as stocks continued their descent well into 2003. Nevertheless, as Figure 5-8 suggests, for a simple, back-of-the-envelope type of forecast, the tool isn't too bad a predictor of stock market returns.

Regional economists and all those who are looking for a more detailed, targeted representation of manufacturing conditions are encouraged to visit the ISM's website and view the various regional business survey reports. These surveys are conducted by the many local purchasing management associations, and should not be confused with the national survey that has been examined in this chapter. Some of the more popular regional reports observed by Wall Street include the Arizona, Austin, Buffalo, Chicago, Cleveland, Dallas, Denver, Georgia, Houston, New York, Northwest Ohio, Pittsburgh, and Western Washington reports.

These reports have helped many Wall Street economic departments create a mock Beige Book. The real Beige Book, so called by the Street because of the color of its cover, is one of the three books that the Federal Reserve creates and uses during its eight-times-a-year monetary policy deliberations. It is the only information at those meetings released to the public; this generally occurs two weeks prior to the Fed's Open Market Committee meeting.

Formally known as the Summary of Commentary on Current Economic Conditions by Federal Reserve District, the Beige Book contains anecdotal commentary that has been accumulated by each of the twelve Federal Reserve districts. The regional ISM surveys are frequent providers of information to those surveys and generally offer excellent insight as to the manufacturing and economic climate in each region.

Manufacturers' Shipments, Inventories, and Orders 6

T HE MANUFACTURERS' SHIPMENTS, INVENTORIES, AND ORDERS, or M3, survey is one of the most respected economic indicators on Wall Street. Published monthly by the U.S. Department of Commerce's Census Bureau, the report measures current activity and future commitments in the U.S. manufacturing sector. Using data supplied by some 4,700 reporting units of businesses in eighty-nine industry categories, it provides statistics on the value of factories' shipments, new orders, unfilled orders, and inventories. The survey is closely followed by economists, members of the business community, and various government organizations, including the Bureau of Economic Analysis (BEA), which employs the survey's figures in preparing its gross domestic product, or GDP, report, particularly the investment and inventory sections.

The M3 survey is published in two parts. The Advance Report on Durable Goods is released about four weeks after the reference month, on about the eighteenth business day of the month (the date varies somewhat to avoid overlapping with other economic releases). The revised and more comprehensive Manufacturers' Shipments, Inventories, and Orders appears about a week later and provides greater detail about production, by industry group, as well as including for the first time information about nondurable, in addition to durable, goods. In both the advance and the later report, it is the orders component that garners the most attention from market participants.

Manufacturing orders constitute a leading economic indicator, because they reflect decisions about optimal inventory levels given the demand businesses anticipate based on their economic forecasts. In this regard, new orders for durable goods have proved to be particularly accurate predictors, because demand for such products is especially dependent on economic health.

Manufacturing is an important sector of the U.S. economy, accounting for roughly 20 percent of GDP and about the same percentage of overall employment. But the significance of the demand and pace of production figures for trading floor economists and traders is even greater than those percentages imply. Trends in production are usually experienced as well by the services sectors associated with shipments of manufactures and can be quite accurate in marking turning points in the overall economy. For that reason, the Conference Board's index of leading indicators (LEI) includes components of the M3 survey: manufacturer's new orders for non-defense capital goods and manufacturers' new orders for consumer goods and materials.

The M3 survey can be found on the Census Bureau's website, at www.census.gov/indicator/www/M3/index.html, together with the historical series for all its components. Larger increases—of the magnitude of 1.0 percent or more—in the monthly percent change of new orders for durable or factory-produced goods are usually interpreted as positive for equity markets and somewhat undesirable for fixed income security holders. Businesses only order if they expect demand to increase. Conversely, declines in new orders are perceived as slower times to come, which generally cause the stock market to decline and bond prices to rally. Investors must keep in mind that both reports are extremely volatile and hard to predict, so the markets may not always place the utmost emphasis on the month-to-month postings.

EVOLUTION OF AN INDICATOR

The M3 survey grew out of the Department of Commerce's Current Industrial Report (CIR) program, in place since 1904. In 1939, the Commerce Department's Office of Business Economics, working through the CIR program, established the first monthly

Industry Survey. The forerunner of the M3 survey, it contained broad-based measures of inventory changes and information about the ratio of new and unfilled orders to current sales. In following years, various changes were made in how the data were calculated and presented, as well as in which industry groups were represented and their composition. Revisions instituted from 1947 to 1963, for example, included adding seasonally adjusted dollar estimates of the data to better reveal non-seasonal features, distinguishing durable from nondurable and household from business-related goods, and breaking down market categories into final products and materials. Seasonal effects include a decline in motor vehicle production during summer months as factories retool for the new model year, and the increase in the production of heating oil during September ahead of the winter special season.

In 1997, as part of a broader revision involving many Commerce Department economic reports, the Census Bureau responded to the development of new products and industries by switching the M3 series of data to the more current and generally accepted North American Industry Classification System (NAICS) from the outdated Standard Industrial Classification (SIC) system. These systems are simply uniform systems of classification. By adopting the NAICS, manufacturing, trade, and inventory data can be compared throughout all of North America, rather than just the United States. The NAICS system resulted in a number of regroupings. For example, some activities that were not previously classified as manufacturing under the SIC system—such as bottled spring water, retail bakeries, and software reproduction—are now formally counted under the new NAICS system. During this benchmark reclassification, data were revised only back to February 1992, when the U.S. economy was in the process of emerging from the 1990–91 recession. Because the NAICS data are only available from that date and previous data are classified by different, SIC industries, historical analysis is limited.

DIGGING FOR THE DATA

The Census Bureau obtains its data on domestic manufacturing through surveys of manufacturing companies with annual shipments totaling $500 million or more. Participation is voluntary, and responses may be submitted over the Internet, by telephone, or by fax. Relevant data received by the eighteenth day of the month following the month covered by the survey are included in the Advance Report on Durable Goods. Additional data, collected through the thirtieth of the month, are consolidated with the previously reported data and included in the more complete Manufacturers' Shipments, Inventories, and Orders.

The reports contain both seasonally adjusted and nonadjusted figures for the record month and for the previous three months, together with percentage changes from month to month. All the values are nominal, given in constant-dollar terms.

The Department of Commerce's Census Bureau presents the collected data both by industry category, such as industrial machinery and computers, and by topical series. Topical series aggregate industries into broad market groupings, such as home goods and apparel, and into special series, such as nondefense capital goods and defense capital goods. For example, the nondefense capital goods series includes small arms; farm machinery and construction equipment; turbines, generators, pumps, and compressors; oil- and gas-field machinery; computer storage devices; office and institutional furniture; and medical equipment and supplies. Wall Street industry analysts monitor the topical series carefully. Aerospace and defense analysts, for instance, watch defense capital goods closely, whereas hardware and peripheral equipment analysts scrutinize the information technology series.

DURABLE GOODS REPORT

Durable goods are goods expected to last three years or more. They include lumber and wood products; furniture and fixtures; stone, clay, and glass products; and industrial machinery and equipment. These products tend to be quite pricey and are not usually purchased on a regular basis. As a result, data connected to their manufacture fluctuate significantly from month to month and are difficult to predict. This is particularly true with regard to defense-related goods, such as ships and aircraft, whose valuation is exceptionally complex.

The Advance Report on Durable Goods contains four categories of data: shipments, new orders, unfilled orders, and inventories. The table in **FIGURE 6-1**, from the May 2003 report, illustrates how the seasonally adjusted data (and the monthly percentage change) for shipments and new orders of durable goods in different sectors are reported. Another table in the report (not shown) presents the same breakdown for unfilled orders and total inventories.

Shipments comprise products actually sold by establishments. The dollar figures reported are the net sales values of domestically manufactured goods shipped to distributors during the record month. (For larger goods with lengthy fabrication schedules, such as aircraft and tanks, the reported figures are estimates of the value of work performed during the survey period.)

Some of the larger categories of shipments include capital goods (products, such as machinery, that are used to make other products), which amount to 37.3 percent of the total; of transportation products, representing 29 percent; and of machinery, 13 percent. (The percentages don't add up to 100 percent because the categories overlap, i.e., both nondefense capital goods and machinery include textile and paper industry machinery.)

New orders are product orders received during the record month, including both those to be filled during the month and those for goods to be delivered some time in the future. Because these figures indicate businesses' intentions with regard to purchases, they are the most forward-looking in the release. **Unfilled orders** are orders that haven't yet been shipped or reported as sold. They are a measure of order backlog.

Businesses understandably want to keep information regarding the level of new orders close to their vests. Because some survey participants (in this voluntary survey) are reluctant to provide this

Figure 6-1   Manufacturers' Shipments and New Orders for Durable Goods

Item	Seasonally Adjusted					
	Monthly			Percent Change		
	Apr 2003	Mar 2003*	Feb 2003	Mar–Apr	Feb–Mar *	Jan–Feb
DURABLE GOODS						
Total						
Shipments	$170,294	$171,564	$170,675	–0.7	0.5	–1.9
New orders	168,929	173,159	170,833	–2.4	1.4	–1.1
Excluding transportation						
Shipments.	120,546	120,393	118,694	0.1	1.4	–3.0
New orders	119,331	120,745	119,485	–1.2	1.1	–2.3
Excluding defense						
Shipments	161,426	163,060	161,964	–1.0	0.7	–2.1
New orders	158,903	161,365	160,283	–1.5	0.7	–2.9
Manufacturing with unfilled orders						
Shipments	118,998	119,382	118,902	–0.3	0.4	–1.6
New orders	117,633	120,977	119,060	–2.8	1.6	–0.4
Primary metals						
Shipments	10,719	10,957	10,985	–2.2	–0.3	–3.2
New orders	10,553	10,363	10,871	1.8	–4.7	–2.8
Fabricated metal products						
Shipments	20,408	20,641	20,606	–1.1	0.2	–1.3
New orders	20,236	20,496	20,247	–1.3	1.2	–1.7
Machinery						
Shipments	22,296	22,320	21,905	–0.1	1.9	–2.2
New orders	21,849	22,686	21,836	–3.7	3.9	–2.5
Computers and electronic products						
Shipments	27,023	26,075	25,492	3.6	2.3	–4.7
New orders	26,829	26,824	26,177	0.0	2.5	–4.2
Computers and related products						
Shipments	7,489	6,233	6,608	20.2	–5.7	–14.0
New orders	7,415	6,431	6,451	15.3	–0.3	–13.1
Communications equipment						
Shipments	5,473	5,595	5,496	–2.2	1.8	–1.6
New orders	6,039	6,365	6,371	–5.1	-0.1	0.8

Source: U.S. Department of Commerce, Bureau of Census

Figure 6-1   (continued)

	Seasonally Adjusted					
	Monthly			Percent Change		
Item	Apr 2003	Mar 2003*	Feb 2003	Mar– Apr	Feb– Mar *	Jan– Feb
Computers and electronic products (continued)						
Semiconductors						
Shipments	(NA)	(NA)	(NA)	(NA)	(NA)	(NA)
New orders	(NA)	(NA)	(NA)	(NA)	(NA)	(NA)
Electrical equipment, appliances, and components						
Shipments	$ 8,609	$ 8,644	$ 8,568	–0.4	0.9	–4.3
New orders	8,553	8,871	8,574	–3.6	3.5	–1.7
Transportation equipment						
Shipments	49,748	51,171	51,981	–2.8	–1.6	0.8
New orders	49,598	52,414	51,348	–5.4	2.1	1.8
Motor vehicles and parts						
Shipments	35,538	36,655	37,013	–3.0	–1.0	–2.6
New orders	35,412	36,515	37,117	–3.0	–1.6	–2.2
Nondefense aircraft and parts						
Shipments	5,306	5,980	6,071	–11.3	–1.5	28.0
New orders	4,427	2,980	3,588	48.6	–16.9	–30.5
Defense aircraft and parts						
Shipments	3,362	3,299	3,249	1.9	1.5	0.4
New orders	4,285	5,822	2,449	–26.4	137.7	3.4
All other durable goods						
Shipments	31,491	31,756	31,138	–0.8	2.0	–2.7
New orders	31,311	31,505	31,780	–0.6	–0.9	–0.9
Capital goods						
Shipments	63,567	62,997	62,328	0.9	1.1	–1.2
New orders	64,404	66,665	63,431	–3.4	5.1	–0.4
Nondefense capital goods						
Shipments	56,121	55,817	55,035	0.5	1.4	–1.4
New orders	55,644	55,801	54,098	–0.3	3.1	–4.9
Excluding aircraft						
Shipments	54,042	53,155	52,193	1.7	1.8	–3.5
New orders	53,874	55,516	53,006	–3.0	4.7	–2.4
Defense capital goods						
Shipments	7,446	7,180	7,293	3.7	–1.5	0.5
New orders	8,760	10,864	9,333	–19.4	16.4	37.4

NA Not Available   * Revised

information, Commerce Department's Bureau of the Census is forced to estimate the level of new orders.

New orders numbers are derived by adding together the dollar values of shipments and of unfilled orders from the current month and subtracting the value of unfilled orders from the previous month (which can't be "new"). For example, in April 2003, the value of durable goods shipments was $169.791 billion and that of unfilled orders was $477.388 billion, for a total of $647.179 billion. Subtracting March's $478.035 billion of unfilled orders yielded a new orders number for April of $169.144 billion. (For nondurable goods, new orders and shipments are generally the same. Because many of these products are perishable, they are usually shipped, and in many cases, consumed, as soon as they are ordered.)

The monthly inventory postings in the M3 report indicate the dollar value of goods stockpiled at factories and in sales branches, regardless of the stage of fabrication. These manufacturing inventories account for about 40 percent of the total U.S. inventories. (The total business inventory position is discussed in detail in Chapter 7.)

FACTORY ORDERS REPORT

The more comprehensive factory orders report contains revisions to the Advance Report on Durable Goods, as well as the first presentation of nondurable goods data and greater detail on all of these data by stage of fabrication.

What's a **nondurable good?** An old economist friend once gave the following nontechnical definition: If you leave it outdoors in the elements and after three years it disappears, it's a good bet that it was a nondurable good. Included in this category are foods and beverages, tobacco products, textiles, apparel, paper and allied products, chemicals and allied products, and petroleum and coal products.

Nondurables don't enjoy the headline status of their cousins, durables. Durable goods such as turbines, engines, household appliances, and machinery are sexier and easier to visualize as factor-produced manufactures than are nondurables such as pesticides, tobacco, and paints. That doesn't mean they aren't an integral part of the economy, however. Nondurable goods account for just a little less than half of total manufacturing industry shipments. In April 2003, for example, nondurables made up 46.95 percent of total shipments, compared with 52.95 percent for durables.

In addition to industry category and topical series, the factory orders report also groups data by stage of fabrication: materials and supplies, work in process, or finished goods. Most economists like to look at the work in progress stage, because it includes material already in the pipeline. About three-quarters of the products at this stage of fabrication are durable goods. The fabrication of short-lived nondurables tends to be similarly short; these goods are heavily represented in the finished-goods numbers.

WHAT DOES IT ALL MEAN?

The M3 report is a gold mine of economic information for investors, traders, analysts, and economists. The durable new orders data represent a particularly rich lode, because of the insight they provide into a large component of personal-consumption and capital expenditures.

DURABLE GOODS REPORT

The equity market reacts positively to increases in new orders for durables, because they indicate new demand and an optimistic economic outlook. Conversely, a slowdown or decline in new orders implies a softer economic climate and less likelihood of a pickup in corporate profitability, which generally hurts the value of stock. In the land of fixed income, the situation is reversed: Strong monthly postings fuel worries about inflation, which erodes the value of coupon payments and sends interest rates higher, both of which depress bond prices and push yields up. The bond market welcomes weaker data, because they are generally associated with a benign inflationary environment.

Interpretation of these data is complicated, however, by their ex-

Figure 6-2   Month-to-Month Percentage Change in New Orders for Durable Goods

Source: U.S. Department of Commerce, Bureau of the Census

treme volatility. Postings in the durable goods and factory orders reports whipsaw from month to month. This is illustrated by the chart in **FIGURE 6-2,** which shows the monthly changes in new orders for durable goods. Virtually all the new orders data, whether for fabricated metals, communications equipment, or machinery, exhibit this type of irregular behavior, which inhibits accurate trend spotting.

To correct for this instability, economists adopt two approaches. One is to look at the data without the most volatile components: the defense and transportation sectors. Demand for goods such as ships, military armored vehicles, and guided missiles is highly unpredictable and unstable, especially on a monthly basis; an unforeseen order for twenty-five commercial airplanes can really blow an economic forecast. The other approach is to apply some smoothing techniques, such as moving averages, to the data. To compute a moving average, you start by averaging the data over a certain period—for a three-month moving average, for example, you would add together the figures (new orders, say) from three monthly reports and divide by three. To make this average *move*, you recalculate it each month, dropping the oldest data point and adding the newest one. Another smoothing technique is to look at year-over-year (rather than month-to-month) changes.

Figure 6-3   New Orders for Durable Goods

Sources: U.S. Department of Commerce, Bureau of the Census; NBER

The chart in **FIGURE 6-3** illustrates the smoothing effects of two approaches: eliminating the volatile transportation sector and taking the longer, year-over-year view. Although the data still reveal plenty of volatility, the sharp swings are minimized.

The chart illustrates another point: the importance of using additional sources of information, such as business reports in newspapers and on TV, in interpreting the data. In Figure 6-3, the line graphing new orders bottoms out in October, one of the final months of the 2001 recession, and heads higher during the year's final quarter. Anyone following the economic news would know that this recovery was prompted by the zero percent financing that automakers introduced for several makes and models in October 2001. This move sparked the highest automotive demand, production, and sales in history: In October alone, some 21.1 million cars and lightweight trucks were sold. In the period of sluggish economic growth that followed the 2001 recession, big-name retailers such as Home Depot and Sears also offered zero percent financing for up to eighteen months on large durable goods such as washing machines, refrigerators, carpeting, and lawn mowers. These actions served not only to spur activity in the sectors directly involved but also to boost aggregate demand in 2001 and so help keep the recession mild and short-lived. Economists and analysts who took the extra step of investigating the automakers' and retailers' business decisions were able to forecast economic activity more accurately and perhaps avoid being overoptimistic about any continuing impetus from the auto sector, since its strength is somewhat artificial, built on unsustainable zero financing and discounts that in effect cannibalized its future sales.

Of the categories represented in the durable goods report, the primary metals sector—which includes iron, steel, aluminum, and copper production—is among those most closely watched by economists. Although shipments of these products represent a relatively small slice of the total for durable goods (about 6 percent in April 2003, as shown in Figure 6-1), the materials are vital ingredients in the manufacturing process. Consequently, increases in new orders for the metals generally hint at greater future manufacturing activity.

Most of the other categories in the durable goods report involve manufacturing. The goods produced by these sectors are generally expensive, and buyers of them (whether individuals or companies) usually need to finance their purchases. New orders for and shipments of these products are thus very sensitive to interest rates. High rates mean lower numbers. Lower rates, in contrast, boost the figures, by making it easier for consumers to buy furniture, appliances, automobiles, and personal computers and for businesses to buy machinery, power transmission generators, and capital equipment. When the Federal Reserve reduces its overnight borrowing target, it is attempting to stimulate these sectors.

FACTORY ORDERS REPORT

By the time the report on factory orders comes out, the markets have had time to absorb and react to the critical data in the durable goods report, released a week earlier. The more detailed information on inventories and unfilled orders contained in the later report doesn't exactly light a fire under traders. Therefore the markets don't move much when it is released. The report contains several components, however, that provide important measures of current and future demand and so bear careful monitoring.

Unfilled orders are a reasonably accurate gauge of the strength of demand for the particular industry, and so of the strength of the underlying economy. Economists view a rising backlog as a sign of accelerating demand and economic strength and a declining backlog as an indication of a weakening economy. The story behind this relationship is somewhat complicated. When the economy is expanding rapidly, businesses tend to be optimistic about the future and place large numbers of new orders for goods. They want the products on their shelves and in their showrooms when consumers come calling. The manufacturers of these goods attempt to fill as many of the orders as possible but often can't do so expeditiously with their existing staff levels. Most employers put off hiring new workers until they see demand increasing. Companies adopt this "just-in-time" approach to hiring because of the expenses related to employment and employees—perhaps their greatest business costs. Manufacturing is largely unionized, and specialized craftsmen with finely honed skills are often needed to fill skyrocketing new orders. Manufacturers must consult union officials, adopting specific pay rates and working schedules. They are often forced to hire a minimum number of workers. If the economy turns south, triggering widespread order cancellations, the companies are saddled with newly hired workers standing around idled machinery. Only when the union-negotiated contracts expire are they free to eliminate staff. No wonder they're reluctant to add employees until demand makes it necessary. But the process of advertising for, interviewing, hiring, and training new workers is lengthy. In the meantime, backlogs of unfilled orders thus pile up.

HOW TO USE WHAT YOU SEE

The basic trading strategy related to the M3 report involves identifying potential turning points in demand for U.S. manufactures and related products. Obviously, the greater the volume of shipments, the greater the strength of current demand. For future demand, the

Figure 6-4   Shipments of Nondefense Capital Goods Excluding Aircraft
Versus Software and Equipment Investment

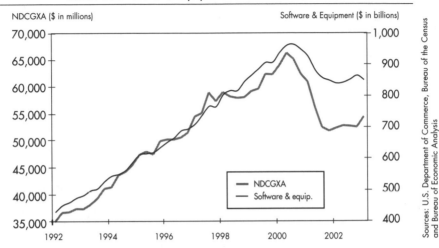

reasoning is similar: The higher the number of new orders for goods, the greater the probability of strong activity down the road; the lower the number, the bleaker the outlook. Particularly potent in predicting the future are manufacturers' new orders of consumer goods and materials and of nondefense capital goods. These components have proved so accurate that the Conference Board includes them in its index of leading economic indicators. Remember, however, that in applying this approach, it is best to look at year-over-year percentage changes as opposed to the monthly figures, which, as noted above, are too volatile to allow accurate trend spotting.

TRICK FROM THE TRENCHES

This chapter's trick is to watch the value of nondefense capital goods spending excluding aircraft (NDCGXA). The BEA uses the reports' figures for shipments of NDCGXA in determining the equipment and software investment component of the GDP report. As **FIGURE 6-4** shows, the volume of NDCGXA shipments shows a high correlation with the level of software and equipment spending.

Because of this relationship, shipments of nondefense capi-

Figure 6-5   New Orders for Nondefense Capital Goods Excluding Aircraft
Versus Capital Spending

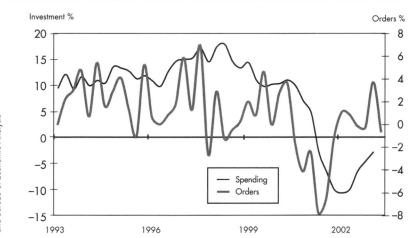

Sources: U.S. Department of Commerce, Bureau of the Census
and Bureau of Economic Analysis

tal goods excluding aircraft can serve as a proxy for the level of
total nonresidential business investment in the GDP report, also
referred to as capital goods investment. This is very useful; because
investment in capital drives economic activity, economists want
to spot trends in this component as early as possible. But capital-
investment figures are available only on a quarterly basis, in the
GDP report, and three months is a very long time to wait. NDC-
GXA shipments are among the few monthly surrogates for this
important indicator—and the only one that is given in dollar-
denominated values, rather than as a representative index, like the
industrial-production or the Institute for Supply Management New
Orders diffusion indices.

As mentioned above, shipments data paint a picture of current
demand; for future trends you have to look at new orders. New orders for nondefense capital goods excluding aircraft are particularly
significant. Only when businesses are confident about the economic
outlook and future demand will they make costly investments in
new machinery and innovative processes. As **FIGURE 6-5** illustrates,
NDCGXA new orders anticipate this investment by about three
to six months. On a macroeconomic level, prior to the commence-

ment of the recession in April 2001, for instance, new orders began a sharp decline in July of 2000 replicated by capital spending during the fourth quarter of 2000.

So watch for trends in the NDCGXA data. These reveal corporate perceptions of the near-term economic outlook and so can help you to predict manufacturing activity and overall economic growth.

Manufacturing and Trade Inventories and Sales

7

T ALK ABOUT THE RED-HEADED STEPCHILD of economic indicators! Few investors, either professional or lay, pay much attention to inventories. Even popular economics texts largely ignore them. Not so corporate managers and economists. Both these groups are well aware of the importance of inventory levels—and of the dangers of miscalculating them.

Business inventories are "waiting room" goods—products that have been manufactured, processed, or mined but have not yet been sold to a final user. As such, they are very important in the calculation of the Gross Domestic Product report (see Chapter 1). GDP is the total amount of final goods and services produced in an economy in a given period. That includes goods that haven't found a final purchaser—in other words, inventory. Accordingly, the Bureau of Economic Analysis incorporates inventories in the aggregate expenditure formula—$C + I + G + (X\text{–}M)$—used to calculate GDP. The I in the formula stands for gross private domestic investment, which includes businesses' spending on inventories. That's one reason economists keep close track of this factor. Miscalculating the value of inventories can throw off an estimate of economic growth by up to two percentage points—a mistake that can ruin a Wall Street economist's career.

But inventories' role in the GDP calculation is not the sole reason economists and managements monitor them carefully. Failure to balance inventories against demand can, and has, hurt businesses and destabilized the economy. Companies that overstock their shelves in anticipation of orders that fail to materialize find themselves in a hole, forced to cut production and lay off workers. Some prominent economists have even implied that the Great Crash of 1929 was provoked, at least in part, by the misalignment of inventory positions. Businesses whose inventories are too lean, on the other hand, miss potential profit during a boom. To avoid such opportunity loss, companies with low stocks may pick up the pace of new orders, spurring manufacture and boosting the economy. Because of their relation to production activity, inventory levels are also of interest to traders. Falling levels, with their promise of increased production and thus higher earnings, can boost equity prices. Fixed-income prices, meanwhile, may decline because of fear of heightened inflation that often accompanies an accelerating economy. On the other hand, rising inventories, implying slowing production, depresses stocks and buoys bonds.

Several economic reports address the inventory position of U.S. companies, but the most comprehensive is the monthly Manufacturing and Trade Inventories and Sales report. The MTIS report, also referred to on the Street as the total business inventories report, contains the most recent available inventory data for the manufacturing, wholesale, and retail sectors. It is assembled by the U.S. Department of Commerce's Census Bureau and released at 8:30 a.m. ET, about six weeks after the reference month. The report for June 2003, for example, was distributed on August 13. Both the current report and historical data are available on the Census Bureau's website at www.census.gov/mtis/www/current.html.

Despite the importance of inventories to GDP and business management, the monthly MTIS report is generally ignored by the investment community and the business media. One reason is that all the sales statistics it contains and two-thirds of the inventory data—those for manufacturing and wholesalers—have already been reported elsewhere. The only new information is on retail inventories, and all the figures are a month and a half old.

Another reason for the MTIS report's lukewarm reception is the difficulty of making the historical comparisons necessary for extensive analyses. The numbers presented are only for the record month and the preceding one. Moreover, because all the data were converted to the North American Industry Classification System (NAICS) in 2001, the statistical history extends only to 1992.

These drawbacks notwithstanding, the MTIS report is definitely worth a careful read. Beyond presenting the first monthly numbers for retail inventories, it contains the very useful inventories-to-sales ratios. And its breakdown and presentation of the data make it relatively easy to trace trends and evaluate the significance of movements.

EVOLUTION OF AN INDICATOR

The MTIS survey was originally implemented and the results published and analyzed by the Department of Commerce's Bureau of Economic Analysis. The Census Bureau took on those duties in March 1979, with the release of the January inventory and sales data of that year. In 1997 the bureau, responding to the scores of new products and industries that needed to be catalogued, decided to convert to the NAICS from the outdated Standard Industrial Classification (SIC) system. It wasn't until 2001 that the data contained in the MTIS report was converted to NAICS. This necessitated some adjustment of data reported under the old system, so that historical comparisons could be made. But the adjustment has been completed back to only 1992.

DIGGING FOR THE DATA

The MTIS report compiles sales data previously reported in the Census Bureau's Advance Monthly Sales for Retail Trade and Food Services report (see Chapter 10) together with inventory and sales information from its Wholesale Trade Survey and its Manufacturers' Shipments, Inventories, and Orders survey (see Chapter 6). The only new information, as noted earlier, is on retail inventories, which is obtained from retail firms regarding the value of their end-of-month inventories.

Figure 7-1   Estimated Monthly Sales and Inventories for Manufacturers,
Retailers, and Merchant Wholesalers

| | Sales ($ in millions) | | |
	June 2003 (p)	May 2003 (r)	June 2002
Total business	**$845,230**	**$835,780**	**$819,478**
Manufacturers	324,611	321,153	320,810
Retailers	283,096	280,578	270,093
Merchant wholesalers	237,523	234,049	228,575

(p) Preliminary, (r) Revised

The report organizes the data into three tables. Table 1 contains sales and inventory numbers and inventories-to-sales ratios for business as a whole as well as for the three primary subgroups: manufacturers, retailers, and merchant wholesalers. The numbers are given, in both seasonally adjusted and nonadjusted form, for the reference month and the month preceding, as well as for the same month a year earlier. **FIGURE 7-1** shows part of Table 1 from the June 2003 report, released in August. In this table, manufacturing accounts for 38 percent of total inventories, retailers for about 37 percent, and merchant wholesalers about 25 percent. These percentages tend to remain relatively stable, although they can be expected to change somewhat as the composition of the American economy evolves.

Table 2 from the report shows the month-over-month and year-over-year percent changes in sales and inventories (both seasonally adjusted and not) for the reference month and the month-over-month changes for the month preceding. Table 3 presents the detail for the retail sector, breaking down the inventory and sales numbers, percent changes, and ratios by retail business: motor vehicle and parts dealers; furniture, home furnishing, electronics, and appliance stores; building materials, garden equipment, and supplies stores; food and beverage stores; general merchandise stores; and, within the last category, department stores excluding leased stores. It also gives two totals: for the retail sector as a whole and for the sector excluding motor vehicles and parts dealers.

Inventories ($ in millions)			Inventories/Sales Ratio		
June 2003 (p)	May 2003 (r)	June 2002	June 2003 (p)	May 2003 (r)	June 2002
$1,168,312	$1,167,232	$1,130,803	1.38	1.40	1.38
430,508	431,356	428,230	1.33	1.34	1.33
448,755	446,914	418,653	1.59	1.59	1.55
289,049	288,962	283,920	1.22	1.23	1.24

Source: U.S. Department of Commerce, Bureau of the Census

WHAT DOES IT ALL MEAN?

What do the levels of inventories tell economists? The simple answer is, plenty. Low inventory positions may signal an impending acceleration in production and manufacturing activity. Conversely, very high inventories may portend a recession and widespread layoffs. Wall Street equity analysts likewise can learn much from inventories. By monitoring the levels in the industries they cover, they can identify developing imbalances and potential troubles that other indicators may not reveal.

Inventories are informative because they are central to the production process, which in turn is key to the health of individual businesses, sectors, and the broader economy. As an illustration, consider the recent history of the telecommunications industry.

During the dot-com heyday of the late 1990s and early 2000s, companies desperate to keep up with the twenty-first-century zeitgeist were continually upgrading their Internet infrastructure with the newest telecom technologies. Communications and fiber-optic equipment went from blueprint to development and production on what seemed a monthly basis, and businesses and consumers eagerly bought up the new products. Competing telecom-equipment makers, greedy for market share, dropped prices. They also boosted production, both to make up for their shrinking margins and to keep ahead of soaring demand. Then the bubble burst. Everyone had upgraded as far as they needed or could afford to, and the telecom manufacturers were left with massive inventories. The only way to deplete these was by selling stock at deep discounts. The resulting downward price spiral squeezed profits. Companies slashed orders for goods they couldn't sell, leading to pullbacks in production and the layoff of thousands of idled workers. Stock prices collapsed, credit deteriorated, companies declared bankruptcy—and the economy fell into recession.

An interested observer could have identified the potential formulation of a bubble in the telecommunications equipment industry by merely observing this sharp increase in inventories. The graph in **FIGURE 7-2** shows that inventories in the nondefense communications industry increased steadily but evenly during the boom time of the mid-1990s, as manufacturers managed to keep just ahead of heavy demand. Around the turn of the century, though, inventories suddenly shot up, reflecting the steep reduction in consumer purchases. The following period of recession was marked by companies slowly clearing their shelves.

Not all accumulation or depletion of inventories is economically significant; some degree of growth or shrinkage is part of the normal course of business. The significance of a change in inventory level depends in part on its cause—whether it was planned or unplanned. The smart economist determines this by talking with corporate officers in the industry experiencing these run-ups or depletions.

Figure 7-2   Inventories of Telecommunication Equipment Manufactures

Source: U.S. Department of Commerce, Bureau of the Census

INVENTORIES AND THE BUSINESS CYCLE

Inventories are obviously closely tied to economic activity. But are they a lagging, coincident, or leading indicator? The answer is: It depends on how you look at them. The *level* of inventory investment is generally considered a lagging indicator. This is because businesses have traditionally been slow to recognize that demand is drying up and their back stock getting dangerously high and thus don't start to draw down inventory until an economic slowdown is already under way. Once they begin, however, the decline in inventory investment from business cycle peak to trough can be staggering, sometimes actually exceeding that in aggregate demand. At the other end of the cycle, businesses have generally delayed ramping up production and restocking their shelves until they're certain a recovery is underway.

Much of this lagging association can be identified in **FIGURE 7-3**, which depicts the month-over-month *change* in manufacturing and trade inventories.

Changes in inventory levels lead the business cycle insofar as they reflect business expectations. If managements anticipate solid economic growth down the road, they beef up their stocks. Alter-

Figure 7-3   Month-to-Month Dollar Change in Inventories

natively, if they foresee lackluster demand, they permit current sales to draw down their existing inventories. The object is to maximize inventory levels with respect to anticipated demand. Achieving this goal has become easier in recent years with the advent of technologies such as electronic scanners and supply-chain and related inventory management systems. These innovations have improved businesses' ability to monitor merchandise levels, so that they don't overorder or understock, and have given them greater control over inventory movements. The result has been a gentler business cycle with recessions that are both shorter and milder.

The rate of change in total business inventories is a useful tool in predicting business cycle turning points. But it can be calibrated to an even finer instrument by looking at the numbers for individual industries, some of which have much more relevance than others to economic activity. Inventory levels of nondurable goods such as food, for instance, don't offer much insight into the general economic situation. The demand for these goods is fairly stable, whether recession is imminent or not, and because the products are, by definition, perishable, they never sit long on the shelf. Much more revelatory are the inventory levels of more cyclical sectors such as nondefense capital goods, automobiles, and consumer durable goods.

INVENTORIES-TO-SALES RATIOS

Among the most useful numbers in the MTIS report are the inventories-to-sales ratios. They indicate how many months it will take, at the current sales pace, until inventories are entirely liquidated—that is, until nothing is left to be sold. An I/S ratio of 1.40, for example, means that at the current sales rate, businesses have 1.40 months of inventories left on their shelves. From 1992 through 2002, the average ratio of total business inventory to sales was 1.45.

Because different types of goods have varied shelf lives, production schedules, and sales rates, the inventories-to-sales ratios for different industries normally move within separate ranges. This is clearly illustrated in **FIGURE 7-4**, which graphs the ratios for the

Figure 7-4   Inventory-to-Sales Ratios: Retail, Wholesale, Manufacturing

Sources: U.S. Department of Commerce, Bureau of the Census; NBER

manufacturing, retail, and wholesale sectors. The chart shows that from 1992 through 2003, retailers had the highest ratios of the three groups, followed by manufacturers and then wholesale merchants. Security analysts who are aware of the range for their area of specialization can check the MTIS report to see where the current ratio fits within it.

HOW TO USE WHAT YOU SEE

Because the data in the MTIS are dated, it is more productive to look at long-term trends in the inventory numbers than to try to analyze those contained in individual reports. Many Wall Street economists maintain running databases of inventories, sales, and the inventories-to-sales ratios from the reports, updating the numbers with each release. This practice can be a bit tedious, but it is well worth the undertaking.

The economics departments at most Wall Street research institutions provide monthly chartbooks to their security analysts. These chartbooks inventory data in the Manufacturing and Trade Inventories and Sales report so that potential production changes can be identified. A sustained, abnormal run-up in monthly automobile inventory levels, for instance, could mean a manufacturing slowdown in the industry down the road, together with slashed prices or staff reductions. An analyst or economist noticing such a trend might talk with automotive industry insiders to confirm or refute the apparent production overhangs and identify their causes. It's always useful to have a Rolodex of insiders' numbers.

TRICK FROM THE TRENCHES

The trick for this chapter involves a different way of looking at data that are there in the MTIS report for anyone to see: the inventories-to-sales ratios. As was noted, these have long been considered good indicators of future economic activity. In the period before the conversion to NAICS, an I/S ratio between 1.55 and 1.60 was taken to mean that recession was imminent. That indication no longer seems to be the case. As also was noted, innovations such as just-in-time inventory and supply-chain management systems have given businesses a better grasp of appropriate inventory levels and better control over the production-shipment-inventory process. As a result, no specific I/S number can be an accurate recession signal.

Instead, economists look for pronounced movements in the ratio that are sustained over several months, such as the rapid run-up from 1.38 in March 2000 to 1.46 in April 2001. When the I/S ratio rises over time, it means that sales are not strong enough to reduce inventories or that goods are being accumulated at too fast a pace. The bottom line is that sales are slower than companies had anticipated. This is a bad sign for the economy. As **FIGURE 7-5** shows, a recession soon followed the 2000–2001 buildup. Conversely, when the ratio of inventories to sales falls over several months, it means that sales are growing faster than inventories and that manufacturers may soon have to boost production. This, of course, is good for overall economic activity.

Figure 7-5   Total Business Inventory-to-Sales Ratio

Sources: U.S. Department of Commerce, Bureau of the Census; NBER

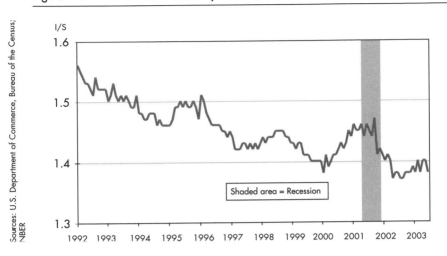

New Residential Construction 8

I F YOU LEARN ONE LESSON from this book, let it be this: never underestimate the economic importance of housing. The realization of the American Dream of home ownership is one of the primary drivers of the economy. Housing activity affects the investment (I) component of the aggregate expenditure formula for calculating gross domestic product (see Chapter 1): $C + I + G + (X–M)$. The construction of new, privately owned residential structures, particularly single-family homes, is very informative about consumer sentiment and the health of the economy. After all, a purchase of this magnitude requires the utmost confidence in one's personal financial situation, including employment security and earnings prospects. It also implies favorable conditions in the broader economy. Beyond personal income, the primary influences on housing activity are the level of interest rates and demographics. When these factors are aligned correctly, a buoyant housing market can boost total economic activity; when they're not, a slumping market can drag the overall economy into deep recession.

How can new housing construction, which accounts directly for only 3 percent of GDP, influence the economy so profoundly? Because of the multiplier effect of related spending and other indirect contributions. Once a home is bought, it must be furnished and decorated. All of this activity means new jobs for construction workers, retail salespeople, and manufacturers; increased tax revenues for local and state municipalities; and greater spending on goods such as carpeting, furniture, and appliances. Of course, these jobs and revenues fail to materialize if unfavorable conditions, such as rising interest rates, stifle demand for new homes.

Several important housing indicators exist, including the Census Bureau's new home sales and the National Association of Realtors' existing home sales. The most influential, however, are new-housing starts and building permits. These statistics are contained in New Residential Construction, which is released jointly by the U.S. Department of Commerce's Census Bureau and the U.S. Department of Housing and Urban Development, at 8:30 a.m. ET on approximately the fifteenth day of the month following the reference month. The release, as well as detail on the different stages of the construction process and a description of the methodology used, is available on the Census Bureau's website, at www.census.gov/const/www/newrcsconstindex.html. The data contained in New Residential Construction, informally called "housing starts" by market participants, are among the most respected economic indicators on Wall Street and should be included in any serious model of U.S. economic activity.

EVOLUTION OF AN INDICATOR

Information regarding the origins of the new residential construction report is limited. Truth be told, there is little meaningful history to speak of. The Commerce Department's U.S. Census Bureau assumed the responsibilities of the collection of housing starts data back in 1959. Previously, the duties of aggregating, calculating, and distributing the starts and permits data belonged to the Department of Labor's Bureau of Labor Statistics (BLS). The data that the BLS had gathered dated back to 1889.

The report has remained basically the same, in form and methodology, since 1959. A few minor changes have occurred along the way, such as the inclusion of farm housing and the exclusion of public housing. Some definitions have also been modified. In the wake of Hurricane Andrew in 1992, for instance, the meaning of "housing starts" was expanded to include rebuilding on existing foundations. In the 1990s, a correction was made so that starts without legal permits would be included, resulting in a break in the series. This break has had minor consequence on the continuity of the series. In 1968, the bureau began reporting detailed housing characteristics, such as completions. For the most part, however, any and all of these changes have had a negligible effect on the monthly reports.

DIGGING FOR THE DATA

The New Residential Construction report contains data on privately owned residential structures, both single family and multifamily. Each unit in the multifamily structures is counted separately; so a building with ten apartments, for example, is counted as ten units. Excluded are public housing and hotels, motels, group residential structures such as college dormitories and nursing homes, and mobile homes.

The release consists of a summary of the month's figures followed by five tables. Each table corresponds to five stages in the residential construction process. The first contains data on the number of new, privately owned housing units for which applications for building permits, required for construction in most U.S. regions, have been filed. The figures are compiled from responses to mail surveys sent to building permit officials in 8,500 permit-issuing localities, out of a universe of some 19,000.

The Census Bureau derives a sample of 900 permit-issuing places in the Survey of Construction (SOC), which is the source for the Housing Units Authorized, but Not Started; Housing Starts; Housing Units Under Construction; and Housing Completions (Tables 2 through 5) data. This sample is chosen with respect to the labor force, race/ethnic origin, population change, and family and housing characteristics in the respective permit-issuing place. Census Bureau field representatives canvass these 900 places, as well as the less than 3 percent of areas that don't require permits, and estimate the characteristics of the several stages of construction (i.e., was the unit started, completed, and so forth).

The second table contains data for units whose construction has been authorized but not yet begun. The Census Bureau produced this table because the majority of new construction typically begins during the month of permit issuance, and is included in Table 1. The difference between the two tables is the number of housing units that have been authorized by zoning or building permit, where construction was and wasn't started.

The third table presents the number of housing starts—that is, the number of units for which excavation of the footings or foundation has begun. This is the headliner of the *New Residential Construction* report. By this stage, money has generally been exchanged, implying that owners are committed to the construction project. The fourth table includes units "under construction"—that is, where work has begun but not yet been completed. These data closely parallel the changes in residential construction figures contained in the Commerce Department's *Value of Construction Put in Place* report, referred to on the Street as construction spending.

The fifth table analyzes completions.

By breaking down the numbers according to stages in the housing construction process, the tables allow economists, investors, and other market participants to pinpoint where the strengths and weaknesses lie. For example, should permits, starts, and construction all pick up but completions remain flat, homebuilders may be running up against troubling economic conditions such as an increase in the unemployment rate that could hinder would-be home buyers from purchasing a new home. Also, a rising interest rate environment could create difficulties for those buyers attempting to obtain financing at reasonable terms.

The tables present twelve months of data—preliminary figures for the record month, revisions for the two previous ones, and final figures going back a year—in both seasonally adjusted annualized form and as unadjusted monthly numbers. They also include the unadjusted annual numbers for the previous two years and the year-to-date totals for the current year and the one before, as well as the adjusted annualized percent changes between the record month and the previous month and between the record month and year-earlier one.

The numbers of units at each stage of construction are given for the entire United States as well as for four regions: Northeast, Midwest, South, and West. The figures for the entire country are broken down by size of structure, into single-family dwellings, residences with two to four units, and those with five or more units.

WHAT DOES IT ALL MEAN

Residential housing investment has a ripple effect on the overall economy that is far greater than its direct contribution to GDP. This is because of the amount of labor and the number and volume of products involved in constructing and furnishing a home. Just consider the following list, from the National Association of Home Builders (NAHB), of resources used in an average 2,000-square-foot single-family home:

- 13,127 board feet of framing lumber
- 6,212 square feet of sheathing
- 13.97 tons of concrete
- 2,325 square feet of exterior siding material
- 3,100 square feet of roofing material
- 3,061 square feet of insulation
- 6,144 square feet of interior wall material
- 120 linear feet of ducting
- 15 windows
- 13 kitchen cabinets, 2 other cabinets
- 1 kitchen sink
- 12 interior doors
- 7 closet doors
- 2 exterior doors
- 1 patio door
- 2 garage doors
- 1 fireplace
- 3 toilets, 2 bathtubs, 1 shower stall
- 3 bathroom sinks
- 2,085 square feet of flooring material, such as carpeting, resilient sheet, resilient tile, ceramic tile, or wood plank
- 1 range, 1 refrigerator, 1 dishwasher, 1 garbage disposal, 1 range hood
- 1 washer, 1 dryer

Of course, those timbers have to be joined, the concrete poured, the sheathing, siding, roofing, wall material, and insulation applied, and the windows, doors, appliances, and other amenities installed. The NAHB has concluded that building 1,000 single-family homes generates 2,448 full-time jobs, $79.4 million in wages, and $42.5 million in government revenues.

Even after houses are built and furnished, they can continue to stimulate economic activity—and not just through remodeling and other forms of upgrading. People's homes are often their largest asset, and thus their largest potential source of capital. When mortgage rates fall, home owners refinance at the lower rates, either reducing their monthly payments or increasing the amount of their loans, or some combination of the two.

Research has shown that most of the savings realized are poured back into the home. It should thus come as no surprise that do-it-yourself home centers such as Home Depot and Lowe's Corporation performed so well during the mortgage refinancing boom of the late 1990s and early 2000s. Furthermore, because consumer spending is a large component of GDP, the entire economy benefits from this activity. In fact, many economists credit the mildness of the recent recession to the surge in mortgage refinancings driven by the low interest rates during the period.

INFLUENCES ON RESIDENTIAL CONSTRUCTION

Clearly, housing investment has a profound effect on the economy. The reverse is also true: Residential construction is one of the most economically sensitive and cyclical sectors. Two important influences on housing are interest rates and demographics.

Because their homes are the most expensive purchases that most people make, borrowing is almost a certainty—unless, of course, they're big lottery winners. It's not surprising, therefore, that housing starts are correlated with the level of interest rates: the lower the 30-year fixed mortgage rate, the rate at which most wannabe home owners borrow, the less onerous the loan and the higher the number of starts. **FIGURE 8-1** shows the relationship between mortgage rates

Figure 8-1   Single-Family Housing Starts and the 30-Year Fixed Mortgage Rate

and starts (an inverse one—note the inverted right-hand scale). A general rule of thumb is that as long as income and employment are both growing steadily and home prices remain reasonable, rates of 7.25 percent or lower will boost housing activity.

Because it indirectly influences the 30-year rate, the Federal Reserve has the power to boost or dampen housing activity. When economic growth threatens to spark high inflation, the Fed may attempt to slow things down by raising its overnight borrowing rate (see Chapter 1). This increase usually travels along the maturity spectrum, eventually resulting in higher mortgage rates. The consequent reduction in house building and sales, combined with retrenchments in other capital spending caused by the Fed tightening, slows economic growth. If the Fed is overzealous and raises interest rates too high, a recession can set in. On the other hand, when the economy is sluggish, the Fed often acts to stimulate it by lowering its overnight target rate, which bolsters demand for and construction of new homes.

Also important in determining housing activity are the size and composition of the population. Obviously, the more people there are of home-buying age, the greater the potential activity. Economists have found that the number of people between 30 and 59 has the strongest correlation with the number of new and existing home sales, as well as with the pace of single-family residential construction. Remember, it generally takes a while after graduation for individuals to accumulate enough money for a down payment on a home. Furthermore, earnings for individuals in their 20s generally don't amount to much.

People between 20 and 25 and those 60 and above are more closely linked to multiple-unit construction, because recent graduates and the elderly tend to reside in multifamily structures, such as apartment buildings. The first of the 77 million or so baby boomers— Americans born between 1946 and 1964—reached the average home-purchasing age, 32, in 1978. This demographic shift not only boosted the housing market over the past quarter century, but also played an integral role in greater economic activity in general.

Immigration increases the population and thus the demand for housing. The Federal National Mortgage Association (FNMA) has found that newcomers to the United States typically realize the American Dream about ten to fifteen years after arriving. Given the incredible improvement in immigrant incomes and the interest rate environment, recent immigrants might become first-time home owners a bit quicker than that. Already, the tsunami of immigration in the late 1900s and early 2000s has buoyed new construction activity, with some homebuilders crediting the housing boom of late as being related more to improvements in immigrant welfare than to the near-record low interest rate environment.

Because of their sensitivity to interest rates, demographics, and other factors, such as taxes and weather, monthly housing data are very volatile. To discern trends more easily, economists smooth out this volatility by looking at new construction activity on a quarterly or a trending three-month basis.

REGIONAL DIFFERENCES

Many of the factors that can affect construction activity vary considerably from region to region across the United States. Midwestern agricultural communities, for instance, will typically suffer disturbances in employment and income growth at different times and

Figure 8-2 Regional Composition of New Residential Construction (1990–2003)

Source: U.S. Department of Commerce, Bureau of the Census

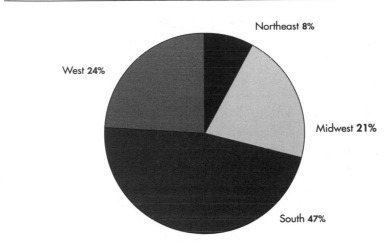

Northeast 8%

West 24%

Midwest 21%

South 47%

under different economic conditions than areas with more manu-facturing industries, such as the Rust Belt, and the West Coast with its concentration of technology companies. Weather conditions also vary regionally, with hurricanes in the Southeast, cold winters in the Northeast and Midwest, and flooding and drought in the South and Southwest. Furthermore, although monetary policy, which deter-mines interest rates, is national, other policy matters, such as tax in-centives, differ from state to state. Not surprisingly, then, there is a great disparity among the housing statistics for the different regions represented in the New Residential Construction report.

As shown in **FIGURE 8-2**, throughout the 1990s and the early 2000s, the Northeast has accounted for less than 10 percent of the total of new private housing starts. The Midwest, West, and South, meanwhile, have contributed approximately 20, 25, and 45 percent, respectively.

HOUSING AND THE BUSINESS CYCLE

The preceding sections described the close two-way relationship be-tween housing and the economy. But what does housing activity—and, more precisely, the statistics contained in the new construction report—tell us about different stages and turning points in the business cycle?

Housing's relationship with the business cycle may best be described as FIFO, or first in, first out: Housing is one of the first industries to head south before a downturn and among the first to pull out of recession. In other words, it is somewhat of a leading indicator. Not all the stages of construction, however, have the same predictive power, nor do they receive the same attention.

The number of permit applications is the most forward-looking of all the statistics in this report. It is so forward-looking, in fact, that the Conference Board includes it in the index of leading economic indicators (see Chapter 2). Although permit applications don't always result in starts, economists assume that contractors won't go through the trouble, time, and expense of applying for a permit unless they are very serious about building a home. Because this statistic is a gauge of future demand for construction and housing, equity analysts covering the home builders and real estate investment trust (REIT) markets should keep an eye on it.

Economists have found that privately-owned housing units authorized by building permits generally precede housing starts by about one month and sales by about three. The number of permit applications peaks as much as twelve months before the onset of a recession and bottoms out, for the most part, almost simultaneously with the overall economy.

The number of units authorized for construction, representing a later stage in the process, is slightly more accurate than the number of applications as a measure of future building activity. Economists have found that this indicator leads new starts by about two months. Units under construction depict the current state of construction activity, construction-industry employment, and the demand for building materials.

Housing completions can point to problems brewing in the economy. A significant gap between units under construction and the number completed may be due to inclement weather—hurricanes in the South and blizzards in the Northeast and West frequently cause lengthy delays in the building process. But a lag in completions can also mean that a large number of builders or buyers cannot afford to finish their projects. That in turn may signal financial weakness in the overall economy.

SINGLE-FAMILY HOUSING STARTS

Although the statistics for the other stages of construction are informative, the headliner of the New Residential Construction report is the number of housing starts—more specifically, those relating to single-unit structures. Wall Street focuses on single-family residences rather than multiunit ones because the figures for the latter are more volatile. Multiunit structures typically include apartments, condominiums, and townhouses. As noted earlier, each apartment in one of these buildings is counted as a separate unit. So when construction of a 500-apartment building is started or canceled, 500 units at a time are added to or eliminated from the monthly tally. This can cause extreme month-to-month swings.

Multiunit housing is also more sensitive to tax policy. The U.S. government, for instance, provides the incentives for building in underdeveloped neighborhoods; these incentives usually involve multi- rather than single-unit structures. Because such incentives change with the political landscape, they can add to the volatility of the multiunit numbers. Finally, the pace of multiunit construction may be partly a function of the growth rate of single-family housing. In the late 1990s and early 2000s, for instance, many apartment dwellers left them to buy single-family homes, which had become much more affordable. This boosted single-unit numbers and depressed multiunit ones.

Single-family starts, as illustrated in **FIGURE 8-3**, typically account for close to 80 percent of all new private housing starts. This statistic may be the ultimate gauge of consumer confidence; and because consumer activity accounts for upwards of 70 percent of total U.S. economic output, single-family starts deserve the attention they get.

Why is the level of single-family housing starts such an excellent barometer of the health of the consumer sector? Simply put, when people are concerned about their economic situation, they may

Figure 8-3 Total and Single-Family Housing Starts

Units in thousands

Source: U.S. Department of Commerce, Bureau of the Census

still spend on other products but they won't even consider buying homes. This is another reason why the housing market is such an excellent indicator of business cycle activity.

Before the 2001 recession, housing starts were the most reliable and accurate measure of U.S. economic health. Every post–World War II economic recession was accompanied by a precipitous decline in new housing starts and housing activity in general, which triggered similar reductions in consumer expenditures for related goods and in the employment of workers in associated industries.

The 2001 recession broke this pattern. Housing starts remained strong during the downturn because historically low inflation kept mortgage rates low. Multidecade lows in the unemployment rate and soaring personal incomes from the torrid pace of payroll growth during the 1990s helped fuel future (i.e., recession-period) home and related purchases. The same factors—plus the mortgage refinancing mentioned earlier—kept consumer spending in positive territory. In fact, the worst showing for expenditures, occurring during the second quarter of 2001, was a 1.4 percent increase. Not coincidentally, a great deal of this spending was on home-related goods, along with renovations, additions, and other home improvements. All this kept the 2001 recession very mild.

Another reason that home purchases and related spending remained strong during the recession and through 2002 was the dismal performance of the stock market. Recognizing that they could do little or nothing to improve their portfolios' value, people worked to increase the value of their greatest asset, their home. It is important to remember that at this time, home owners (at 67 percent) outnumbered shareholders (50 percent of U.S. households) in the United States. Home ownership is defined by the Census Bureau as the proportion of the number of households that are owners to the total number of households. After the September 11, 2001, attacks, moreover, Americans became nesters, vacationing within 100 miles of their homes and eliminating unnecessary business travel. They also started buying second homes as getaways from primary residences in, or near, big cities. Many of the purchasers were baby boomers looking toward retirement, whose second homes could become their primary post-retirement residences.

How to Use What You See

As always, one of the goals for market pros is to get a jump on the most market-moving statistics in the report. In the case of the New Residential Construction report, one strategy would be to gather anecdotal evidence from the home builders themselves. Many of the nation's largest builders—including K&B Homes, MDC Holdings, Pulte Homes, Inc., Toll Brothers, Lennar Corporation, Ryland Group, Hovnanian Enterprises, Engle Homes, and Beazer Homes USA—talk about the issues they are facing in their quarterly statements or in frequent presentations, which are available on their websites. In addition, the NAHB provides excellent statistical measures of the housing market, remodeling trends, and housing affordability. The Mortgage Bankers Association (MBA) has created a few of the Street's most respected economic indicators on mortgage applications for purchases and refinancings. It's also a good idea to keep an eye on the loan and default data on the Federal Reserve's website, which can provide early signals of troubles in the industry. Reluctance by loan officers to extend housing credit may signal that banks are having problems collecting on extended loans. Specifically, interested readers should watch the household detail in the Federal Reserve's Senior Loan Officer Opinion Survey on Bank Lending Practices. It is available on their website, www.federalreserve.gov.

TRICKS FROM THE TRENCHES

Economists have found that the difference between the number of total privately-owned housing starts and the number of privately-owned housing units authorized by building permits yields a crude gauge of housing activity that is more informative than the number of starts by itself. Permits here can be seen as a proxy for housing demand and starts as a proxy for housing supply. The resulting "spread" is most useful as an indicator of boom conditions in the housing sector.

A negative spread, with permits lagging behind starts, is characteristic of normal or even moderately expansionary housing market. As **FIGURE 8-4** shows, such a spread existed from 1992 to 1997. During this six-year period, new housing starts averaged about 1.4 million units (annualized), a reasonably strong pace by historical standards.

Figure 8-4 Difference Between Housing Permits and Starts

In thousands

Source: U.S. Department of Commerce, Bureau of the Census

Positive spreads, when permits exceed starts, existed from 1998 to mid-2002. Economists interpreted these as signals of a boom in future housing activity. When housing demand exceeds supply by a significant amount, prices generally rise. From 1998 to 2002, median new home prices advanced 28 percent. A boom generally occurs when all economic cylinders are firing, inflation and interest rates are low, and incomes and employment are on the rise.

Conference Board Consumer Confidence and University of Michigan Consumer Sentiment Indices

9

M OST, PROBABLY, OF OUR DECISIONS to do something positive, the full consequences of which will be drawn out over many days to come, can only be taken as a result of animal spirits—of a spontaneous urge to action rather than inaction, and not as the outcome of a weighted average of quantitative benefits multiplied by quantitative probabilities." These words—by pioneering economic theorist John Maynard Keynes in his 1936 opus, *The General Theory of Employment, Interest, and Money*—may be the first written recognition of the importance of consumer sentiment in economics. The need to quantify these "animal spirits" is the motivating force behind the consumer confidence measures of today.

When it comes to the economy, consumers are king, accounting for roughly two-thirds of gross domestic product through their spending on items from abacuses to Zip disks. It is always good to know how the king is feeling. When people feel confident about their financial situation and future, they are usually reacting to some positive economic fundamental, such as solid employment growth or rising personal incomes. It is not surprising, then, that measures of consumer attitude have produced an impressive record of predicting economic turning points.

Many surveys of consumer confidence and sentiment exist. Some research institutions and investment firms have even created their own, to get the data into their systems and transformed into forecasts and strategies as quickly as possible. Although differing in specifics, the various surveys share one crucial characteristic: They ask everyday people from different walks of life simple questions that probe their feelings about the current and future state of the economy, inflation, and their plans for vehicle and home purchases. The survey participants may not know the difference between recession and depression, but their answers provide insights into the likelihood of these situations occurring.

Of all the surveys and measures, the best known and most respected are the Conference Board's Consumer Confidence Index and the University of Michigan's Index of Consumer Sentiment. (The weekly ABC News/*Money* Magazine Consumer Comfort Index is another outstanding measure with exceptional links to consumer retail sales activity, but it is less popular than the other two, possibly because its weekly schedule makes it extremely volatile and therefore less market-moving.)

The Conference Board's confidence index is generally released on the last Tuesday of each month and made available to the investing public (in a limited version) on the Conference Board's website at www.conference-board.org. A more detailed version, as well as its history, is available by subscription directly from the Conference Board.

The University of Michigan usually issues its sentiment index on the second to last Friday of each month, followed by the revised *final* estimate two weeks later. This survey is available by subscription only. An historical series of the Sentiment Index and the Inflation Expectation Index is available at the Federal Reserve Bank of St. Louis website at http://research.stlouisfed.org/fred2/. The results that come across the newswires or are posted at the more popular business news websites are sufficient for most readers' purposes.

Every Wall Street economics department that is serious about forecasting growth subscribes to these surveys. They are also frequently cited by Federal Reserve and White House officials and are the object of countless studies by government agencies seeking to determine if economic policies are working as intended. After the Federal Reserve lowers the overnight interest rate, for instance, it will want to know if this move has encouraged consumers to buy interest-rate-sensitive goods, such as houses and automobiles. The answer could well determine whether the Fed will lower rates further or not.

The markets generally react most sharply to the confidence measures when the business cycle is close to a turning point. The indices won't indicate how much the economy may grow or fall back. But when they decline sharply, you can bet on tough economic sledding ahead. Conversely, when the indices spike upward, you can look forward to more prosperous times.

EVOLUTION OF AN INDICATOR

George Katona, a Hungarian-born psychologist and economist with the Survey Research Center of the University of Michigan, started asking questions about consumer intentions in the 1940s. The university began conducting its survey in 1946, using many of the same questions that it does today. The survey, originally an annual event, switched to a quarterly schedule in 1960 and then a monthly one in 1978.

Throughout the 1940s and 1950s, Katona and University of Michigan economics professor Eva Mueller were virtually alone in the field, together producing a weighty corpus of studies of consumer attitudes, incomes, and spending habits. The Conference Board started conducting bimonthly surveys of consumer attitudes only in 1967. It, too, converted to a monthly schedule ten years later, in June 1977.

DIGGING FOR THE DATA

Although both the Conference Board's and the University of Michigan's indices measure consumer confidence and expectations, the underlying surveys pose different questions and poll sample groups of different size and breadth. For its indices, the University of Michigan's Survey Research Center polls 500 households in the lower forty-eight states by telephone, asking participants about their personal finances, general business conditions, and planned purchases. The entire survey consists of more than two dozen core questions, which serve as the basis for several indices. The Index of Consumer Sentiment (ICS) is created from the responses to five of the questions, those asking respondents (1) if they're better or worse off financially than a year ago; (2) whether the year to come will be better or worse for them financially; (3) how businesses will fare in the next twelve months; (4) whether the country during the next five years or so will experience good times or widespread unemployment and depression; and (5) whether it is a good or bad time to buy major household items. Responses are classified as positive, neutral, or negative. Two sub-indices are formed from different subsets of the five responses: the Index of Current Economic Conditions (ICC), from replies to questions 1 and 5, and the Index of Consumer Expectations (ICE), from 2, 3, and 4.

The ICS, ICC, and ICE are all constructed using diffusion methodology: The positive responses are added up and the result divided by the sum of positive and negative responses to yield a relative value. The index values are calculated relative to a base month of January 1966, whose value is set at 100. The Center generally releases preliminary indices on the second Friday of the month following the record month and issues final versions within two weeks after that.

The survey on which the Conference Board bases its indices is conducted by Greenwich, Connecticut–based NFO Research. NFO polls a panel of about 5,000 households on their assessment of current economic conditions, their expectations for the future, and their plans for major purchases in the next six months. Like Michigan's Survey Research Center, the Conference Board constructs three diffusion indices from the responses to five of these questions. These five ask respondents (1) how they rate general business conditions in their area; (2) what conditions they foresee in six months; (3) how they would characterize current job availability in their area; (4) how they think availability will compare in six months; and (5) how they think their family income in six months will compare with their current income. The Consumer Confidence Index is constructed from the responses to all five questions; the Present Situation Index from answers to 1 and 3; and the

Expectations Index from 2, 4, and 5. All three indices are calculated relative to the base year 1985, whose value is set at 100. Unlike the Survey Research Center, the Conference Board adjusts the survey statistics for seasonal variations.

The Conference Board receives preliminary results eighteen to twenty-one days into the record month, so the indices reflect the conditions of the month's first three weeks. Any late surveys are retained and used in the revision contained in the next month's release. The index numbers in the monthly report are kept secret until the official release. The only exceptions are for the Conference Board officials charged with writing the accompanying commentary, the Federal Reserve, and the White House's Council of Economic Advisors. The Fed and the CEA receive the report after 4:00 p.m. ET the day before the official release. The Conference Board also releases, separately, consumer confidence data for nine geographical regions.

WHAT DOES IT ALL MEAN?

The differences in the methodologies used by University of Michigan's Survey Research Center and the Conference Board are small but still important enough to produce indices with somewhat divergent characteristics and strengths. On the one hand, many economists feel that the larger pool sampled in the NFO survey makes the Conference Board's indices more significant statistically. They also believe that eliciting expectations for the next six months, as the NFO survey does, is more realistic than the Michigan survey's practice of asking for a five-year perspective. On the other hand, the longer history and the twice-monthly reporting of the sentiment indices make the University of Michigan report one of Wall Street's favorites. Serious investors would be best served by subscribing to both surveys.

That said, the similarities between the two sets of indices are in many ways more important than their differences. The most obvious similarity is that they all move in a close association with the business cycle.

Figure 9-1 University of Michigan Consumer Sentiment Index and Conference
Board Coincident Index

FIGURE 9-1 shows the University of Michigan's Index of Consumer
Sentiment charted against the Conference Board's coincident indicators index. As explained in Chapter 2, the coincident index reflects the current condition of the economy; it rises during periods
of expanding economic activity and declines during recessions or
periods of retarded growth. Note that current economic activity, as
measured by the coincident index, flat-lines or declines each time
the University of Michigan's Index of Consumer Sentiment falls
below 80. When the index is below that level for a sustained period,
the economy is extremely sluggish. Such was the case from late 1978
through early 1983. During that stretch, the economy was mired in
recession, plagued by some of the poorest economic fundamentals
in history: Inflation topped 14 percent, unemployment broke 10
percent, and both the prime and the Fed funds rate exceeded 20
percent. No wonder consumer confidence tumbled. Consecutive
index readings above 90, conversely, coincide with periods of relative prosperity, marked by a rising trend in the coincident index.

The picture is similar for the Conference Board's Consumer
Confidence Index. Lynn Franco, the director of the Conference
Board's Consumer Research Center, says that a reading of 100 or

Figure 9-2   Conference Board's Consumer Confidence Index and Recessions

above indicates the economy is expanding. During the 120 months from April 1991 through March 2001, which marked the longest economic expansion in U.S. history, the confidence index stood above 100 for 69 months and above 90 for 81. At the onset of a recession, in contrast, the index usually dips below 80. This is illustrated in **FIGURE 9-2**, which shows the confidence index overlaid by highlighted bars representing recessions, as identified by the National Bureau of Economic Research (NBER), the official arbiter of U.S. business cycles. Note that during the 1981–82 recession, the index was below 80 for fifteen of the sixteen months, and during the 1990–91 recession for five of the eight months.

Figures 9-1 and 9-2 also illustrate one drawback of the two indices as economic indicators: Because of their strong links to consumer activity, they may fail to identify turning points that are not consumer-driven. Figure 9-1, for example, shows that the Michigan sentiment index badly lagged the 1991 economic recovery, remaining in the 60s and 70s even as the economy was steadily improving. This "hangover" reflects the fact that the job market remained stagnant for more than two years after the official end of the recession in March 1991. Labor conditions have a profound effect on consumer attitudes.

The Conference Board's confidence index has also missed the mark from time to time, as witness its behavior during the 2001–02 recession, represented in Figure 9-2. During the entire seven months from April 2001 to November 2001 that the economy was in recession, the index never fell below 80. In fact, its lowest reading during the recession was 84.9, recorded in November 2001. This reflects the fact that unlike other post–World War II downturns, the recession of 2001 was the result of a precipitous decline in business investment rather than a retrenchment in consumer spending. In fact, spending was buoyed by low, 4.6 percent unemployment, mild 2.5 percent inflation, and similarly low interest rates.

Another potential source of misleading sentiment readings is the lag that occurs between conducting the surveys and releasing the indices. The Conference Board indices reflect the conditions of the first three weeks of the month. Any earth-shattering news occurring after the twenty-first of the month will not be reflected in the confidence level recorded in the release. A dramatic example of this was the stock market crash of 1987. Black Monday, when the Dow Jones Industrial Average tumbled a record 508 points, was October 19. Many responses to the NFO survey were elicited before this date. As a result, the Confidence Index fell a mere 0.6 points in October, to 115.1 from 115.7 in September. By November, everyone was aware of the crash, and the index declined nearly fifteen points, to 100.8. Of course, 100 is still far from 80, the usual recession level. The Confidence Index was thus one of the few indicators that accurately predicted economic prosperity after the stock market crash.

THE EXPECTATION INDICES

Although the overall confidence and sentiment indices possess moderate predictive power, as illustrated in the preceding example, they are more likely to move in synchrony with the business cycle. The true powerhouses of predictability are the two expectations indices constructed by the Conference Board and University of Michigan. In fact, the University of Michigan's Index of Consumer Expectations (ICE) is included in the Conference Board's leading economic indicators index (LEI). The University of Michigan's Sentiment Index predates the Conference Board's measure and was used in the LEI prior to the Conference Board's formal acceptance of the calculation, publication, and caretaking responsibilities of the Business Cycle Indicators in 1996.

Before a recession, the two expectations indices typically experience considerable declines for about five to six months. There is no specific reading or percentage drop associated with either index that signals a definitive downturn. However, momentous declines in either index pretty much alert the analyst of a probable economic downturn. For example, prior to the commencement of the August 1990 recession, the Conference Board's Expectations Index tumbled from a reading of 100.3 in May to 74.2 in August. The Index continued to decline into the 50s throughout the remainder of the year. Declines in the Conference Board's Expectations Index of this magnitude have historically preceded downturns in the economy by an average of about three months, and the University of Michigan's ICE by two months. The longest lead for both indices was six months, before the beginning of the downturn in April 2001.

The indices are most accurate in predicting recessions when their movements over an entire year are considered. The expectations indices of the Conference Board and the University of Michigan tumbled an average of 24 percent and 18 percent, respectively, over the twelve months leading up to the 1980, 1990, and 2001 recessions. Interestingly, the total confidence and sentiment indices are also strongly predictive when looked at in this way. In the twelve months before those same recessions, the Conference Board's index declined 20.9 percent on average and the University of Michigan's index 14.4 percent.

The expectations indices tend to possess less predictive powers when it comes to recoveries. For example, when the 1990–91 recession ended in March 1991, the Conference Board's Expectations Index bottomed in January 1991 with a reading of 5.3, and followed with gains in February to 63.3 and a tremendous surge in March to 100.7. Similarly, the Conference Board's Expectations Index bottomed in October 2001 with a reading of 70.7, a month before the "official" end of the recession in November when the Expectations Index had a reading of 92.4. The expectations indices clearly identify recoveries, but with little lead time.

CONFIDENCE AND DURABLES SPENDING

People generally buy big-ticket durable goods, such as stoves, refrigerators, and autos, on credit, which means committing to principal and interest payments over a long period. In making such purchases, therefore, consumers need to take stock of their financial future. That entails considering their employment status, potential income growth—even the state of the economy. These are the very considerations covered in the forward-looking questions of the Conference Board and University of Michigan surveys. It's hardly surprising, then, that the two expectations measures possess a strong parallel relationship with durable goods purchases, as illustrated in **FIGURE 9-3**.

Recognizing this relationship, the big automakers, producers of some of the priciest durable goods, keep a watchful eye on the consumer indices. Ford Motor Company's sales analysis manager

Figure 9-3 Conference Board's Expectations Index Versus Consumer Spending: Durable Goods

Figure 9-4 University of Michigan Index of Consumer Sentiment and Federal Reserve's Industrial Production Index of Auto Production

Sources: University of Michigan; Board of Governors of the Federal Reserve System

underlined the importance given these numbers in the industry when he told *The Wall Street Journal* in January 2001 that the drop in the University of Michigan's sentiment index in that month's report to 93.6 from 98.4 the previous month had "played an important role" in the company's decision to cut back on North American production.

The automakers' close reading of the indices is reflected in **FIGURE 9-4**, which shows that for much of the 1980s and especially in the 1990s, automobile production paralleled the sentiment index. This relationship broke down a bit in the 2000s because of the zero percent financing deals that automakers offered in fall 2001. Consumers simply could not ignore such incredible deals. Still, this relationship is steady over time and all analysts are encouraged to keep this index in their toolkits.

HOW TO USE WHAT YOU SEE

Any indicator becomes a more useful tool when you understand the factors that affect it. Such knowledge can aid in both interpreting and anticipating the indicator's readings. The task is different with measures of consumer attitude than it is with other indicators, because the former deal not with something tangible—such as the number of computers produced, the level of aircraft orders, or the value of construction put in place—but with psychology. Wielding consumer sentiment measures thus entails knowing how consumers' emotions are brought into play and whether these emotions are sufficiently strong to change spending habits and so have an impact on the general economy.

EMPLOYMENT AND SENTIMENT

In the United States, employment status has deep psychological resonance. You are what you do. When people meet at a cocktail party or at a bar, their first question after exchanging names is usually, "Where do you work?" Not having a proper response can be upsetting.

People who are uncertain about their job security or hear of relatives or neighbors being laid off become pessimistic, the depth of pessimism depending on the breadth of job losses and the length of unemployment. During a recession, jobless claims and widespread layoff announcements usually garner headlines, producing anxiety even among those that still have jobs. All this is reflected in the consumer confidence and sentiment indices. As **FIGURE 9-5** illustrates, confidence falls steeply when nonfarm payroll growth slows and plummets when that measure moves into negative territory. Watching the employment numbers can thus help you anticipate the next month's sentiment numbers or, just as important, interpret current readings. As the confidence index's behavior during the 1991 recovery illustrates, high unemployment can keep confidence low even when other fundamentals are picking up.

NONECONOMIC INFLUENCES ON SENTIMENT

Consumers react to many things besides employment and perceptions of general economic health. War, peace, and politics can all shake or bolster consumer confidence. The emotional ride is particularly turbulent today, because of the tremendous growth

Figure 9-5 Consumer Confidence Index and Nonfarm Payroll Growth

Sources: U.S. Department of Labor, Bureau of Labor Statistics; The Conference Board

in news outlets on the Internet and cable and the almost instantaneous dissemination of information over these channels. The result is often a false economic signal. Economists, analysts, and traders must learn to differentiate between news that will stimulate or stop spending and information that consumers will simply find uplifting or irritating.

Consider the 1990s. The flood of investment advice, technical and fundamental information, and live securities prices flowing through financial websites and news channels fed stock market fever in the general populace. Not surprisingly, consumer attitudes closely paralleled monthly changes in stock prices. While consumers frequently misassociate stock market activity with economic activity, differentiating between the two can be difficult for those analysts interpreting the confidence measures. Rather than look at the mounting excesses in the underlying economy and the irrational stock market valuations, consumers clung to the false sense of enthusiasm generated by business journalists that were attempting to scoop one another with respect to new investment trends. It was this subsequent rising stock market wealth that was reflected in the rising confidence measures of the 1990s, not the heavily burdened economic foundations.

News, of course, affects confidence in both directions. Just as the dot-com news festival propelled sentiment to some of the highest levels ever recorded, so too did reports of President Bill Clinton's possible impeachment, the "hanging chad" presidential election of 2000, and the anthrax terrorist scares of 2001 drive the confidence numbers down into the cellar.

When President Clinton was threatened with impeachment in December 1998, Americans were gravely concerned about the leadership of the nation, its direction, and the possible consequences this action would have on their personal situations. The same holds true for the 2000 presidential election, when Al Gore won the popular vote and George W. Bush the electoral vote. There were suspicions of widespread scandal in Florida's ballot counting and doubts about the legitimacy of the electoral process. Both events affected consumer sentiment negatively, but because neither really had anything to do with the economy, economic activity was generally unaffected.

Impeachment and election uncertainty are mild disturbances compared with war and terrorism. These can have devastating effects on consumers' confidence. The Iraqi invasion of Kuwait in August 1990, which sparked the first Gulf war in January 1991, sent fear of casualties throughout U.S. households. The Oklahoma City bombing in 1995, with its unexpected threat of domestic terrorism, similarly shocked the country. These episodes rattled confidence but didn't constrain spending.

Even more psychologically crushing were the attacks of September 11, 2001. Americans feared for their safety, their finances, and their jobs. The U.S. financial markets and banking system were closed for the greater part of a week, prompting fears about their soundness. In the face of all this, consumer confidence slumped to a six-year low. The drop was interpreted as a recession signal, especially given the economic context, with the nation's airports, borders, ports, and terminals shut down; domestic and international commerce brought to a screeching halt; and workers idled in hundreds of industries. Miraculously, however, recession was actually a month away from ending, not beginning.

The moral is that not every crisis of confidence presages an economic downturn, nor every swell of optimism an economic expansion. This is not a problem for the indices. Rather it is a challenge to the interpreter, who must learn to distinguish between changes in confidence that affect consumer spending and those that leave it untouched.

TRICKS FROM THE TRENCHES

One way economists use the sets of consumer sentiment indices to predict economic peaks and troughs is to chart the spread, or difference, between the Conference Board's Expectations and Present Situation indices. The reasoning behind this strategy is simple: If the Expectations Index is higher than the Present Situation Index, generating a negative spread, the implication is that people are happier with where they are now than with where they see themselves in the near future. That attitude is bound to constrain spending and so dampen economic growth. Conversely, a positive spread implies belief that greater prosperity lies just around the corner, a good sign for spending and the economy. The wider the spread in either direction, the drearier or dreamier future conditions are expected to be relative to the present.

As **FIGURE 9-6** shows, the Expectations–Present Situation spread generally bottoms out just before a recession begins and peaks just after it ends. In February 2001, the spread widened considerably, putting it into record negative territory. Apparently consumers were spot-on with their concerns, because a recession began two months later and lingered eight months, to November 2001. Consumers retrenched, as their incomes dwindled and stock markets fizzled. In response, the Bush Administration instituted immediate tax relief in the form of individual tax rebates ($300 per worker, up to $600 per working family) and longer-term relief through reductions in the marginal tax rate.

Also in many economists' bag of tricks is another index based on the same survey as the University of Michigan's sentiment index and its associated sub-indices but constructed from a different subset of

Figure 9-6 The Expectations–Current Situation Spread and Recessions

Sources: The Conference Board; NBER

responses. The Price Expectations Index is based on two questions, asking respondents whether they believe prices will rise, fall, or remain stable in the next twelve months and by what percentage they expect them to change. The end product, as **FIGURE 9-7** demonstrates, is a highly accurate predictor of near-term inflation. Because inflation influences both consumer spending and the fixed-income market, this is a very useful and highly respected indicator.

Throughout the twenty-five years covered by the graph, growth in the Price Expectations Index was almost identical to growth in the Consumer Price Index, a proxy for inflation. Only in 1979–81 and 1990–91 did the actual inflation rate differ significantly from consumers' expectations. During both periods, the U.S. economy was mired in recession. In the first, inflation unexpectedly topped 10 percent. At the time, no economist on Wall Street foresaw price growth of that magnitude, so consumers' predictive failure shouldn't be surprising.

Figure 9-7 Change in the Price Expectations and Consumer Price Indices

Sources: University of Michigan; U.S. Department of Labor, Bureau of Labor Statistics

Advance Monthly Sales for Retail Trade and Food Services **10**

T HE CENSUS BUREAU of the U.S. Department of Commerce releases the Advance Monthly Sales for Retail Trade and Food
Services report, known on the Street simply as the retail sales report,
about two weeks after the end of the record month, at 8:30 a.m. ET.
The report, which presents preliminary estimates of the nominal
(non-inflation-adjusted) dollar value of sales for the retail sector,
as well as the month-to-month change in that value, is available
on the Census Bureau's website, at www.census.gov/svsd/www/
fullpub.html. These releases are avidly followed by economists and
analysts and have been known to generate serious jolts to the financial markets.

The reason for the intense interest in the retail sales report is that
retail spending provides a great deal of insight into personal consumption expenditures—the largest contributor to gross domestic
product (GDP)—both in the aggregate and with respect to several
industries and sectors. These data, moreover, are available up to two
weeks before the Bureau of Economic Analysis releases its monthly
Personal Income and Outlays report, the source for the consumption
expenditure statistics incorporated into the GDP report (see Chapter
11). The retail sales report, despite covering a narrower range of data
than the Personal Income and Outlays report, is therefore a timely
index of current and future economic health.

Not surprisingly, the report has a significant effect on the financial markets. Stocks react favorably when it shows an increase
in total retail sales, which generally equates to greater corporate
profitability. Higher sales numbers may also, however, imply higher

prices. Because inflation erodes the value of fixed-income coupon and principal payments, a strong report depresses bond prices and boosts bond yields, which move inversely to price. Sluggish retail sales activity, on the other hand, portends weak profit performance and few inflationary pressures. In this situation, stocks slump, bonds rise, and yields fall.

If the total retail sales numbers are significant for the markets as a whole, the figures for various components of the report can move related sectors or even individual stocks. Noteworthy increases in retail sales at electronics and appliances stores, for example, may lift the shares of Best Buy and Circuit City, whereas lower postings at clothing and accessory stores may hurt Ann Taylor and Talbots.

EVOLUTION OF AN INDICATOR

The Census Bureau began collecting data on retail sales in the early 1950s. The first Monthly Retail Trade Report, published in March 1952, contained estimates of sales at retail stores beginning with January 1951.

In mid-1997, the Census Bureau significantly modified its collection procedures. Hoping to reduce the size of revisions necessary between preliminary and final statistics, the bureau redefined the sample used in its surveys based on the results of the 1992 Census of Retail Sales and instituted a system of polling all the 13,000 companies included each month. Previously, only the largest companies were surveyed monthly, with smaller companies divided into three rotating panels, each of which was polled once every three months. In mid-2001, the Census Bureau instituted another major change, converting the data for this report, as it had for other of its economic reports and surveys, from the old Standard Industrial Classification (SIC) system to the North American Industry Classification System (NAICS). The goal was to facilitate comparisons of retail numbers for the whole continent. Because of the size of the task, however, data were converted to the new system back only to 1992, thus reducing the scope of possible historical comparisons and analyses.

DIGGING FOR THE DATA

The Census Bureau compiles the Advance Monthly Sales for Retail Trade and Food Services report from responses to a survey it mails out to approximately 5,000 companies about five working days before the end of the reporting month. These 5,000 are a subsample of the 13,000 or so companies polled for the later Monthly Retail Trade report. The principal business of all the survey participants is selling goods that are intended for personal or household consumption.

Replies, which are weighted and benchmarked to give an accurate representation of the more than 3 million retail and food services companies in the United States, indicate what these establishments earned during the record month from merchandise sales and for providing services that, as the Census Bureau puts it, are "incidental to the sale of the merchandise." In other words, repairs offered at auto retailers are included but not life insurance or taxi rides. In this respect, the retail sales figures paint a less complete picture of consumer spending than the Personal Income and Outlays report, which does incorporate service expenditures.

Included in the retail sales receipts are excise taxes—such as those levied on alcohol, tobacco, and gasoline—that are paid by the manufacturer or wholesaler, passed along to the retailer, and bundled into the price of the good. Excluded are sales taxes paid by customers.

The bureau aggregates the survey data into total sales figures for the month. It also breaks down some of the numbers by type of business, using the NAICS categories and subcategories, similar to the table shown in FIGURE 10-1, and by two subgroupings: total sales excluding motor vehicles and parts and GAFO (an acronym for general merchandise, apparel, furniture, and other).

All the figures are given both unadjusted and adjusted for seasonal, holiday, and trading-day variations. The report consists of a short summary of the survey findings followed by several charts and tables. These present retail sales, adjusted and unadjusted,

Figure 10-1 Major Categories of Retail and Food Services Companies, With Percentage Each Contributes to Total Sales

Major Category Percentages of Total Retail and Food Services Sales*
Total retail and food services sales

Motor vehicle and parts dealers		**24.51%**
Automobile and other motor vehicle dealers	*22.46%*	
Auto parts, accessories, and tire stores	*2.06%*	
Furniture, home furnishings, electronics and appliances		**5.07%**
Furniture and home furnishings stores	*2.60%*	
Electronics and appliance stores	*2.47%*	
Computer and software stores	*0.67%*	
Building material and garden equipment and supplies		**8.27%**
Building material and supplies dealers	*7.27%*	
Food and beverage stores		**13.32%**
Grocery stores	*12.00%*	
Beer, wine, and liquor stores	*0.86%*	
Health and personal care stores		**4.97%**
Pharmacies and drug stores	*4.21%*	
Gasoline stations		**6.95%**
Clothing and clothing accessory stores		**4.75%**
Clothing	*3.42%*	
Men's clothing stores	*0.27%*	
Women's clothing stores	*0.96%*	
Shoe stores	*0.59%*	
Jewelry stores	*0.70%*	
Sporting goods, hobby, book and music stores		**2.23%**
General merchandise stores		**12.57%**
Department stores (excluding leased departments)	*5.97%*	
Other general merchandise stores	*6.59%*	
Warehouse clubs and superstores	*5.59%*	
All other general merchandise stores	*1.01%*	
Miscellaneous store retailers		**2.82%**
Nonstore retailers		**5.16%**
Electronic shopping and mail-order houses	*3.25%*	
Fuel dealers	*0.85%*	
Food services and drinking places		**9.39%**
PERCENTAGE OF TOTAL RETAIL AND FOOD SERVICES SALES		**100.00%**

* percentages a/o December 2002

The percentage contributions are for September 2002. Note that those italicized subcategories do not add up to 100 percent because the entire detail for them is not provided in this abbreviated table. The bold figures of the major subcategories, however, do total 100 percent.

Source: U.S. Department of Commerce, Bureau of the Census

both in nominal dollars and as percent changes from the previous month and the previous year. In addition to total sales, figures for all the categories, subcategories, and subgroupings are given—advance figures for the record month, preliminary ones for the previous month, and final ones for the month before that. The report also contains revised year-earlier numbers for the record and previous months.

In its breakdown of sales numbers according to NAICS business classification, the retail sales report differs from the Personal Income and Outlays report, which categorizes spending activity not by where it was done but for what it was used—whether a service, or durable or nondurable good. To illustrate, the purchase of a refrigerator from Best Buy would be included in durable goods spending in the income and spending report but recorded as a sale at an electronics and appliance store in the retail sales report.

Organizing the retail data according to the NAICS business classification simplifies the survey process for the respondents. A reporting company simply records its total sales for the period and sends the form back; no need to break receipts down by type of merchandise or service involved. Unfortunately, the easiest collection method doesn't necessarily produce the most informative data. Consider that refrigerator purchase again. It happened to be made at an electronics and appliance store. But a consumer could just as well buy a refrigerator at a furniture store, a building material and supplies center, a warehouse club, a department store, or an Internet site or mail-order house. Because the report organizes sales data by point of purchase, it reveals nothing about the level of refrigerator sales each month.

That said, analyzing sales numbers by business classification can be very informative for retail equity analysts. Economists, moreover, can glean important insights into consumer attitudes by looking at the numbers for the retail subgroupings. In the immediate aftermath of the 2001 recession, for instance, consumer confidence surveys slipped, suggesting economic frailty. At the same time, however, sales at food services and drinking places remained strong. Seeing this, savvy economists concluded that confidence was not really that low: If consumers are truly upset about the economic future and their personal financial situations, they don't head out to restaurants and bars.

SURGING SUBCATEGORIES: SUPERSTORES AND E-COMMERCE

In just a few years, new business models can significantly alter the retail landscape. Two such models are represented in a couple of retail subclassifications: warehouse clubs and superstores, and electronic shopping and mail-order houses.

In the past decade, discount wholesalers have had a profound impact on the economy as a whole, and on retail prices in particular. The percentage that warehouse clubs and superstores contribute to total retail sales excluding motor vehicles and parts nearly tripled from 2.6 percent in 1992 to 8.8 percent in 2003. This is testament to the growing popularity of stores such as Costco, BJ's Warehouse, and Sam's Club.

According to Leonard Nakamura, a research adviser at the Federal Reserve Bank of Philadelphia, conventional supermarkets accounted for 73 percent of supermarket sales in 1980. By 1994, this share had tumbled to a mere 28 percent. Dominance was lost to superstores (stores with in-store butchers, bakeries, pharmacies, and so forth) and warehouses (large discount supermarkets).

The Internet and Web shopping sites have also upended traditional business models, with significant effects on both the retail sector and on the broad economy. Census Bureau statistics show that e-commerce made up about 1.3 percent of total retail sales in 2002. This may seem a small contribution, but it is still significant and it is growing.

According to the Census Bureau, the number of American households with access to the Internet has soared in recent years—from 26 percent of all households in 1998 to approximately 44 million (42 percent of all households) in August 2000. There's no doubt that these numbers have climbed considerably in the four years since the survey was conducted, given the increased affordability of personal computers. Many schools and libraries provide free access. With a few keystrokes on their computers, consumers are now able to locate hard-to-find merchandise, search thousands of stores, and compare prices, any time of day and any day of the week. All retailers want to make their merchandise known to as many potential buyers as possible, and e-commerce allows them to do just that: They can post their entire universe of products on their websites, together with the latest prices and availability, inform consumers of sales and new arrivals, and maintain up-to-the second inventory levels, all at an incredibly low cost. The result: a several-fold increase in profitability.

Because of the growing importance of this sales channel, the Census Bureau in 1999 began issuing the quarterly Retail E-Commerce report. This enumerates all sales of goods and services that are negotiated over an online system (whether they're paid for online or through traditional channels). The methodology for the Retail E-Commerce report is basically the same as that used for the monthly retail sales report, except that only electronically sold merchandise is counted. As you can see in **FIGURE 10-2**, the total estimated value of quarterly e-commerce retail sales has rocketed from approximately $5.3 billion in the last quarter of 1999 to about $12.5 billion in the second quarter of 2003.

Figure 10-2 Retail E-Commerce Sales

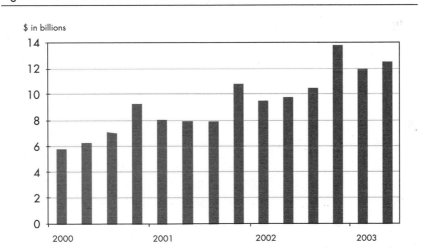

Source: U.S. Department of Commerce, Bureau of the Census

E-commerce has transformed retailers' way of doing business. It has also had beneficial effects on inflation. Using the Internet, consumers can search for the least expensive set of tires, shortwave radio, or hockey stick in a matter of minutes. Companies from Bangkok to Boston have been compelled to either reduce prices or risk losing business. This has undoubtedly played a vital role in suppressing price rises during the later half of the 1990s and the early 2000s.

WHAT DOES IT ALL MEAN?

As was noted, the sales figures for individual business classifications are a rich lode of information for those conducting retail equity analysis. Economists mine the whole report for precious insights. The Street, however, focuses on two numbers: the monthly percentage changes in total retail and food service sales and the change in total sales excluding motor vehicles and parts.

TOTAL RETAIL AND FOOD SERVICE SALES, NOMINAL AND REAL FIGURES

As noted earlier, the advance retail sales total creates a stir in the markets because of the insight it provides into consumer spending, one of the major forces driving the U.S. economy. Traders focus on the month-to-month percentage change in the total, and in the total ex-auto retail sales, rather than the monthly change in the dollar amount. The primary reason is that a $10 million monthly increase in 1993 isn't the same as a $10 million advance in 2003. Analysis of monthly percent change eliminates this distortion. For the determination of longer trends, and a further refinement of month-to-month swings, analysts look at the year-over-year percentage change.

The picture it paints of general economic activity is a bit distorted, however. Beyond the fact that retail sales don't include expenditures on certain services, they are also given in nominal terms. Because the numbers are unadjusted for inflation, it is impossible to determine if growth is the result of larger sales volumes or of price

Figure 10-3 Growth in Real and Nominal Retail Sales

Sources: U.S. Department of Commerce, Bureau of the Census; Federal Reserve Bank of St. Louis

hikes. For this reason, some economists adjust the retail sales data for inflation by subtracting the year-over-year percentage change in the Consumer Price Index (CPI; see Chapter 12). As shown by **FIGURE 10-3**, the real growth rate in retail sales is generally lower than the nominal one, even dropping into negative territory during the economically difficult early 2000s.

The Consumer Price Index has a significant flaw as an inflation deflator for retail sales—namely, it includes expenditures for services such as health care, education, transportation, and housing (the largest component of the CPI), all of which are largely absent from the retail sales data. Still, CPI-adjusted sales figures produce economically sensible estimates of real growth.

TOTAL SALES EXCLUDING MOTOR VEHICLES AND PARTS

Motor vehicle and parts dealers are responsible for a very large portion of retail sales, ranging from 20 to 27 percent since 1992. The advance retail sales total is thus heavily influenced by the numbers generated at auto shops. Because motor vehicle sales, like those of all expensive goods, can vary considerably from month to month, the total retail numbers including these sales are also highly vola-

Figure 10-4 Growth in Total Retail Sales and in Total Sales Excluding Autos

Source: U.S. Department of Commerce, Bureau of the Census

tile. This extreme volatility makes it difficult to discern long-term trends in the retail numbers. Accordingly, economists often focus on total sales excluding motor vehicles. As **FIGURE 10-4** illustrates, the total "ex-autos" year-over-year growth trend is relatively smooth, eliminating, for instance, the extreme spikes and dips manifested by the total sales numbers in late 2001 and late 2002.

GAFO

The motor vehicle business is not the only one represented in the retail sales figures that is subject to wide price swings. Similar volatility afflicts building materials dealers, health and personal care stores, food and beverage purveyors, and gasoline stations, whose dollar sales figures rise and fall with the highly mutable markets for lumber, pharmaceuticals, food, and petroleum. As an example, consider petroleum. Should the government decide to raise the gasoline tax or require additives in the summer months to reduce pollution, the dollar value of service station sales will rise. The cause of the increase is higher prices, not greater demand, but this would be hard to price out from the numbers. Because the components of the consumer price index and its associated weights differ greatly from those of the retail sales report, "deflating" the retail sales report with the CPI is not a perfect process. The same issue arises with sales of building materials and health and personal care products. In addition, as with auto sales, the volatility of these components is transferred to the sales total, making trends hard to read.

The solution: GAFO. GAFO excludes the volatile sectors just discussed, in addition to motor vehicle sales. Also omitted are food services and drinking establishments, because they are considered for this purpose services rather than goods. Sales growth in the GAFO businesses—which include furniture and home furnishings stores; electronics and appliances shops; clothing and clothing accessories purveyors; sporting goods, hobby, book, and music stores; general merchandise stores; and office supplies, stationary, and gift stores—is considered the "core" retail growth rate, similar to the core inflation rate (see Chapter 12). As shown by **FIGURE 10-5**, the trend line of year-over-year growth in GAFO sales is noticeably smoother than the jittery movements in the total retail and food service sales and the retail sales excluding motor vehicles and parts.

Figure 10-5   Growth in GAFO Sales

Source: U.S. Department of Commerce, Bureau of the Census

How to Use What You See

As with the indicators discussed in other chapters, analysts and traders strive to get an early lock on the retail sales numbers. Forecasting these figures is difficult, largely because of a paucity of information. Several sources do exist, however, that may give insight into what the report will show and definitely help in interpreting the figures when they do appear.

To gain a more accurate perspective on industry-specific activity and trends, economists and retail equity analysts often supplement the data in the monthly retail sales report with anecdotal evidence. As baseball legend Yogi Berra once said, "You can see a lot just by observing." Many analysts and traders head out to malls and shopping centers every Saturday and Sunday during the crucial Christmas holiday season to get an idea of how strong, or weak, the pace of spending is. Some count cars or empty parking spaces. That's obviously a very crude measure, however. People frequent malls for reasons other than shopping—teenagers go to hang out, for instance, and elderly "mall walkers" go to get some exercise protected from extreme heat or cold. Many shoppers, moreover, take mass transportation rather than private cars. Even if the car count reflected the real number of shoppers, moreover, it wouldn't indicate which types of stores were being patronized. Short of actually consulting with store managers and asking what's selling and what's not, the most effective mall sales-estimate method is to count the number of bags that consumers are carrying, noting the store logos on them. People don't generally carry unnecessary baggage, so the presence of a bag implies that a purchase has been made.

Analysts and economists also consult chain store announcements, looking for advance insights into consumer activity. Early each month—often as much as two weeks before the retail sales report—and in some cases every week, retail chain stores report on their sales activity. In addition to indications of individual retailers' strengths or weaknesses, perspectives on total economic activity can be gleaned from the comments of giant retailers such as Wal-Mart. Because of their growing popularity, wholesale discounters also provide important indices of retail activity. Finally, retail trade groups such as the National Retail Federation, the International Council of Shopping Centers, and the International Mass Merchants Association issue informative reports on seasonal spending patterns and trends, most of which are available on their websites.

In interpreting these data, climate should be taken into account. Hazardous storms close stores, disrupt transportation routes, and reduce hours worked. All of this means lost retail business, offset somewhat by increased sales of shovels, generators, snow blowers, and related merchandise. That said, the role of nature has been reduced by the advent of the Internet, which enables consumers who can't get to the store to pursue their shopping online.

SAME-STORE SALES

Early each month, usually during the first week, the nation's largest retailers announce their same-store sales, or "comps," for the preceding month. These announcements can be useful in forecasting what trends the advance retail sales report will reveal for major business categories. For instance, it's a fair bet that the building materials and suppliers group will post activity in the advance report similar to that announced earlier by Home Depot and Lowe's—not the same magnitude necessarily but the same vector, or direction. In like manner, announcements made by companies such as Ann Taylor, The Sports Authority, and CVS provide clues to the retail sales numbers for the clothing, sporting goods, and health and personal care categories, respectively.

Same-store sales figures do have some drawbacks as predictive tools. For one thing, they don't include sales by stores that have been open less than a year. This is an important omission. New outlets are carefully sited and heavily promoted by the parent companies and consequently often show the strongest sales activity. Second, only year-over-year growth is reported, so the figures provide little insight into the monthly activity reflected in the retail sales report. To interpret same-store sales, moreover, you must know what retail conditions prevailed in the comparison, or base, month. For instance, if sales were at all-time highs in December 2002, lower numbers in December 2003 wouldn't necessarily mean that activity was sluggish in that month, just slower than the record pace of a year earlier.

SEASONALITY

It should come as no surprise that many retail sectors cycle with the season, all of which are accounted for in the seasonally adjusted data. Apparel and accessories sales, for instance, usually surge in August and September, when young kids are heading back to school and older ones off to college. College freshmen, in particular, need to stock up on new clothes, personal computers, and other electronic must-haves. Similarly, February shows strong candy, cards, flowers, and restaurant sales. The reason, of course, is Valentine's Day. In fact, a very large portion of retail activity is holiday-related. A good or bad holiday season can make or break the entire year for a retail sector. No wonder economists and retail analysts keep an eye on where in the calendar movable fetes like Thanksgiving and Easter are scheduled to occur.

Timing is important. Easter, for instance, may fall either in March or in April, boosting retail sales that month, particularly at apparel stores. This can make for misleading comparisons. Say Easter occurs in March one year and in April the next. By comparison with year-earlier numbers, the sales for March in the second year will appear weak, whereas those in April will seem strong.

The timing of Thanksgiving is also important, because the following Friday is the unofficial start of the Christmas shopping season. Because Thanksgiving always falls on the fourth Thursday of November, this season ranges between twenty-six and thirty-two days. The assumption is that the longer the stretch, the stronger the holiday sales numbers will be. Of course, most people must buy a particular number of presents, whether they have twenty-seven or thirty shopping days in which to do so. But the longer time span (together with expanded holiday hours) does mean more spending on everyday items, such as gasoline, groceries, and bar and restaurant visits.

TRICKS FROM THE TRENCHES

Holiday sales are good gauges of economic health and consumer well-being. If the numbers are robust, people are probably feeling secure both financially and in their jobs. A pullback, on the other hand, may reflect consumers' fears about finances and the labor market. The sales numbers for Thanksgiving, Easter, and even Halloween and Valentine's Day are all significant in this regard. But not surprisingly, the real make-or-break shopping season is Christmas.

Because of the importance of the Christmas sales, economists, analysts, and traders have developed different ways of estimating these numbers from the monthly retail sales reports. Some extrapolate holiday sales from the total for November and December. Others use the total excluding motor vehicles and parts—a reasonable approach, because few autos appear under the Christmas tree (at least outside Mercedes Benz commercials). Still others look only at the December figures, reasoning that in many years November contains only a few real holiday shopping days and that most Americans every year wait until the last moment to buy their presents. The two most popular holiday-sales proxies, however, seem to be the combined November and December totals excluding autos and food services, and the two months' combined GAFO sales.

Which is the better proxy? It depends on your definition of "holiday sales." If you believe that spending at motor vehicles and parts shops is not holiday related but that sales of gasoline, food and beverages, health and personal care items, and building materials and garden equipment are, the first approach is for you. If you think only purchases of general merchandise qualify, the GAFO method is more realistic.

Most economists favor the GAFO proxy. After all, how many Santa wish lists include oak paneling, carpeting, or prescription drugs? On the other hand, the hot housing and refinancing markets of the late 1990s and early 2000s did create a ravenous demand for home-improvement equipment, tools, and do-it-yourself merchandise, and many of these items may have been Christmas gifts. All the parties given in November and December undoubtedly beef

Figure 10-6 Holiday Retail Sales Estimates Using GAFO Approach

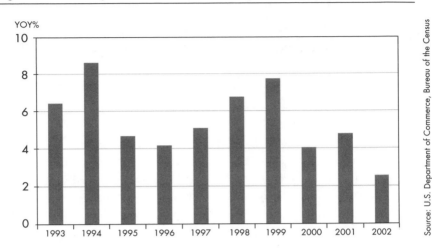

up food and beverage store sales as well as restaurant and bar sales. Finally, if not for stores like Walgreens, CVS, Rite-Aid, Brooks Pharmacy, The Body Shop, and Sephora, where would people get their perfume and cosmetics stocking stuffers?

Whatever method they choose, economists estimate holiday sales because of the relationship they bear to the broader economy. This relationship is illustrated in **FIGURE 10-6**, which charts the year-over-year growth in holiday sales, estimated using the GAFO approach. Note that sales increased steadily in the last half of the 1990s. In this period, GDP was growing strongly and the stock market surging. Sales then fell off sharply in 2000, at a time when consumers were struggling with recession and a jobless recovery.

Personal Income and Outlays 11

T HE MONTHLY PERSONAL INCOME AND OUTLAYS report, produced by the Bureau of Economic Analysis (BEA), contains
incredible detail on income-related measures, as well as spending
data for virtually every imaginable good and service. Commonly referred to on the Street as "income and spending," it consists largely
of income statistics, but the underlying detail on spending may just
be the most comprehensive of all economics statistics.

What more could an economist—and those who trade on economic news—ask for in an economic indicator than timely detail on
what consumers earn and what they spend their earnings on? And
all on a monthly basis: The Personal Income and Outlays report
is released about four weeks after the record month, on the first
business day following the release of the Gross Domestic Product
(GDP) report, at 8:30 a.m. ET. It's available on the BEA website
(www.bea.gov) within minutes after the formal release, and is extremely helpful in the analysis of macroeconomic trends.

Because spending and income data are coincident indicators, they
don't rank high as market movers. Unexpected postings, however,
have occasionally given the financial markets a considerable jolt.

The BEA uses the spending data in the report in compiling the
consumption expenditures portion of the GDP report. Consumer
expenditures, as noted in Chapter 1, account for about 70 percent
of all economic activity in the United States. Strong spending is
a sign of an expansionary climate; slower spending signals softer
economic conditions. The income data, meanwhile, provide insight
into future spending and thus future economic activity.

While economists generally draw the inference that rising incomes eventually result in greater spending, quantifying this relationship is less clear-cut. Conceptually, the income-spending relationship is somewhat leading, yet graphically that relationship is more of a coincident association. Strong income growth usually means an expanding economy, whereas declining income may signal weaker times ahead. Disposable income (what's left of wages and salaries after personal-tax and nontax payments) is particularly important in identifying the likelihood of greater spending. Rising income from transfer payments, such as unemployment benefit insurance, can signal an economy that is spinning its wheels. (The report also contains personal savings data, derived by subtracting expenditures from income, but this is generally less revelatory than the other information.)

The market reaction to the monthly percent change in the income and spending figures is generally subdued, unless of course they deviate greatly from the Street expectations. Stronger than expected increases in both the incomes or spending are a sign of a strengthening economy, which would bode well for the general economic climate, corporate profitability, and subsequently the valuation of stock prices. Weaker spending and incomes generally result in softer stock prices. The bond market usually reacts unfavorably to strong postings in income and consumption and favorably to sluggish income and spending growth. Considerably strong releases spark unease in the stock and bond markets because of the fear of a possible tightening in fed policy.

EVOLUTION OF AN INDICATOR

Because the GDP report draws on data in the monthly Personal Income and Outlays report, you might expect the two to have similar origins. Well, they do. The birth of the income and spending report, however, lies a little further back in time, in the 1920s. In 1921 Wesley Clair Mitchell, together with his staff at the National Bureau of Economic Research (NBER), which he helped found and for which he served as its first director of research, published

Income in the United States: Its Amount and Distribution 1909–1919. This two-volume work set out a framework for measuring national income and quantitatively describing its composition, industrial sources, and distribution. The data used in the report were collected from sources as obscure as American Telephone and Telegraph town rent surveys and the Department of Agriculture's annual crop estimates. It was an impressive achievement, especially because the NBER received its charter only in 1920. The calculations, however, were relatively crude, and the reports available only on an annual basis. It was up to Simon Kuznets, a student of Mitchell's, to bring the project to maturity. In the 1930s, Kuznets, as described in Chapter 1, created the National Income and Product Accounts, from which comes the GDP report, for the Department of Commerce. The department published the first national income statistics in 1934.

It wasn't until the comprehensive revision of 1958 that quarterly estimates began to appear and both income and outlays data were formally presented. Over the next four decades there have been several revisions, modifications, and definitional improvements that have served to make the Personal Income and Outlays report a first-class gauge of household activity.

DIGGING FOR THE DATA

Like the GDP report, the monthly Personal Income and Outlays report contains data from both the income and the production sides of the economy. Every month, these data are analyzed and displayed in typically about eleven tables, one of which (from the May 2003 report) partially appears in **FIGURE 11-1**. The tables show personal income and its disposition—that is, how it is distributed among tax and nontax payments; personal outlays; and personal savings—in terms of both dollar amounts and percent changes from previous months, quarters, and years. Expenditures and disposable income are expressed in current (nominal) and chained (real) dollars. (See Chapter 1 for a discussion of *chained*, *nominal*, and *real* values.)

Figure 11-1   Personal Income and Outlays
             ($ in billions; months seasonally adjusted at annual rates)

	Mar 2003 (r)	Apr 2003 (r)	May 2003 (p)
Personal income	$9,119.2	$9,136.6	$9,163.7
Wage and salary disbursements	5,083.4	5,083.4	5,091.0
Private industries	4,198.4	4,195.7	4,202.6
Goods-producing industries	1,113.5	1,110.9	1,114.0
Manufacturing	752.9	748.5	748.9
Distributive industries	1,118.5	1,118.7	1,120.6
Service industries	1,966.4	1,966.0	1,968.0
Government	885.0	887.7	888.4
Other labor income	641.1	642.9	645.0
Proprietors' income with inventory valuation and capital consumption adjustments	787.7	796.5	804.1
Farm	15.9	16.5	17.7
Nonfarm	771.7	780.0	786.4
Rental income of persons with capital consumption adjustment	126.2	120.5	113.6
Personal dividend income	453.7	456.4	459.1
Personal interest income	1,072.2	1,076.4	1,080.6
Transfer payments to persons	1,348.9	1,354.6	1,365.1
Old-age, survivors, disability, and health insurance benefits	727.1	728.8	735.7
Government unemployment insurance benefits	63.6	64.8	65.8
Other	558.1	561.1	563.6
Less: Personal contributions for social insurance	394.0	394.1	394.8
Less: Personal tax and nontax payments	1,083.1	1,085.5	1,090.2
Equals: Disposable personal income	8,036.1	8,051.1	8,073.6
Less: Personal outlays	7,769.8	7,779.6	7,790.2
Personal consumption expenditures	7,553.9	7,564.2	7,575.2
Durable goods	871.7	895.2	889.1
Nondurable goods	2,223.3	2,194.6	2,191.4
Services	4,458.9	4,474.4	4,494.7
Interest paid by persons	182.5	182.0	181.6
Personal transfer payments to the rest of the world (net)	33.4	33.4	33.4
Equals: Personal saving	266.4	271.5	283.4

(p) Preliminary, (r) Revised

Revisions include changes to series affected by the introduction of revised wage and salary estimates for the fourth quarter of 2002.

Source: U.S. Department of Commerce, Bureau of Economic Analysis

PERSONAL INCOME

The BEA calculates **personal income** by adding together income from seven major sources and then subtracting personal contributions for unemployment, disability, hospital, and old-age survivors' insurance. The largest income source is wages and salaries, which account for about 55 percent of the total. The BEA obtains data for this category from Internal Revenue Service (IRS) reports. Transfer payments—government disbursements such as Social Security payments, veteran's benefits, and food stamps—usually constitute about 15 percent of total income. The Social Security Administration and the Bureau of Labor Statistics supply the data for this category. The remaining 30 percent or so of total monthly income comes from personal interest income, which contributes 11 percent; proprietors' income, 8 percent; other labor income (such as group health insurance and pension and profit-sharing), 7 percent; personal dividend income, 5 percent; and rental income, 1 percent. (The actual percentages vary somewhat from month to month but remain relatively close to the levels indicated here.)

By subtracting personal tax and nontax payments such as donations, fees, and fines from personal income, you arrive at **disposable personal income**. This figure is generally regarded as more useful than personal income pure and simple, because it represents the money that households have available to spend or to save.

PERSONAL CONSUMPTION EXPENDITURES

The BEA defines **personal consumption expenditures** as the goods and services individuals buy, the operating expenses of nonprofit institutions serving individuals, and the value of food, fuel, clothing, rentals, and financial services that individuals receive in kind. The primary source for these data is the Census Bureau's monthly retail sales report.

The largest portion of consumer expenditures, accounting for 55 percent of the total, is for services. The U.S. economy is service-dominated. Approximately 80 percent of all workers in the United

States are employed in a service profession. U.S. consumers spend incredible amounts on insurance, repair, transportation, investment advice, and medical care. Legal services are involved in virtually every aspect of America life, from buying a home to getting a divorce to writing a will. Entrepreneurial endeavors, such as setting up a small business or writing a book, require accounting and legal advice. Other service expenditures include school tuition, spending on hotel and motel accommodations, on sporting and theater events, and on telephone and cable television service.

The next-largest category, representing 30 percent of total expenditures, is spending on nondurable goods. Nondurable goods are products with relatively short life spans. They are divided into four major groups: food; clothing and shoes; gasoline, fuel oil, and other energy goods; and the catchall "other," which encompasses products such as perfumes, cleaning preparations, film, and greeting cards. Durable goods, which account for the remaining 15 percent of expenditures, are those intended to last a minimum of three years. (Most do, and if they don't, they contribute to services spending through the contracts for repairing them.) Durables include automobiles, refrigerators, washing machines, televisions, furniture, and other big-ticket items, such as jewelry, sporting equipment, and guns. Because durables are expensive and (because of their "durability") are purchased infrequently, spending on these items as a percentage of total expenditures can vary considerably from month to month.

Personal outlays are one of the subcategories of the personal income report. To compute personal outlays, the BEA adds net transfers to the rest of the world and personal interest expense to personal consumption expenditures. **Net transfers** include payments sent abroad by U.S. residents, such as remittances from foreign workers to their home countries. **Interest expense** comprises what consumers pay on credit cards and on auto and personal loans (but not mortgage interest, because housing is regarded as an investment).

PERSONAL SAVINGS

The BEA includes personal savings and the personal savings rate in Table 1 of the income and spending report. **Personal savings** are defined as the difference between consumers' disposable incomes—the money they have available to spend—and what they actually spend, their personal outlays. This figure expressed as a percentage of disposable income is the **personal savings rate**. The May 2003 computation of the personal savings rate, for example, was:

Disposable personal income	$8,073.6 billion
less Personal outlays	– $7,790.2 billion
equals Personal savings	= $ 283.4 billion
expressed as % of disposable personal income	

$$\$283.4 \div \$8,073.6 \times 100$$

equals Personal savings rate	approximately 3.5%

WHAT DOES IT ALL MEAN?

The two top attention-getters from the income and spending report are the monthly percent changes in nominal personal income and nominal personal consumption expenditures. These month-to-month changes receive the most attention of any number in the report from the financial markets. Because the dollar values of these two series are so large—in the trillions—they tend not to fluctuate too greatly from month to month. In other words, the month-to-month changes tend to be of the magnitude of 0.1, 0.2, or 0.3 percent. Therefore, monthly 0.2 percent announcements in personal income or consumption can, as a result, be a bit of a wet firecracker. The real story is in the detail, however, specifically that underlying the income and consumption numbers. By analyzing those details and the relationships among the personal income and expenditure figures, economists and investors are able to identify possible turning points and developing trends in the economy.

PERSONAL INCOME

The financial media tend to pay less attention to income than to expense data. You are more likely to hear a business journalist comment on the monthly increase in services spending, for example, than on an unexpected gain in dividend income. The reason for this lack of interest is most likely due to the indirect effect of incomes on the economy. Incomes don't always have to be spent—they may be saved. Conversely, the spending data are quite telling about what consumers are actually doing with those incomes. Another reason for the preference of expenditures data over incomes is that stock market traders can directly determine what consumers are spending on. The income data don't provide market traders with such detailed information. That doesn't mean personal income data are less meaningful, however. On the contrary, they provide important insights into the financial health of consumers, a group that, as we have seen, has tremendous impact on all sectors of the economy.

Because some level of income is necessary for all economic activity, trends in income growth should theoretically permit inferences about future spending patterns. Unfortunately, theory doesn't always mesh with reality. As the chart in **FIGURE 11-2** illustrates, personal income tends to move in sync with, rather than lead, expenditures.

One reason for this synchronicity is that wages and salaries burn a hole in most Americans' pockets. Many people live paycheck to paycheck, spending their earnings immediately and saving smaller and smaller amounts. In addition, personal income includes not only wages and salaries but also dividend and interest income and transfer payments, such as health insurance and unemployment benefits. These crucial disbursements of unemployment benefits are generally spent immediately on basic necessities, such as food or rent.

Because these payments are spent on necessities rather than on durable goods and services, they have relatively little influence on macroeconomic activity. Economists trying to judge economic strength therefore focus on wage and salary income.

Still another explanation for the coincidence of income and spending growth may lie in a source of income that is not included

Figure 11-2   12-Month Changes in Personal Incomes and Consumption
Expenditures

Source: U.S. Department of Commerce, Bureau of Economic Analysis

in the monthly report: consumer credit. Consumer credit is a critical source of income in the United States, capable of altering the amount of spending in the economy. It's not exactly clear how wide or narrow the gap between income and spending growth would be without a formal credit channel. Perhaps income growth would assume a more leading nature because consumers could not make as many purchases with only wages and salaries. The existence of the credit transmission mechanism permits greater access to funds, enhancing spending without respect to wage and salary growth. No doubt, consumer credit plays some role in the leading/lagging quality of incomes. Because of this important economic role, economists, retail analysts, and money managers keep a keen eye on the section of the Federal Reserve's Board of Governors' monthly release that shows the current amount of outstanding consumer credit, including personal, auto, and education loans, as well as the amount of revolving credit on credit cards. The Fed's consumer credit report doesn't contain consumer loans secured by real estate, such as mortgages or home equity lines of credit. All these data and their histories are available on the Federal Reserve's website at www.federalreserve.gov.

Another factor that influences personal income but is not included in the monthly reports is mortgage refinancing. During the late 1990s and into the early 2000s, mortgage rates plunged to their lowest levels in recorded history. Americans refinanced their existing mortgages—some doing so two or three times—to reduce their interest burden. The sky-rocketing pace of mortgage rates affected economic activity in two respects: first, it freed up income that had previously been earmarked for interest payments. Second, several homeowners took advantage of the equity that they had already paid off in their original loans, permitting them to take out even bigger loans—and purchase larger homes—yet make the same monthly payment as the pre-refinancing loan. The savings and capital thus created, which amounted to hundreds of billions of dollars, were not recorded as income. But they did fuel spending. This, too, has caused some discrepancy between the leading/lagging characteristic of incomes.

Consumer credit and mortgage refinancings can thus increase consumption expenditures. Nevertheless, the amount of income from these two sources—and, consequently, the influence they exert on spending—is tiny compared with total personal income as measured in the BEA reports. To predict the economically crucial consumption expenditures figure, it is necessary to understand the factors that influence the level and growth rate of total income—in particular, total disposable income. The most important of these factors are employment, tax structure, and the general economic climate.

As noted earlier, wage and salary disbursements are the largest sources of personal income. To earn a salary, one must generally perform some service. (OK, some people manage to receive compensation for doing absolutely nothing, but let's just consider the overwhelming majority of Americans.) So job growth should be an important determinant of income growth. The associated chart in **FIGURE 11-3** highlights some incongruities, which may be credited to a number of factors including changes in tax policy and the come-uppance of non-wage sources of income like stock distribution and stock options.

Figure 11-3   Disposable Personal Incomes and Employment

Sources: U.S. Department of Commerce, Bureau of Economic Analysis; U.S. Department of Labor, Bureau of Labor Statistics

Growth in payrolls encourages spending not only by increasing disposable income but also by lifting consumers' spirits. Another important influence on consumer expenditures is the taxation level. When marginal tax rates are low, disposable personal incomes rise. With more of their earned income left over, people have a greater propensity to spend; and because consumer spending accounts for almost 70 percent of all economic activity, and the United States is traditionally a nation of spenders, economic growth will expand.

CONSUMER SPENDING

The connection between consumer expenditures and economic growth has already been well established. But not all spending is equally revealing of economic trends. Spending on nondurable goods such as food and home-heating fuel tends to be fairly constant, remaining positive even in trying economic times. In contrast, spending on durable goods, which are relatively expensive and long-lived, requires good economic conditions to flourish. In less flush times, consumers aren't going to head out to buy stereos, furniture, or new china. Therefore, of all the subcomponents in the Personal Incomes and Outlays report, durable goods spending

Figure 11-4   Spending on Consumer Durables and Recessions

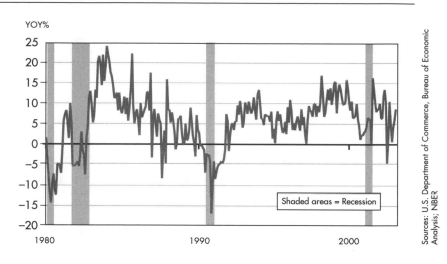

Sources: U.S. Department of Commerce, Bureau of Economic Analysis; NBER

might be considered the most effective in calling turning points in the economy.

The chart in **FIGURE 11-4** shows that three of the last four recessions identified by the National Bureau of Economic Research—1981–82, 1990–91, and 2001—were accompanied by simultaneous declines in the growth rate in consumer spending on durable goods. The 2001 recession broke this pattern, as automakers and certain other retail giants kept consumers buying their products by offering zero percent financing, hefty discounts, and other incentives.

PERSONAL SAVINGS RATE

Americans spend. The nation as a whole just can't seem to "save for a rainy day," despite the warnings of previous generations. As the chart in **FIGURE 11-5** illustrates, this propensity has worsened in the past five years.

Americans' declining savings rate can be explained in part by demographics. Baby boomers—people born between 1946 and 1964—are the first generation that stands to inherit a significant amount of wealth. The baby boomers' grandparents, born in the late nineteenth century, lost most of their accumulated assets during the

Figure 11-5   Personal Savings as a Percentage of Disposable Personal Income

Source: U.S. Department of Commerce, Bureau of Economic Analysis

Great Depression. Even when the economy picked up, they retained memories of the hardscrabble times and raised their children in households of frugality, saving everything they could. As the Depression survivors began to die off in the mid-1990s, their children, the boomers, inherited the homes, investments, jewelry, cars, autographed baseballs, and other assets they had amassed. This was occurring during some of the best economic conditions in about five decades—rock-bottom unemployment of around 3.9 percent, virtually nonexistent inflation, and a skyrocketing stock market. No wonder the boomers didn't find savings crucial.

Economists generally worry when the personal savings rate slows. This usually signals that consumers are dipping into their savings to make ends meet. Depleted savings are most disturbing during soft economic times, such as those of the early 2000s when unemployment was on the rise. The hardships posed by the loss of a job—and of its associated income—are exacerbated when the worker is already overextended. That is why it is important to keep an eye on the pace of consumer credit. If it is rising during a weak economy, a very dangerous situation may be developing, which could result in a double-dip recession as the consumer spending that initially brought the economy out of the recession disappears.

How to Use What You See

The data in the monthly Personal Income and Outlays reports supply the raw material for the analyses in the quarterly GDP report. To come up with the quarterly figures, the BEA simply averages the monthly numbers recorded for each data category. Because the GDP report isn't published until about a month after the end of the record quarter, analysts, money managers, and economists (as well as some analysts and money managers) keep a running tab of the monthly consumer spending figures to approximate the value of this important contributor to economic activity.

Because personal incomes and expenditures are so critical to the overall pace of economic activity, economists attempt to predict what the report will show before it is released. One way they do this is to go straight to the data sources. The largest source for monthly expenditures information is the Advance Monthly Sales for Retail Trade and Food Services report. Spending on some retail goods, though, is more significant than that on others. Durable goods, as noted above, are more economically sensitive than nondurables. Among durable goods, some are better as predictors of macroeconomic conditions. Wall Streeters, for instance, watch the "RV Indicator." Recreational vehicles, or RVs, are usually purchased out of discretionary or unessential income. When expenditures on these vehicles slump, it's a good bet that the economy will soon slow. Conversely, when sales begin to accelerate, the economy is expected to expand.

RVs may still be regarded as luxuries by many Americans. Cars, in general, are not. Every teenager dreams of owning a sports car, and virtually every adult has fond memories of his or her first automobile. (For the record, my first was my grandfather's 1965 forest green Chevy Impala with a 283—the best engine GM ever made.) It's not surprising, then, that purchases of motor vehicles and parts constitute one of the largest components of consumer spending. As the chart in **FIGURE 11-6** shows, motor vehicle spending accounts for a great deal of durable goods spending. In fact, at least since 1997, this component never accounted for anything less than 40 percent of total durable goods spending.

Source: U.S. Department of Commerce, Bureau of Economic Analysis

Figure 11-6   Spending on Motor Vehicles as a Percentage of Durable Goods Expenditures

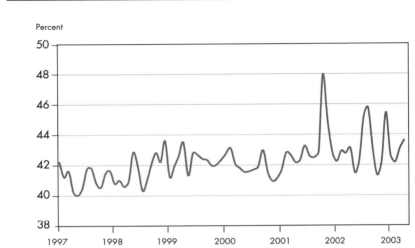

Knowing this, economists like to look at the monthly pace of auto sales. Several indicators of motor vehicle demand exist. The most relevant are contained in the advance retail sales report, because they are a measure of spending, and the monthly sales reports of individual car companies (available on their websites). By assessing the pace of automotive sales, investors are able to get a good idea of activity in durable goods as a whole and thus of consumer spending in general and of overall economic conditions.

TRICKS FROM THE TRENCHES

This chapter's tricks involve factors that influence levels of spending and that economists and investors can use to foretell what those levels will be. What determines how much consumers spend? What doesn't? Some people spend because it's Saturday night. Gloomy days often prompt spirit-boosting trips to malls. But rain crimps sales at the beaches and shores, and blizzards keep everyone inside, preventing even determined shoppers from getting to a store and spending. Meanwhile, closed stores prevent hourly workers from earning income. Weather, time of week, time of year, and many other factors affect spending. For economists, however, three influences are predominant: wealth, prices, and employment.

The Wealth Effect

Many economists identify a **wealth effect**: As individuals' wealth rises, the reasoning goes, so does the level of spending. This seems logical. But how do you measure individuals' wealth? One way is to look at the Federal Reserve's quarterly Flow of Funds report (available on the Fed's website, www.federalreserve.gov/releases/ Z1/), which tracks financial and physical asset flows in the U.S. economy. The Fed's report contains detailed information regarding outstanding levels of household ownership of several types of assets such as U.S. government securities, mutual fund shares, and corporate equities. Unfortunately, these data are provided solely on a quarterly basis and delayed for about three months, rendering them useless for analyzing monthly trends. First quarter data, for example, are not released until the middle of June—and they undergo wide-ranging revisions.

Given these drawbacks, economists have developed their own, more timely way of measuring the consumer confidence implied by the wealth effect. They divide the dollar value of the Wilshire 5000—a stock market index composed of the equities of all the companies headquartered in the United States—as of the end of the quarter by the level of disposable personal income. When the ratio of the Wilshire 5000 to disposal personal income—our proxy for wealth—rises, the stock market wealth is on the rise. This increase makes consumers feel wealthier and so willing to spend more. Through econometric analysis, some economists have determined that for every $1.00 increase in the level of stock market wealth, consumer spending increases by $0.03 to $0.07 per year.

Some economists argue against the wealth effect, pointing out that only about 50 percent of American households have a link (direct or indirect) to the stock market. In other words, our proxy

Figure 11-7 Wealth Ratio Versus Consumer Spending

Sources: U.S. Department of Commerce, Bureau of Economic Analysis; Bloomberg LP

would only explain the gain or loss in wealth for about 50 percent of all households. This might explain the disconnect between the two series prior to 1997 and after 2002 in **FIGURE 11-7**. Because our wealth-effect ratio does parallel trends in year-over-year growth rate of consumer spending for the better portion of 1997 through 2001, when stock prices sky-rocketed, and then tumbled, it might be the case that the wealth effect only works during periods of high stock market participation. It seems reasonable, though, that even people who don't invest in equities feed off of the positive atmosphere of a rising market and pick up the pace of spending. Newspapers, evening news programs, and radio stations broadcast the daily stock market gains and the reasons for them—usually upbeat signals about the economy given by the indicators described in this book. Higher stock market valuations result from higher earnings expectations, which in turn imply increased business spending and the increased likelihood of hiring. When job creation increases, consumers are more upbeat, and incomes and spending rise.

Prices

Another obvious relationship exists between spending and prices. This is summed up in one of the first laws that every economics student learns: the law of demand. In rough terms, this states that the higher the price of a good is, the lower the demand for it will be, and conversely, the lower the price, the greater the demand. Consider gasoline. When the price of a gallon rises to $2.00 or more, consumers demand less of it. Commuters who usually drive to work may carpool or use alternative means of transportation, like the bus, train, or ferry. Families might postpone vacation plans until fuel prices recede to more affordable levels. **FIGURE 11-8** illustrates the inverse relationship between price and demand. The time span covered includes three periods of high inflation in gasoline prices: 1990, 2000, and 2003. During all three of these episodes, the growth rate of consumer spending on the fuel declined. Readers can obtain these data—in amazing detail—from the BEA's website, http://www.bea.gov/bea/dn1.htm.

Investors should get into the habit of knowing the underlying price trends for several major spending categories such as healthcare, medicine, apparel, food, housing, tuition, and transportation.

Figure 11-8   Growth in Real Consumer Spending on Gasoline Versus Growth in Consumer Price of Gasoline

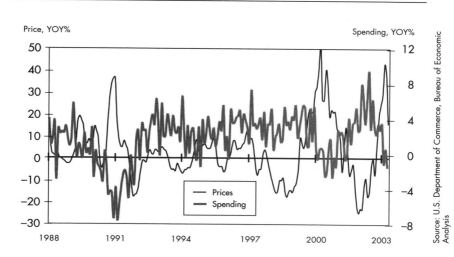

Source: U.S. Department of Commerce, Bureau of Economic Analysis

Obviously the higher the price of these goods, in many cases necessities, the less money there will be available for spending on other things. The detail regarding all of these consumer prices of goods and services—and thousands more—are available at the Bureau of Labor Statistics website (www.bls.gov). The price measures will be discussed in Chapter 12.

Employment

Stock market losses and rising prices may dampen consumers' enthusiasm, but they tend to slow spending growth rather than stop it altogether. There's one influence that will cause consumers to virtually cease all nonessential spending. That's the loss of a job.

FIGURE 11-9 illustrates the incredibly tight relationship between the growth rate of nonfarm jobs and the rate of spending. Nothing is as economically depressing as the loss of employment or the fear of losing a job. It isn't just that unemployed people don't have earned income to spend. They may also despair of finding a job any time in the near future. This is particularly true during weak economic times, when several hundred people might be applying for the same advertised position. When consumer confidence mea-

Figure 11-9   Growth in Real Consumer Spending Versus Payroll Growth

Sources: U.S. Department of Commerce, Bureau of Economic Analysis; U.S. Department of Labor, Bureau of Labor Statistics

sures tumble before and during recessions, they are capturing this discouragement. The feeling can paralyze spending.

Figure 11-9 shows a bit of disconnect in 2001 to 2002 when payroll growth was contracting, yet spending registered some reasonable solid gains. This is a rarity; the 2001 recession was the first in post–World War II history during which consumer spending did not decline. This anomaly can be credited to the sound implementation of fiscal and monetary policy. Expeditious tax cuts by the Bush administration and the pre-emptive lowering of interest rates by the Greenspan Fed fueled incomes and kept spending on the rise.

Knowing that the level of employment is critical in the determination of spending, investors should always keep an eye on the pace of job creation. The stronger the rate of growth in employment, the stronger the pace of spending will be. Employment data and its detail can also be found at the Bureau of Labor Statistics website. The employment situation is discussed in detail in Chapter 3.

Consumer and Producer Price Indices **12**

W HEN THE PRICES OF goods and services rise, it is called inflation. A certain level of inflation in the economy is normal,
even healthy. Accelerating inflation, however, can cause severe
problems, sometimes sparking recession. No wonder the financial
markets keep a close eye on price measures and their growth rates.
For this purpose, many traders and economists, including those at
the Federal Reserve, favor the implicit price deflators contained in
the Gross Domestic Product (GDP) report (see Chapter 1). That
report appears only quarterly, however. For more timely—and
detailed—inflation indicators, most market participants turn to
the reports on the Consumer Price Index (CPI) and the Producer
Price Index (PPI).

The Bureau of Labor Statistics (BLS) calculates, maintains, and
reports on the CPI and the PPI. (The bureau also produces a third
set of indices in the international import and export price report,
but the market doesn't react to these, so they will not be discussed
in this book.) The CPI and PPI reports are released around the
middle of the month following the record month, the PPI usually
at least one business day before the CPI. The releases—which hit
the newswires at 8:30 a.m. ET and are available on the BLS website,
www.bls.gov—often create quite a stir in the financial world, especially the fixed-income market.

The **CPI** tracks the change in price, at the consumer level, of a
weighted basket of a few hundred goods and services. The composition of this basket reflects households' typical monthly purchases,
as revealed in the Consumer Expenditure Survey (CEX), which the

Census Bureau conducts for the Bureau of Labor Statistics. The weight given each item is determined by its percentage of total household expenditures. The index reading represents how much the basket has increased in value since 1984, the base year. A reading of 130, for instance, denotes that the current average cost of the goods and services is 30 percent greater than it was twenty years ago.

The CPI has two basic versions: the CPI-U, which reflects the buying habits of all urban consumers, and the older CPI-W, which relates only to urban households that include a wage earner or clerical worker. The two versions employ data from the same survey and are constructed using the same methodology. They differ only in the weight given certain basket components. The CPI-W is used by the private sector in contract price-escalation clauses and by the government in computing cost-of-living adjustments, or COLAs, for Social Security. The Street and the media focus on the CPI-U, because it represents roughly 87 percent of the noninstitutionalized population, against the CPI-W's mere 32 percent. National and local governments, businesses, and organizations employ the CPI-U in forming and implementing policies. Economists use it to adjust nominal-based indicators, such as retail sales, for inflation. All of the discussions of CPI in this book refer to the CPI-U.

The **PPI**, also known as the wholesale price index, tracks changes in the selling prices of some 3,450 items, at various stages of manufacture, that are received by the producers of those items. Price figures are collected monthly and, for the most part, are those recorded on the Tuesday of the week containing the thirteenth day of the record month. Components are weighted according to their contribution to the GDP. As for the CPI, readings represent price changes from the base year 1984.

The Producer Price Index incorporates data about prices before the retail level is determined. It covers items not in the CPI, such as raw materials and intermediate goods. Economists looking at the PPI data can thus see how far in the production process inflation pressures have traveled and how close they are to emerging in the retail or consumer sector. They can also get a feel for whether any rise in business costs is driven by demand or by supply.

Because of these characteristics, and because of its earlier release date, the PPI is used by some analysts to predict CPI readings. This can be misleading, however. The two indices are very different, both in the way they are constructed and in the items they include. The PPI, for instance, doesn't contain any information on prices for services, the largest part of the U.S. economy. On the other hand, it does incorporate information about the prices of raw materials, which are extremely sensitive to weather conditions. As a result, the PPI's monthly readings are extremely volatile and can be quite different from those of the CPI, although the two indices do show a high degree of correlation over the longer term.

EVOLUTION OF AN INDICATOR

The origins of the PPI and CPI, unlike their release dates, are widely separated in time. They were created not only at different times but to serve different purposes, and so each index evolved quite differently.

PRODUCER PRICE INDEX

In the late 19th century the United States Senate authorized the Bureau of Labor Statistics to start collecting and reporting wholesale prices, so that it could assess the economic effects of tariff laws. The first Wholesale Price Index (WPI), the index's official name for nearly eight decades, was published in 1902. It was an unweighted index of about 250 commodity prices, covering the period from 1890 through 1901. A weighting scheme was adopted in 1914; it was later refined in 1952 and 1967.

The index's original purpose was to reveal price activity at the earliest stage of production. It was believed that this was best accomplished by compiling the prices that domestic producers or importers of the goods and commodities received for them. The original method, unfortunately, involved skewed sampling techniques where responses from large companies dominated the sample. Over time, this resulted in a misrepresentation of goods prices. This initial method had an overemphasis on prices of goods produced by the larger firms and under-representation of goods produced by smaller firms. By the 1940s, moreover, the original weighting schema was outdated, giving too little importance to certain mining and manufactured products that by then accounted for about half (in dollar value) of all goods used in the production process. These wrinkles were eventually ironed out through the recategorization of data and constant revision to sampling methods and weighing systems.

In 1978, the BLS overhauled the index again, emphasizing the categorization of prices by stage of processing, rather than by commodity or industry, and stressing finished goods over those at other stages. The bureau also changed the name of the index at this time, from "wholesale" to "producer" price index.

CONSUMER PRICE INDEX

Compared with the PPI, the CPI is a newcomer. Prices on the consumer level were first collected during World War I, to estimate cost-of-living adjustments to wages. From 1917 through 1919, the BLS collected data from ninety-two industrialized population centers and analyzed spending patterns to create weighted indices of consumer expenditures.

Profound changes in consumer buying habits, particularly during the Roaring Twenties and the Great Depression in the 1930s, led to a comprehensive overhaul of the weights and composition of the indices in 1940. World War II–related rationing and shortages necessitated similar revisions. In 1953, the CPI underwent its greatest makeover up to that time, including improvements in methodology and collection procedures, as well as new sources of data and a more representative list of items. This process of refinement and restructuring continued through the late 1990s.

In December 1996, a commission created by the Senate Finance committee to study the CPI and its framework released a highly publicized report concluding that the CPI, as currently constituted, overstated the true level of inflation by about 1.1 percentage points and suggesting several remedies. The Boskin Report (so-called after the commission chair, Michael Boskin) set the financial world abuzz: Because cost of living adjustments in employee compensation and pensions are linked to the growth rate of the CPI, a reduction in the index's growth rate would lower disbursements to retirees, Social Security recipients, and civil service workers and so restrict their spending power. Due to the political, economical, and social nature of these findings, there hasn't been any serious adjustment to the consumer price measures.

DIGGING FOR THE DATA

As do the indices' origins, the data sources of the CPI and PPI and the methodologies used in compiling them differ considerably.

CONSUMER PRICE INDEX DATA SOURCES

The CPI represents prices on the retail, or demand side, of the economy. To gather the data used to compose the index, field economists from the BLS visit supermarkets, department stores, gasoline filling stations, hospitals, and other establishments in eighty-seven urban areas all around the nation, recording prices of food, fuel, beverages, apparel, health care, and other goods and services. Additional prices are obtained via mail survey.

The prices gathered are organized into eight expenditure categories: housing, transportation, food and beverages, recreation, medical care, education and communication, apparel, and "other," which includes such items as personal-care products and tobacco. The goods and services included in the survey are determined by the results of the Consumer Expenditure Survey, as are the weights given to their categories in computing the index. These weights, which reflect the portion of their incomes that consumers spend on the items in the category, range from 40.8 percent for housing and 17.3 percent for transportation, through 5.7 percent for education and communication to 4.3 percent for "other" and 4.2 percent for apparel (see **FIGURE 12-1**).

Figure 12-1   Composition of the CPI-U

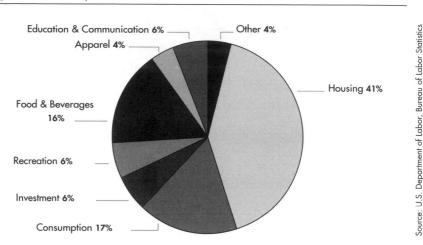

Source: U.S. Department of Labor, Bureau of Labor Statistics

The index's basket of goods and services does not, of course, capture every individual's or every group's consumption pattern. The elderly, for instance, probably spend more of their monthly allowances on medical costs, whereas the younger generation lays out more on tuition and apparel. The categories and their weights, however, present a fairly accurate picture of Americans' average monthly spending habits.

Calculating the average prices for items and categories isn't as simple as it may sound. For goods like toothpaste, alcoholic beverages, tires, or a ticket to a sporting event, the process is straightforward. Services are a different matter. Housing, the largest component of the CPI, is particularly complex. The index measures the cost of using services, not of obtaining assets, such as condos or Cape Cods. The BLS accordingly recognizes two categories of housing costs: residential rent and owners' equivalent of residential rent. The BLS defines the latter as "the cost of renting housing services equivalent to those services provided by owner-occupied housing." This definition removes the investment component of ownership. Price information for the housing category is obtained through interviews with landlords, tenants, and owner-occupants.

From the monthly pricing data, the BLS calculates values for the headliner all-items index (covering the entire basket) and for various subindices, including one for each of the eight expenditure categories and several "special" subindices. Tables throughout the report present values for the various indices and subindices, both adjusted and unadjusted for seasonal variations. What draw the most attention are the percentage changes—from month to month, year over year, and over a three-month period—which represent inflation rates for the relevant periods and categories of items.

The top three special indices are for energy, food, and all goods and services except food and energy. The last of these, referred to as core CPI, is particularly influential.

Energy and food prices are extremely volatile. Tensions in the Middle East, unusually cold or hot weather, changes in production schedules, particularly among OPEC countries, are just a few factors that can send oil and gas prices soaring or plummeting. Similarly, food prices can move violently on news of droughts, storms, or late frosts that destroy crops. Removing these components and their erratic movements makes it easier to discern longer-term inflationary trends. The result is termed "core inflation." (Economists at the Federal Reserve Bank of Cleveland have gone one step further in reducing CPI "noise," lopping off those components showing the biggest gains or declines in a given month; the so-called Median Index—also referred to as the Cleveland Fed Index, the Median CPI, or the Cleveland Fed's Median CPI—is available on the Cleveland Fed's website, www.clevelandfed.org, and has become a Wall Street favorite.)

PRODUCER PRICE INDEX DATA SOURCES

The PPI tracks price trends from a seller's, or supply-side, perspective. Every month, the BLS collects prices for about 100,000 goods at various stages of production from voluntary surveys completed by some 30,000 businesses. Using these prices, it compiles around 10,000 indices, which fall into three major categories: commodity indices, which organize data according to end use or material composition (farm products, textiles and apparel, transportation equipment, for instance); industry indices, which are organized according to Standard Industrial Classification (SIC) and weight their components by "net output," or the value of shipments outside the industry (railroads, the U.S. Postal Service, tour operators); and stage-of-processing indices, which are grouped by the amount of processing of the good and the purchaser's class. The last category is the focus of the PPI report and the one most often cited in the business press and on trading floors.

The stage-of-processing system classifies items as crude materials for further processing, intermediate components, or finished goods. *Crude materials* are commodities that have not been refined or processed, such as raw cotton, hides and skins, and copper and aluminum base scrap. *Intermediate materials* have undergone some processing but have not completed the fabrication process. Popular goods in this category include industrial textile products, leather, glass containers, and synthetic rubber. *Finished goods* are ready to be sold to the final user (consumers and businesses) without further refinement.

The stage of processing category is divided into two major groups, with weights in line with respect to the contributions to total economic activity in the national income and product accounts: *consumer goods*, which are weighted in line with the composition of personal consumer expenditures (accounting for approximately three-quarters of all finished goods) and are themselves divided into food and nonfood items; and *capital equipment*, a representation of the value of business purchases. (**FIGURE 12-2** shows the finished goods components and subcomponents.) Finished goods include apparel, roasted coffee, textile machinery, commercial furniture, and railroad equipment. Because these items are the closest to the retail level, the Street focuses on their price indices. When the media, economists, or analysts refer to producer prices, wholesale prices, or PPI, they are referring to the inflation rate or percentage change in the finished goods indices.

The monthly PPI news release contains only the key aggregate indices of about two hundred or so seasonally adjusted and unadjusted indices. BLS publishes more than five hundred industry price

Figure 12-2   Finished Goods Components

Crude Foods	1.333 %*
Processed Foods	19.339
Finished Consumer Foods	**20.672**
Nondurable Goods less Foods	36.364
Durable Goods	*16.303*
Nonfoods	**52.667**
Finished Consumer Goods	**73.339**
Manufacturing Industries	7.839
Nonmanufacturing Industries	18.822
Capital Equipment	**26.661**
FINISHED GOODS	**100.000**

Source: U.S. Department of Labor, Bureau of Labor Statistics

*All percentages as of July 2003.

indices, ten thousand specific product line and product category subindices, and 3,200 commodity price indices. The complete series of indices, as well as their histories, are on the BLS website and in the BLS's monthly PPI Detailed Report, available by subscription.

CALCULATING THE INFLATION RATE

You can use the following formula to determine the rate of inflation between two periods implied by any of the index values in the CPI or PPI reports:

$R_{Inf} = 100 \times (I_{CP} - I_{PP}) \div I_{PP}$, where R_{Inf} is the rate of inflation, I_{CP} is the current index value, and I_{PP} is the previous index value

To illustrate, say you wanted to figure out the twelve-month inflation rate for copper base as of July 2003. For that month, the unadjusted copper base index value was 123.1, versus 114.2 in July 2002. Plugging those values into the formula, you get

$R_{Inf} = 100 \times (123.1 - 114.2) \div 114.2 = 890 \div 114.2 = 7.79$ percent, or approximately 7.8 percent inflation, year over year.

What Does It All Mean?

The inflation rate can tell us a great deal about economic conditions. When the economy is strengthening, companies experience increased demand for their products and so can charge higher prices for them. As a result, revenues increase, lifting profits and permitting companies to boost capital investment and create new jobs. At the same time, however, the higher prices squeeze consumers, who may have to choose where to allocate limited funds: The more they pay for one good or service, the less they have for others. It's a delicate balance. Too little inflation, and corporate profits tumble, curtailing capital spending and causing unemployment; too much, and consumers can't afford to buy. The results are the same, only the course is different.

That said, the PPI and CPI indices aren't generally considered leading indicators. Changes in the general price level aren't as predictive of business cycle turning points as are many of the indicators discussed in previous chapters. They do tell a great deal about the microeconomic conditions of individual commodities or industries, however. Just don't read too much into a single month's activity. Price indices, even those excluding energy and food, can be affected by any number of influences. Legislation and taxes, for example, can push up prices on items like liquor and tobacco quite dramatically from one month to the next.

Price Trends

Prices can display three trends: **inflation**, or a sustained increase in prices; **disinflation**, a slowing of the rate of increase; and **deflation**, a sustained decrease. FIGURE 12-3 illustrates all three phenomena. First, inflation. The line graphing year-over-year changes in consumer prices remains above zero for the entire chart. That means the inflation rate was positive for the whole period. In other words,

Figure 12-3   Consumer and Producer Price Indices

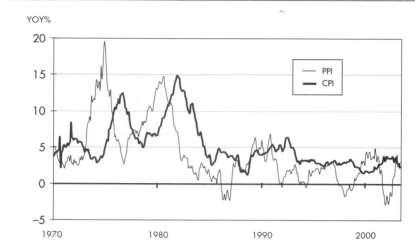

Source: U.S. Department of Labor, Bureau of Labor Statistics

1970 through 2003 saw rising prices for consumer goods. The increases have not been uniform, however. The price-growth line falls sharply from 1972 to 1974, 1975 to 1977, 1980 to mid-1983, and then again from 1991 to 1992. Those drops indicate slower rates of price growth—that is, disinflation—in consumer goods. To see a graphic representation of deflation, you have to turn to the more volatile producer prices (the only serious bout of consumer price deflation that ever occurred in the United States was during the Great Depression). As the PPI-growth graph shows, since 1975 the twelve-month inflation rate in producer prices has fallen into negative—deflationary—territory several times during 1986–87, 1992, 1994, 1997–99, and 2001–03.

Deflation is as damaging to economic health as high inflation. When prices are falling, consumers postpone purchases in anticipation of even lower prices in the future. Without the engine of consumer expenditures (the largest component of GDP), economic growth slows and may even contract if the situation continues. Deflation also hurts corporate profits, causing companies to cut production and reduce staff.

In recent years, economists have fretted about the possibility of deflation in the United States. Growing globalization has sent production facilities to low-wage nations such as China and India, which send incredibly low-priced toys, textiles, computer parts, and foods back to the United States. Prices of nonimported services, such as tuition, medical care, rent, and electricity, however, have been rising. So, although certain industries have experienced deflation, the economy as a whole has not. In a true deflationary period, all prices decline, on both the consumer and the producer level. The only hint of deflation has been in the Producer Price Index. One reason for this is that no services are included in the PPI. Moreover, the core rate of producer price growth—which excludes the volatile food and energy components—has fallen into negative territory only once, and that barely. (Core PPI deflation exists only during prolonged periods of manufacturing weakness.)

PRICE INDICES AND THE MARKETS

To bondholders, inflation is public enemy number one. Bond buyers are actually lending the security's purchase price to the issuer; in return for their loans, they get coupon payments at regular intervals for the life of the bond (unless they sell or it is called). Inflation rates erode the purchasing power of future payments. Say a 10-year bond pays a 6 percent coupon. If inflation rises to 4.5 percent, the investors' real (inflation-adjusted) rate of return is only 1.5 percent—not very good over a ten year period. No wonder that, at the slightest whiff of inflation, investors sell their fixed-income securities, sending prices down and yields (which are inversely related to price) up.

Equity investors generally react very little to the inflation reports. Even stockholders, however, can get exercised when the monthly postings differ greatly from expectations or suggest an inflation rate that could impede consumer spending and disrupt economic growth. A series of high inflation numbers—say, three consecutive monthly increases of 0.7 percent in the CPI or PPI—will have both bond and stock investors anticipating a possible tightening by the Federal Reserve.

To cool the economy down and dampen inflationary pressures, the Fed may raise its target for the Fed funds rate (the rate banks charge each other for overnight loans used to meet reserve requirements; see Chapter 1). Longer-maturity interest rates usually follow suit. High rates discourage consumers from buying assets, such as houses and motor vehicles, whose purchases are financed with loans. Companies may also put off construction and other projects that would necessitate forays into the debt markets. If rates rise to truly restrictive levels, they may be forced to eliminate workers.

PRICE INDICES AND THE BUSINESS CYCLE

As with other price measures, the "core" rate of inflation, computed by excluding the volatile food and energy components, is often used for tracing inflation trends. The BLS calculates core rate for the PPI: The crude nonfood materials less energy index. The core crude PPI, as it is known, is more obscure than the other core indices but very useful in tracking the business cycle.

Raw-material prices historically indicate turning points in the business cycle. Early in a recovery, companies prepare for the anticipated pickup in demand for their products by speeding up their own purchases of commodities they need to begin manufacturing. Conversely, at the first sign of a downturn, they protect against

Figure 12-4   Core Crude PPI Versus S&P 500 Operating EPS

Sources: U.S. Department of Labor, Bureau of Labor Statistics; S&P Corp.; Federal Reserve Bank of St. Louis

slowing demand by reducing their consumption and purchases of crude materials, depressing these items' prices. This relationship is manifested in the correlation, shown in **FIGURE 12-4**, between year-over-year changes in the core crude PPI and the twelve-month growth rate of S&P 500 operating earnings per share.

How to Use What You See

As with other indicators discussed in this book, many of the strategies associated with the inflation reports are aimed at getting a jump on the data in the reports. Economists wishing to predict the CPI and PPI numbers keep a close eye on material and commodity prices. Increases at that stage can lead to price hikes farther down the production pipeline. This is known as cost-push inflation—an industry experiencing rising costs for materials, capital, labor, or land passes the increase on to another sector of the economy by charging higher prices for its own goods or services. When copper prices rise, for instance, homebuilders and buyers feel the pinch. The Copper Development Association, a trade council, estimates that the average single-family home uses about 439 pounds of the metal, in roofing, flanging, gutters, plumbing, circuitry, wire, fillings, valves, appliances, hardware, and lighting fixtures. Builders pass their increased cost for these items along to the buyers. So, when copper prices are on the rise, it's a safe bet that new-housing prices will be rising as well.

The story is similar with natural gas and aluminum. Natural gas not only heats millions of homes in the winter but also is the second-largest resource, behind coal, used in electricity production. One of the most energy-dependent operations is aluminum manufacturing. Higher prices for natural gas can thus push up the price of aluminum. That in turn boosts the prices of goods such as cars, which use aluminum or aluminum derivatives in fenders, motors, axles, bodies, wheels, and other components.

Just about every serious business periodical contains some measure of commodity and raw-materials prices. The *Wall Street Journal*, the *Financial Times*, *Investor's Business Daily*, *The Economist*, *Barron's*, and *Business Week* have detailed listings and usually publish graphs of the most pronounced movements in a select group of goods.

One word of caution: It is not enough to discern movements in commodity and raw-material prices; you must also identify the causes of those movements. Price increases that are due to heightened demand (so-called demand-pull inflation) are more likely to be long term and passed on to end users than those caused by supply-related factors such as strikes, bad weather, factory explosions, and other production disruptions.

TRICKS FROM THE TRENCHES

The price indices are extremely versatile and are employed in a wide array of circumstances. Economists, for instance, use the core rate of CPI as a deflator—subtracting the year-over-year percentage change in core CPI from the twelve-month growth rate in the nominal values of the indicators they track so they can discern trends without the distorting effects of inflation. Sometimes analysts tweak, combine, or compare the inflation indices to produce other findings. The Misery Index is one product of such tweaking.

Aficionados of soprano recitals are familiar with the aria from Antonio Vivaldi's opera *Griselda*—"Agitata Da Due Venti," or "Battered by Two Winds." Economics has its own battering winds: inflation and unemployment. Acknowledging the buffeting these ill winds can give consumers, businesses, and investors, economists have combined the twelve-month growth rate of consumer price inflation with the Bureau of Labor Statistics' unemployment rate to form the Misery Index, shown in **FIGURE 12-5**.

When the Misery Index rises above 13 percent, economic conditions are, well, miserable. During the seven recessions occurring in the forty-plus years covered by the chart, the average index value was 13.25 percent; from mid-1973 through 1984, it was 15.40 percent, with May 1980 recording a dismal 21.9 percent. Expansions, in contrast, are characterized by average Misery Index values of around 9.7 percent. In recent years, the Index has remained mostly in the 6 to 7 percent range.

Figure 12-5   The Misery Index

Source: U.S. Department of Labor, Bureau of Labor Statistics

Yale University economist Ray Fair has shown in several working papers and his book, *Predicting Presidential Elections and Other Things* (Stanford University Press, 2002), that changes in economic conditions, including inflation and unemployment rates, have an effect on voting outcomes. The high levels of the Misery Index registered in May 1980, within months of the presidential election, pretty much guaranteed a loss for incumbent President Jimmy Carter. Americans vote with respect to the economy, and economic conditions during this period were the worst in decades.

References

Introduction

Burns, Arthur F. and Wesley Clair Mitchell. *Measuring Business Cycles.* New York: National Bureau of Economic Research, 1946.

Cottle, Sidney, Roger F. Murray, and Frank E. Block. *Graham and Dodd's Security Analysis.* New York: McGraw-Hill, 1988.

Crescenzi, Anthony. *The Strategic Bond Investor.* New York: McGraw-Hill, 2002.

Goldberg, Linda, and Deborah Leonard. "What Moves Sovereign Bond Markets? The Effects of Economic News on U.S. and German Yields." *Federal Reserve Bank of New York Current Issues in Economics and Finance*, 9, no. 9 (September 2003).

Hagenbaugh, Barbara. "Hints of Optimism Point to Rebound." *USA Today*, 21 August 2003.

Hager, George. "Economists Seek Clues in Daily Life." *USA Today*, 12 February 2001.

Mitchell, Wesley Clair. *Business Cycles: The Problem and Its Setting.* New York: National Bureau of Economic Research, 1927.

National Bureau of Economic Research. *U.S. Business Cycle Expansions and Contractions.* 2003. http://www.nber.org.

Vance, Julia. "Titanium Dioxide's Message." *The Dismal Scientist, Economy.com*, 12 April 2001. http://www.dismal.com/todays_econ/te_041201_2.asp.

Yamarone, Richard. "The Business Economist at Work: Argus Research Corporation." *Business Economics*, July 1999, 65–70.

Chapter 1: Gross Domestic Product

Baumol, William J., and Alan S. Blinder. *Macroeconomics Principles and Policy.* 5th ed. New York: Harcourt Brace Jovanovich, 1991.

Bernanke, Ben S., and Andrew B. Abel. *Macroeconomics.* 3d ed. New York: Addison-Wesley, 1998.

Congressional Budget Office. *The Budget and Economic Outlook: An Update.* July 2000.

———. *CBO's Method for Estimating Potential Output: An Update.* August 2001.

Jones, Charles I. "Using Chain-Weighted NIPA Data." *Federal Reserve Bank of San Francisco Economic Letter,* no. 2002–22 (2 August 2002).

Landefeld, J. Steven. "BEA's Featured Measure of Output and Prices." *National Association of Business Economists: NABE News,* no. 113 (September 1995).

Mankiw, N. Gregory. *Principles of Macroeconomics.* Fort Worth, TX: The Dryden Press, 1998.

Mitchell, Wesley C., ed. *Income in the United States: Its Amount and Distribution 1909–1919.* New York: Harcourt, Brace and Company, 1921.

Okun, Arthur M. "Potential GNP: Its Measurement and Significance." *Proceedings of the Business and Economic Statistics Section of the American Statistical Association* (1962): 98–104.

Popkin, Joel. "The U.S. National Income and Product Accounts." *Journal of Economic Perspectives* 14, no. 2 (spring 2000): 214–224.

Prakken, Joel L., and Lisa T. Guirl. "Macro Modeling & Forecasting with Chain-Type Measures of GDP." *National Association of Business Economists News,* no. 113 (September 1995).

Ruggles, Nancy D., and Richard Ruggles. *National Accounting and Economic Policy.* Cheltenham, UK: Edward Elgar, 1999.

Steindel, Charles. "Chain-Weighting: The New Approach to Measuring GDP." *Federal Reserve Bank of New York: Current Issues in Economics and Finance* 1, no. 9 (December 1995).

United States Department of Commerce, Bureau of Economic Analysis. *An Introduction to National Economic Accounting, Methodology Papers: U.S. National Income and Product Accounts.* Washington, DC, March 1985.

———. *National Income and Product Accounts of the United States, 1929–94: Volume 1, 2.* Washington, DC, April 1998.

———. "GDP: One of the Great Inventions of the 20th Century." *Survey of Current Business* (January 2000): 6–14.

———. *Corporate Profits, Profits Before Tax, Profits Tax Liability and Dividends Methodology Paper.* Washington, DC, September 2002.

———. *Gross Domestic Product Report* (various issues).

———. *Survey of Current Business* (various issues).

———. Website: http://www.bea.doc.gov.

Whelan, Karl. *A Guide to the Use of Chain Aggregated NIPA Data.* Washington, DC: Federal Reserve Board of Governors, June 2000.

Chapter 2: Indices of Leading, Lagging, and Coincident Indicators

Anderson, Gerald H., and John J. Erceg. "Forecasting Turning Points with Leading Indicators." *Federal Reserve Bank of Cleveland Economic Commentary* (1 October 1989).

Burns, Arthur F., and Wesley Clair Mitchell. "Statistical Indicators of Cyclical Revivals." *NBER Bulletin 69* (1938).

———. *Measuring Business Cycles.* New York: National Bureau of Economic Research, 1946.

Diebold, Francis X., and Glenn D. Rudebusch. "Forecasting Output with the Composite Leading Index: A Real Time Analysis." *Journal of the American Statistical Association* 86 (1991): 603–610.

Dueker, Michael J. "Strengthening the Case for the Yield Curve as a Predictor of U.S. Recessions." *Federal Reserve Bank of St. Louis Economic Review* 79, no. 2 (March/April 1997): 41–51.

Duesenberry, James S. *Business Cycles and Economic Growth.* New York: McGraw-Hill, 1958.

Estrella, A., and F. S. Mishkin. "The Yield Curve as a Predictor of U.S. Recessions." *Federal Reserve Bank of New York, Current Issues in Economics and Finance* 2, no. 7 (June 1996).

Gordon, Robert J., ed. *The American Business Cycle.* Chicago: University of Chicago Press, 1986.

Haubrich, Joseph G., and Ann M. Dombrosky. "Predicting Real Growth Using the Yield Curve." *Federal Reserve Bank of Cleveland Economic Review* 32, no. 1 (First Quarter 1996): 26–35.

Kozicki, Sharon. "Predicting Real Growth and Inflation with the Yield Spread." *Federal Reserve Bank of Kansas City Economic Review* (Fourth Quarter 1997): 39–57.

Mankiw, N. Gregory. *Principles of Economics.* Fort Worth, TX: The Dryden Press, 1998.

Mitchell, Wesley C. *Business Cycles, the Problem and Its Setting.* New York: National Bureau of Economic Research, 1954.

Moore, Geoffrey H. *Business Cycles, Inflation and Forecasting.* 2nd ed. Cambridge, MA: Ballinger Publishing, 1983.

———. *Leading Indicators for the 1990s.* Homewood, IL: Dow Jones-Irwin, 1990.

National Bureau of Economic Research. *Conference on Business Cycles.* New York: National Bureau of Economic Research, 1951.

———. *U.S. Business Cycle Expansions and Contractions.* www.nber.orgcycles .html.

Sherman, Howard J. *The Business Cycle: Growth and Crisis Under Capitalism.* Princeton, NJ: Princeton University Press, 1991.

Stock, James H., and Mark W. Watson. *Business Cycles, Indicators, and Forecasting.* Chicago: University of Chicago Press, 1993.

The Conference Board. *Business Cycle Indicators,* New York: The Conference Board, several issues.

———. *U.S. Leading Economic Indicators and Related Composite Indexes.* New York: The Conference Board, several issues.

Zarnowitz, Victor. *Business Cycles.* Chicago: University of Chicago Press, 1992.

Chapter 3: The Employment Situation

Baumol, William J., and Alan S. Blinder. *Macroeconomics Principles and Policy.* 5th ed. New York: Harcourt Brace Jovanovich, 1991.

Dwyer, Jr., Gerald P. and R. W. Hafer. "Interest Rates and Economic Announcements." *Federal Reserve Bank of St. Louis Economic Review* 71, no.2 (March/April 1989): 34–46.

Fleming, Michael J., and Eli M. Remolona. "What Moves the Bond Market?" *Federal Reserve Bank of New York Research Paper,* no. 9706 (February 1997).

Getz, Patricia M., and Mark G. Ulmer. "Diffusion Indexes: A Barometer of the Economy." *Monthly Labor Review.* Washington, DC: U.S. Department of Labor, April 1990.

Hagenbaugh, Barbara. "Part-Time Workforce Grows, Which Is Good and Bad." *USA Today,* 17 June 2003.

Hager, George. "Why Hasn't Today's Jobless Rate Skyrocketed?" *USA Today,* 20 August 2001.

Jossi, Frank. "Temporary Canary." *Federal Reserve Bank of Minneapolis fedgazette* (March 2003).

Leonhardt, David. "A Tale of 2 Totals In the Jobs Report." *New York Times*, 28 January 2001.

Mankiw, N. Gregory. *Principles of Macroeconomics.* Fort Worth, TX: The Dryden Press, 1998.

Miller, Rich. "The Labor Pool: Why Greenspan Is Worried." *Business Week*, 6 December 1999.

Schweitzer, Mark, and Jennifer Ransom. "Measuring Total Employment: Are a Few Million Workers Important?" *Federal Reserve Bank of Cleveland Economic Commentary* (June 1999).

U.S. Department of Labor, Bureau of Labor Statistics. "Labor Force Data Derived from the Current Population Survey." *Handbook of Methods* (April 1997).

―――. "Employment, Hours, and Earnings from the Establishment Survey." *Handbook of Methods.* http://www.bls.gov/opub/hom/pdf/homch2.pdf.

―――. "How the Government Measures Unemployment." July 2001. www.bls .gov/cps/cps_htgm.htm.

―――. *The Employment Situation* (various issues).

Chapter 4: Industrial Production and Capacity Utilization

Board of Governors of the Federal Reserve System. *Industrial Production—1986 Edition with a Description of the Methodology.* Washington, DC, 1986.

―――. Federal Reserve Statistical Release, G.17. *Industrial Production and Capacity Utilization* (various issues).

Corrado, Carol, Charles Gilbert, and Norman Morin. "Industrial Production and Capacity Utilization, The 2001 Annual Revision." *Federal Reserve Bulletin* (March 2002): 173–187.

Corrado, Carol, and Kristen Hamden. "Industrial Production and Capacity Utilization, The 2002 Historical and Annual Revision." *Federal Reserve Bulletin* (April 2003): 151–176.

Emery, Kenneth M., and Chih-Ping Chang. "Is There a Stable Relationship Between Capacity Utilization and Inflation?" *Federal Reserve Bank of Dallas Economic Review* (First Quarter 1997): 14–20.

Finn, Mary G. "Is 'High' Capacity Utilization Inflationary?" *Federal Reserve Bank of Richmond Economic Quarterly* 81 (winter 1995): 1–16.

———. "A Theory of the Capacity Utilization/Inflation Relationship." *Federal Reserve Bank of Richmond Economic Quarterly* 82/3 (summer 1996): 67–86.

Garner, C. Alan. "Capacity Utilization and U.S. Inflation." *Federal Reserve Bank of Kansas City Economic Review* (Fourth Quarter 1994): 1–21.

Gittings, Thomas A. "Capacity Utilization and Inflation." *Federal Reserve Bank of Chicago Economic Perspectives* 13, no. 3 (May/June 1989): 2–9.

Hall, Robert E. *Recessions.* Cambridge, MA: National Bureau of Economic Research, 30 January 2001.

Koenig, Evan F. "Capacity Utilization as a Real-Time Predictor of Manufacturing Output." *Federal Reserve Bank of Dallas Economic Review* (Third Quarter 1996): 16–23.

Rogers, R. Mark. "Forecasting Industrial Production: Purchasing Managers' versus Production-Worker Hours Data." *Federal Reserve Bank of Atlanta Economic Review* (January/February 1992): 25–36.

Shapiro, Matthew D. "Assessing the Federal Reserve's Measures of Capacity and Utilization." *Brookings Papers on Economic Activity,* no. 1 (1989): 181–225.

Chapter 5: Institute for Supply Management Indices

Economic Cycle Research Institute. 2003. Website: www.businesscycle.com.

Harris, Ethan S. "Tracking the Economy with the Purchasing Managers' Index." *Federal Reserve Bank of New York Quarterly Review* (fall 1991): 61, 69.

Institute for Supply Management. *Institute for Supply Management's Manufacturing Report on Business Information Kit* (as of September 2002).

———. *Institute for Supply Management Manufacturing Report on Business* (various issues).

———. *Institute for Supply Management Non-Manufacturing Report on Business* (various issues).

Klein, Philip A., and Geoffrey H. Moore. "N.A.P.M. Business Survey Data: Their Value as a Leading Indicator." *Journal of Purchasing and Materials Management* (winter 1988).

Raedels, Alan. "Forecasting the NAPM Purchasing Managers' Index." *Journal of Purchasing and Materials Management* (fall 1990).

Chapter 6: Manufacturers' Shipments, Inventories, and Orders

Gordon, Robert J. *The Measurement of Durable Goods Prices.* Chicago: The University of Chicago Press, for NBER, 1990.

Harberger, Arnold C., ed. *The Demand for Durable Goods.* Chicago: The University of Chicago Press, 1960.

Klein, L. R. *Studies in Investment Behavior.* New York: Conference on Business Cycles (Universities-National Bureau Committee for Economic Research), 1951.

Mayer, Thomas, and S. Sonenblum. "Lead Times for Fixed Investment." *Review of Economics and Statistics* 37 (August 1955): 300–304.

Roos, C. F. "The Demand for Investment Goods." *American Economic Review* 38 (1948): 311–20.

Stone, J. R. N., and D. A. Rowe. "The Market Demand for Durable Goods." *Econometrica* 25, no. 3 (July 1957): 423–43.

U.S. Department of Commerce, Bureau of the Census. *Manufacturers' Shipments, Inventories, and Orders: 1947–1963 Revised,* Series M3-1. Washington, DC: GPO (October 1963).

———. *Manufacturers' Shipments, Inventories, and Orders: 1992–2001,* M3-1 (01), Washington, DC: GPO (June 2002). Website: www.census.gov/indicator/www/m3/bench/m3-01.pdf.

———. *Instruction Manual for Reporting in Monthly Survey M3,* M3-SD(I). Washington, DC: GPO (21 January 2003). Website: www.census.gov/indicator/www/m3/contactinfo/instructionman.pdf.

———. *Advance Report on Durable Goods Manufacturers' Shipments, Inventories, and Orders* (various issues).

———. *Manufacturers' Shipments, Inventories, and Orders* (various issues).

Zarnowitz, Victor. *Orders, Production, and Investment.* New York Columbia University Press for the National Bureau of Economic Research, 1973.

Chapter 7: Manufacturing and Trade Inventories and Sales

Abramovitz, Moses. *Inventories and Business Cycles: With Special Reference to Manufacturers' Inventories.* New York: National Bureau of Economic Research, 1950.

Allen, Donald S. "Changes in Inventory Management and the Business Cycle." *Federal Reserve Bank of St. Louis Economic Review* 77, no. 4 (July/August 1995): 17–33.

Bils, Mark, and James A. Kahn. "What Inventory Behavior Tells Us about Business Cycles." *Rochester Center for Economic Research Working Paper,* no. 428 (September 1996).

Blanchard, Oliver J. "The Production and Inventory Behavior of the American Automobile Industry." *Journal of Political Economy* 91 (June 1983): 365–400.

Blinder, Alan S. "Retail Inventory Behavior and Business Fluctuations." *Brookings Papers on Economic Activity* 2 (1981): 443–505.

Blinder, Alan S., and Louis J. Maccini. "Taking Stock: A Critical Assessment of Recent Research on Inventories." *Journal of Economic Perspectives* 5, no. 1 (winter 1991): 73–96.

Fair, Ray C. "Production Smoothing Model Is Alive and Well." *Journal of Monetary Economics* 24 (1989): 353–70.

Fitzgerald, Terry J. "Inventories and the Business Cycle: An Overview." *Federal Reserve Bank of Cleveland Economic Review* 33, no. 3 (Third Quarter 1997).

Fitzgerald, Terry J., and Jennifer K. Ransom. "What Happened to the Inventory Overhang?" *Federal Reserve Bank of Cleveland Economic Commentary* 15 (March 1998).

Holmes, Thomas J. "Bar Codes Lead to Frequent Deliveries and Superstores." *Federal Reserve Bank of Minneapolis Research Department Staff Report* 261 (May 1999).

Holt, Charles C., Franco Modigliani, John F. Muth, and Herbert A. Simon. *Planning Production, Inventories and Work Force,* Englewood Cliffs, NJ: Prentice-Hall, 1960.

Huh, Chan. "Just-in-Time Inventory Management: Has It Made a Difference?" *Federal Reserve Bank of San Francisco Weekly Letter,* no. 94–18 (6 May 1994).

Kahn, James A. "Inventories and the Volatility of Production." *American Economic Review* 77 (1987): 667–79.

Little, Jane Sneddon. "Changes in Inventory Management: Implications for the U.S. Recovery." *Federal Reserve Bank of Boston, New England Economic Review* (November/December 1992): 37–65.

McConnell, Margaret M., and Gabriel Perez Quiros. "Output Fluctuations in the United States: What Has Changed Since the Early 1980s?" *Federal Reserve Bank of New York Staff Report,* no. 41 (June 1998).

Metzler, Lloyd A. "The Nature and Stability of Inventory Cycles." *Review of Economic and Statistics* 23 (1941): 113–29.

Morgan, Donald P. "Will Just-in-Time Inventory Techniques Dampen Recessions?" *Federal Reserve Bank of Kansas City Economic Review* (March/April 1991): 21–33.

Ramey, Valerie A. "Inventories as Factors of Production and Economic Fluctuations." *American Economic Review* 79, no. 3 (June 1989): 338–354.

U.S. Department of Commerce, Bureau of the Census. *Census of Retail Trade* (various issues).

———. *Annual Benchmark Report for Wholesale Trade: January 1992 Through February 2002* (May 2002).

———. *Monthly Wholesale Trade: Sales and Inventories* (various issues).

———. *Manufacturing and Trade Inventories and Sales* (various issues).

West, Kenneth D. "The Sources of Fluctuations in Aggregate Inventories and GNP." *Quarterly Journal of Economics* 105, no. 4 (November 1990): 939–971.

Worthington, Paula R. "The Increasing Importance of Retailers' Inventories." *Federal Reserve Bank of Chicago Economic Perspectives* 22, no. 3 (Third Quarter 1998): 2–12.

Zarnowitz, Victor. *Orders, Production, and Investment.* New York: Columbia University Press, for NBER, 1973.

Chapter 8: New Residential Construction

Hagenbaugh, Barbara. "More People Refinance to Wring Cash Out of Their Homes." *USA Today*, Money Section, 28 October 2002.

Hancock, Jay. "Amazing Housing Market Bound to Help the Economy." *The Baltimore Sun*, 27 February 2002.

Mortgage Bankers Association, www.mbaa.org.

National Association of Home Builders. "Housing the Key to Economic Recovery." November 2002. www.nahb.com.

National Association of Realtors, nar.realtor.org.

Smart, Tim. "The Housing Boom Gives the Economy a Boost." *Washington Post*, 9 December 1998.

U.S. Department of Commerce, Bureau of the Census. *Expenditures for Improvements and Repairs of Residential Properties* (Third Quarter 2001).

———., *New Residential Construction* (various issues).

————. *New Residential Construction Documentation.* www.census.gov/const/www/ newresconsdoc.html.

Chapter 9: Conference Board Consumer Confidence and University of Michigan Consumer Sentiment Indices

Bram, Jason, and Sydney Ludvigson. "Does Consumer Confidence Forecast Household Expenditure? A Sentiment Index Horse Race." *Federal Reserve Bank of New York Economic Policy Review* (June 1998): 59–78.

Carroll, Christopher D., Jeffrey C. Fuhrer, and David W. Wilcox. "Does Consumer Sentiment Forecast Household Spending? If So, Why?" *The American Economic Review* 84, no. 5 (December 1994): 1397–1408.

Conference Board. Consumer Confidence Survey. New York: Conference Board, various issues.

Curtin, Richard T. "Indicators of Consumer Behavior: The University of Michigan Surveys of Consumers." *Public Opinion Quarterly* 46 (1982): 340–352.

————. "Index Calculations." University of Michigan. Mimeo.

————. "Surveys of Consumers." University of Michigan. Mimeo.

Friend, Irvin, and F. Gerald Adams. "The Predictive Ability of Consumer Attitudes, Stock Prices, and Non-Attitudinal Variables." *Journal of the American Statistical Association* 89 (December 1964): 987–1005.

Fuhrer, Jeffrey C. "What Role Does Consumer Sentiment Play in the U.S. Macroeconomy?" *Federal Reserve Bank of Boston, New England Economic Review* (January/February 1993): 32–44.

Garner, C. Alan. "Forecasting Consumer Spending: Should Economists Pay Attention to Consumer Confidence Surveys?" *Federal Reserve Bank of Kansas City Economic Review* (May 1991): 57–71.

Graber, Doris A. "Reading Between the Lines of Consumer Confidence Measures." *Public Opinion Quarterly* 46 (1982): 336–339.

Katona, George. *The Powerful Consumer.* New York: McGraw-Hill, 1960.

———— and Eva Mueller. *Consumer Response to Income Increases.* Washington, DC: The Brookings Institution, 1968.

Keynes, John Maynard. *The General Theory of Employment, Interest, and Money.* New York: Harcourt, Brace and Company, 1936.

Kulish, Nicholas. "Michigan's Consumer Sentiment Index for January Fell More Than Expected." *Wall Street Journal,* 22 January 2001.

Lansing, John B., and James N. Morgan. *Economic Survey Methods.* Ann Arbor, MI: The University of Michigan Press, 1980.

Leeper, Eric M. "Consumer Attitudes and Business Cycles." *Federal Reserve Bank of Atlanta Working Paper* 91-11 (August 1991).

———. "Consumer Attitudes: King for a Day." *Federal Reserve Bank of Atlanta Economic Review* 77, no. 4. (July 1992): 1–15.

Linden, Fabian. "The Consumer as Forecaster." *Public Opinion Quarterly* 46 (1982): 353–360.

Matsusaka, John G., and Argia M. Sbordone. "Consumer Confidence and Economic Fluctuations." *Federal Reserve Bank of Chicago Working Paper* 93-13 (November 1993).

Mehra, Yash P. and Elliot W. Martin. "Why Does Consumer Sentiment Predict Household Spending?" *Federal Reserve Bank of Richmond Economic Quarterly* 89, no. 4 (fall 2003): 51–67.

Mishkin, Frederic S. "Consumer Sentiment and Spending on Durable Goods." *Brookings Papers on Economic Activity* 1 (1978): 217–232.

Roper, Burns S. "The Predictive Value of Consumer Confidence Measures." *Public Opinion Quarterly* 46 (1982): 361–367.

Throop, Adrian W. "Consumer Confidence and the Outlook for Consumer Spending." *Federal Reserve Bank of San Francisco Economic Letter,* no. 91–26 (19 July 1991).

Tobin, James. "On the Predictive Value of Consumer Intentions and Attitudes." *The Review of Economics and Statistics* 41 (February 1959): 1–11.

University of Michigan. Surveys of Consumers. Ann Arbor, MI: University of Michigan Survey Research Center, various issues.

Chapter 10: Advance Monthly Sales for Retail Trade and Food Services

Coleman, Calmetta. "Retailers Suffer Sales Slowdown for December." *Wall Street Journal,* 5 January 2001.

Driscoll, Marie. "Monthly Retail Review." *Argus Research Investment Analysis* 68, no. 284 (November 2001).

Harris, Ethan S., and Clara Vega. "What Do Chain Store Sales Tell Us about Consumer Spending?" *Federal Reserve Bank of New York Research Paper,* no. 9614 (June 1996).

Lazear, Edward P. "Retail Pricing and Clearance Sales." *American Economic Review* 76 (March 1986): 14–32.

Mencke, Claire. "Hot Retail Seems to Cinch Rate Hike Even as Producer Prices Stay Tame." *Investor's Business Daily*, April 14, 2000.

Nakamura, Leonard I. "The Retail Revolution and Food-Price Mismeasurement." *Federal Reserve Bank of Philadelphia Business Review* (May/June 1998).

Newberger, Eric C. *Home Computers and Internet Use in the United States:* August 2000. U.S. Department of Commerce, Bureau of the Census, Current Population Reports, P23-207 (September 2001).

U.S. Department of Commerce, Bureau of the Census. *Annual Benchmark Report for Retail Trade and Food Services: January 1992 Through March 2002.* Washington, DC, May 2002.

———. Current Business Reports, Retail e-Commerce Reports, Washington, DC, various issues 1990–2002.

———. Monthly Retail Services Branch. E-Commerce, Frequently Asked Questions (FAQs). http://www.census.gov/mrts/www/efaq.html.

Chapter 11: Personal Income and Outlays

Chow, G. C. 1957. *Demand for Automobiles in the United States ('Contributions to Economic Analysis,')* Vol. XIII, Amsterdam: North-Holland Publishing Co.

Larkins, Daniel. "Note on the Personal Saving Rate." *Survey of Current Business* (February 1999): 8–9.

Leonhardt, David. "Belt Tightening Is Called Threat to the Economy." *New York Times*, 15 July 2001.

Madigan, Kathleen, and David Lindorff. "Consumers Have Money to Burn." *Business Week*, 20 April 1998.

Mitchell, Wesley C., ed. *Income in the United States, Its Amount and Distribution 1909–1919.* New York: Harcourt, Brace and Company, 1921.

Moran, Larry R., and Clinton P. McCully. "Trends in Consumer Spending, 1959–2000." *Survey of Current Business* (March 2001): 15–21.

U.S. Department of Commerce, Bureau of Economic Analysis. *Personal Consumption Expenditures,* Methodology Paper Series MP-6. Washington, DC, June 1990.

———. *National Income and Product Accounts of the United States,* 1929–94: Volume 1, 2. Washington, DC, April 1998.

———. "Personal Income and Outlays." Various issues, 2003. www.bea.gov/bea/rels.htm.

Chapter 12: Consumer and Producer Price Indices

Aluminum Association, Inc. *Industry Overview: From Alumina to Automobiles.* 2003. http://www.aluminum.org.

Bryan, Michael F., and Stephen G. Cecchetti. "The Consumer Price Index as a Measure of Inflation." *Federal Reserve Bank of Cleveland Economic Review* (December 1993): 15–24.

Bryan, Michael F., Stephen G. Cecchetti, and Rodney L. Wiggins II. "Efficient Inflation Estimation." *National Bureau of Economic Research Working Paper Series*, 6183, Cambridge, MA, September 1997.

Bullard, James B., and Charles M. Hokayem. "Deflation, Corrosive and Otherwise." *Federal Reserve Bank of St. Louis National Economic Trends* (July 2003).

Bureau of Labor Statistics. "The Consumer Price Index." Chapter 17 in *BLS Handbook of Methods*, April 1997.

———. "The Producer Price Index." Chapter 16 in *BLS Handbook of Methods*, April 1997.

———. "Measurement Issues in the Consumer Price Index." June 1997. Website: www.bls.gov/cpi/cpigm697.htm.

———. "How Does the Producer Price Index Differ from the Consumer Price Index?" *PPI Program Spotlight*, No. 98-3 (1998).

Cagan, Phillip, and Geoffrey H. Moore. *The Consumer Price Index, Issues and Alternatives.* Washington, DC: The American Enterprise Institute for Public Policy Research, 1981.

Clark, Todd E. "Do Producer Prices Help Predict Consumer Prices?" *Federal Reserve Bank of Kansas City Research Working Paper*, 97-09 (December 1997).

Copper Development Association. *Copper Facts.* 2003. http://www.copper.org.

Fair, Ray C. *Predicting Presidential Elections and Other Things.* Stanford, CA: Stanford University Press, 2002.

———. "Econometrics and Presidential Elections." *The Journal of Economic Perspectives* (Summer 2003): 89–102.

Fuerbringer, Jonathan. "Commodity Costs Soar, But Factories Don't Bustle." *New York Times*, 31 July 2003.

Groshen, Erica L., and Mark E. Schweitzer. "Identifying Inflation's Grease and Sand Effects in the Labor Market," *Federal Reserve Bank of Cleveland Working Paper*, no. 9705 (July 1997).

Hagenbaugh, Barbara. "Fuel Prices 'Cream' Firms." *USA Today*, 6 August 2003.

Hess, Gregory D., and Mark E. Schweitzer. "Does Wage Inflation Cause Price Inflation?" *Federal Reserve Bank of Cleveland Policy Discussion Paper*, no. 1 (April 2000).

Madrick, Jeff. "Economic Scene." *New York Times*, 27 December 2001.

Motley, Brian, and Allison Wallace. "A Better CPI." *Federal Reserve Bank of San Francisco Economic Letter*, no. 99-05 (5 February 1999).

Platt, Gordon. "No Pickup in Inflationary Pressures." *The Journal of Commerce*, 30 July 1998.

Solomon, Jolie. "An Economic Speedometer Gets an Overhaul." *New York Times*, 23 December 2001.

United States Advisory Commission to Study the Consumer Price Index. *Toward a More Accurate Measure of the Cost of Living, Final Report.* 4 December 1996.

Wu, Tao. "Improving the Way We Measure Consumer Prices." *Federal Reserve Bank of San Francisco Economic Letter*, no. 2003–24 (22 August 2003).

Index

Adecco, 85
Advance Monthly Sales for Retail
    Trade and Food Services.
    See Retail Trade and Food
    Services report
after-tax profits, 29
aggregate expenditure equation,
    18–22
American Forest and Paper
    Association, 92
American Staffing Association, 85
Ann Taylor, 205

base year, problem with, 23–24
Beazer Homes USA, 171
Beige Book, 129
BJ's Warehouse, 198
Boeing, 39
book profits, 29
Boskin, Michael, 233
Boskin Report, 233
Briggs & Stratton, 38
building permits for new private
    housing, 57
Bureau of Economic Analysis
    (BEA), 12
  how data is collected, 15–16
  inventories and the aggregate
    expenditure formula, 147
  Personal Income and Outlays
    report, 21, 54, 209–228
Burns, Arthur, 3, 53

Bush, George W., 188
business cycle, 3–5
  housing and, 167–169
  inventories and, 153–154
  price indices and, 241–242
Business Cycle Indicators, 51
  how to use, 66–68

Capacity Utilization: Manufacturing,
    Mining, Utilities and
    Industrial Materials, 91
capacity utilization production, as an
    indicator
  description of, 94–95, 100–104
  evolution of, 90–91
  how to use, 104–105
capital consumption adjustment
    (CCAdj), 28
capital goods, nondefense, 56–57
capital spending, 21, 36–38
Carlyle, Thomas, 11
Carter, Jimmy, 244
Caterpillar, 114
chain weighting, 24
Challenger, Gray and Christmas, 85
Chamber of Commerce, 108
Cleveland Fed Index, 235
Clinton, Bill, 188
coincident economic indicators
    (index), 5, 51–52, 54–55, 60,
    64–65
coincident-to-lagging index, 68

commodity prices, 242–243
Conference Board, 53
   Business Cycle Indicators, 51,
     66–68
   Consumer Confidence Survey,
     176–191
   Help-Wanted Advertising Index,
     85–86
   Index of Coincidental Indicators,
     12
Congressional Budget Office (CBO),
   46
constant dollars, 22–25
consumer confidence and sentiment
   Conference Board's Consumer
     Confidence Survey, 176–191
   durable goods spending and,
     184–185
   employment and, 186
   noneconomic influences on,
     186–189
   University of Michigan's Surveys
     of Consumers, 176–191
Consumer Confidence Survey, 176
   collection of data, 178–179
   evolution of, 177
   how to use, 185–191
   meaning of, 179–185
consumer credit, ratio of personal
   income to, 63–64, 217
Consumer Expenditure Survey
   (CEX), 229–230, 233
consumer goods, manufacturers' new
   orders for, 56–57
Consumer Price Index (CPI), 34, 35,
   64, 201
   business cycle and, 241–242
   CPI-U, 230
   CPI-W, 230
   data sources, 233–235

   evolution of, 232–233
   how to use, 242–244
   inflation rate calculation, 237–
     238
   markets and, 240–241
   meaning of, 238–242
   role of, 229–230
Consumer Sentiment and Current
   Economic Conditions, 61
Consumer Sentiment Index, 82
consumer spending, 19–21, 219–220
consumption
   See also Retail Trade and Food
     Services report
   government, 21–22, 39
   personal, 19–21, 35–36, 213–214
Copper Development Association,
   242
Core PCED, 35
corporate profits, 29–30, 43–45
Costco, 198
Cummins Inc., 38
current dollars, 22–25
Current Employment Statistics
   (CES) (establishment/payroll
     survey), 70, 71, 74–77
Current Industrial Report (CIR), 132
Current Population Survey (CPS)
   (household survey), 70, 71,
     73–74
Curtiss-Wright, 39
CVS, 205
cyclical unemployment, 73

Danaher Corp., 38
Deere & Co., 38
deflation, 33, 238, 239–240
deflators, 25–26, 34–35
diffusion indices, 86–87
   vendor performance, 57

discouraged workers, 73
disinflation, 238, 239
disposable personal income, 213
Dodd, David, 1
Dover Corp., 38
durable goods, 20, 21
    consumer confidence and
        spending on, 184–185
Durable Goods   report, 134–138,
    139–142

Eagle Homes, 171
Eaton Corp., 38, 114
e-commerce, 198–200
Economic Cycle Research Institute,
    123
economic indicators
    classification of, 5
    distribution of reports, 5–6
    evolution of, 13–14, 53
employed, use of term, 72
employee(s)
    compensation, 27–28
    number of, on nonagricultural
        payrolls, 54
employment, as an indicator
    aggregate hours worked index,
        83
    consumer confidence and, 186
    Current Employment Statistics
        (CES) (establishment/payroll
        survey), 70, 71, 74–77
    Current Population Survey (CPS)
        (household survey), 70, 71,
        73–74
    definitions, 72–73
    impact of, 69–70, 77
    relationship of unemployment,
        business cycle and, 78–80
    spending and, 227–228
    state information, 71
    temporary workers, 84–85
Employment Index (ISM), 117–118
employment-population ratio, 73
Employment Situation report (BLS),
    54, 69–70
    collection of data, 72–77
    evolution of, 71–72
    how to use, 85–87
    meaning of, 77–85
establishment/payroll survey, 70, 71,
    74–77

Factory Orders report, 138–139,
    142–143
Fair, Ray, 244
Federal National Mortgage
    Association (FNMA), 166
Federal Reserve
    Flow of Funds, 224
    *Industrial Production and
        Capacity Utilization,* 55,
        89–105
    monetary aggregates, 58
    wealth effect, 224–225
Federal Reserve Bank of New York,
    108
final goods, 16–17
final sales, 41–43
    of domestic product, 42
    to domestic purchasers, 42–43
fixed capital, consumption of, 30
fixed investment, 21, 36–38
fixed-weight approach, 24
Ford Motor Co., 184–185
Franco, Lynn, 180–181
frictional unemployment, 73

GAFO (general merchandise,
    apparel, furniture and other),

195, 202–203
General Dynamics, 39
General Theory of Employment,
Interest, and Money, The
(Keynes), 175
Global Crossing, 99
goods-producing category, 75
goods-providing category, 75
Gore, Al, 188
government consumption
expenditures and gross
investment, 21–22, 39
Graham, Benjamin, 1
Greenspan, Alan, 98, 107
gross domestic product (GDP)
adjustments, 30–32
advance report, 15
benchmark revisions, 16
business cycles and, 5
calculating, 12, 18–22
collection of data, 14–16
composition of, 19
content of reports, 12
defined, 11–12, 16–17
deflators, 25–26, 34–35
evolution of, 13–14
final report, 15
growth, 32–34
how to use, 46–49
meaning of, 32–45
national income, 26–27
nominal (current dollars), 22–25
output gap, 46–49
preliminary report, 15
real (constant dollars), 22–25
versus gross national product,
17–18
gross domestic purchases, 42
gross national product (GNP)
adjustments, 30–32

defined, 11
gross domestic product versus,
17–18
gross private domestic investment,
21
G17 report. *See Industrial*
Production and Capacity
Utilization

Help-Wanted Advertising Index,
85–86
Home Depot, 205
hoot-and-holler task, 6
Hoover, Herbert, 108
household survey, 70, 71, 73–74
housing. *See New Residential*
Construction
Hovnanian Enterprises, 171

Illinois Tool Works, 38
implicit price deflator, 25
Income in the United States: Its
Amount and Distribution
1909–1919 (Mitchell), 211
Indexes of Domestic Business, 90
Index of Coincidental Indicators, 5,
12, 51–52, 54–55, 60, 65
Index of Consumer Expectations
(ICE), 61, 178, 182–183
Index of Consumer Sentiment (ICS),
178, 183
Index of Current Economic
Conditions (ICC), 178
Index of Production in Selected
Basic Industries, 90
indirect business taxes, 30
Industrial Materials Price Index, 123
industrial production, as an indicator
description of, 92–94, 95–99
evolution of, 90–91

how to use, 104–105
Industrial Production and Capacity Utilization (Federal Reserve), 55
collection of data, 91–95
evolution of, 90–91
how to use, 104–105
meaning of, 95–104
role of, 89–90
industrial production index, total, 55
inflation indicators, 80–81, 238–239
inflation measure, 35
inflation rate, calculating annualized, 25–26, 237–238
Ingersoll-Rand, 38, 114
Institute for Supply Management (ISM)
Employment Index, 117–118
Inventories Index, 126
Manufacturing Report on Business, 108
New Orders Index, 126, 127, 128
New Orders minus Inventories Index, 126–127
Non-Manufacturing Report on Business, 123–125
Price Index, 119–121, 127–128
Purchasing Managers' Index (PMI), 57, 97–98, 107–109, 112–117
Supplier Deliveries Index, 121–123
2003 Survey, 110–111
interest expense, 214
interest rate spread, 59–61
Internal Revenue Service, 92
International Council of Shopping Centers, 205
International Mass Merchants Association, 205

International Paper, 114
inventories, 21
See also Manufacturing and Trade Inventories and Sales (MTIS)
business cycle and, 153–154
importance of, 147–148
ratio of manufacturing and trade, to sales, 62
-to-sales ratios, 154–155
inventory valuation adjustment (IVA), 28

job leavers, 72
job losers, 72
Journal of Commerce, 123
judgment trend, 30

K&B Homes, 171
Katona, George, 177
Kelly Services, 85
Keynes, John Maynard, 175
Kuznets, Simon, 13, 211

labor force participation rate, 73
labor pool, available, 81
lagging economic indicators/index, 5, 52, 61–64, 66
layoff announcements, 85
leading economic indicators/index (LEI), 5, 51, 55–61, 65–66, 67
Leggett & Platt, 114
Lennar Corp., 171
loan levels, outstanding commercial and industrial, 63
Lockheed Martin, 39
Lowe's, 205

macroeconomy, 14

Manpower, 85
Manufacturers' Shipments, Inventories, and Orders (M3) survey, 62, 149
  Durable Goods report, 134–138, 139–142
  evolution of, 132–133
  Factory Orders report, 138–139, 142–143
  how to use, 143–146
manufacturing and retail trade sales, 55
Manufacturing and Trade Inventories and Sales (MTIS) report, 55, 62
  business cycle and, 153–154
  collection of data, 149–151
  evolution of, 149
  how to use, 155–157
  importance of, 147–148
  inventories-to-sales ratios, 154–155
  meaning of, 151–155
manufacturing labor cost per unit of output, 62–63
Manufacturing Report on Business, 108
markets, price indices and, 240–241
McGraw-Hill, 91
MDC Holdings, 171
Measuring Business Cycles (Burns and Mitchell), 3
Median Index, 235
Misery Index, 243–244
Mitchell, Wesley C., 3, 53, 210–211
Money, 176
money supply, 58
Monthly Report of Unemployment, 71
Mortgage Bankers Association

(MBA), 171
motor vehicles, 222–223
Mueller, Eva, 177

NAICU (non-accelerating inflationary rate of capacity utilization), 102–103
NAIRU (non-accelerating inflation rate of unemployment), 80, 102
Nakamura, Leonard, 198
National Association of Home Builders (NAHB), 163, 164
National Association of Purchasing Agents, 108
National Association of Purchasing Management, 108
National Association of Realtors, 160
National Bureau of Economic Research (NBER), 3, 13, 53, 89, 90, 95, 181, 210, 220
national defense spending, 39
national income
  accounting, 13
  adjustments, 30–32
  categories of, 27–30
  defined, 26–27
National Income and Product Accounts (NIPAs), 12, 89
  collection of data, 14–16
  evolution of, 13–14, 211
National Retail Federation, 205
net exports, 22, 40–41
net interest, 28
net transfers, 214
new orders, 135
New Orders Index (ISM), 126, 127, 128
New Orders minus Inventories Index (ISM), 126–127

New Residential Construction, 57
  business cycle and, 167–169
  collection of data, 161–163
  evolution of, 160–161
  housing indicators, 160
  how to use, 171–173
  importance of, 159
  influences on, 164–166
  meaning of, 163–171
  regional differences, 166–167
  single-family housing starts 169–171
NFO Research, 178
nominal (current dollars), 22–25
nondefense capital goods
      spending excluding aircraft
      (NDCGXA), 144–146
nondurable goods, 20, 21, 138–139
nonfarm payrolls, 54, 75–77
Non-Manufacturing Report on
      Business (ISM), 123–125
nonresidential investment, 21, 36, 37
North American Industry
      Classification System
      (NAICS), 91, 93, 133, 149
Northrop Grumman, 39

operating profits, 29
Outlook, The, 57
output gap, 46–49

Paccar Inc., 38
Parker-Hannifin Corp., 38
PCEDXF&E, 34
personal consumption expenditures,
      19–21, 35–36, 213–214
personal income
  calculation of, 213
  disposable, 213
  less transfer payments, 54–55

ratio of consumer credit to, 63–64, 217
  use of, 216–219
  wealth effect, 224–225
Personal Income and Outlays report
      (BEA), 21, 54
  collection of data, 211–215
  evolution of, 210–211
  how to use, 222–228
  importance of, 209–210
  meaning of, 215–221
personal outlays, 214
personal savings, 215
personal savings rate, 215, 220–221
Phillips, A. W., 80
Physical Volume of Trade, 90
*Predicting Presidential Elections and
      Other Things* (Fair), 244
pretax profits, 29
Price Expectations Index, 190
Price Index (ISM), 119–121, 127–128
price indices. *See* Consumer Price
      Index (CPI); Producer Price
      Index (PPI)
prices
  role of spending and, 226–227
  trends, 238–240
prime rate, 63
produced goods, 17
Producer Price Index (PPI), 34, 119,
      120
  business cycle and, 241–242
  data sources, 235–237
  evolution of, 231–232
  how to use, 242–244
  inflation rate calculation, 237–238
  markets and, 240–241
  meaning of, 238–242

role of, 229, 230–231
profits
    after-tax, 29
    from current production, 29
    operating, 29
    pretax, 29
proprietors' income, 28–29
Pulte Homes, Inc., 171
Purchasing Managers' Index (PMI),
        57, 97–98, 107–108
    collection of data, 109–113
    description of, 113–117
    evolution of, 108–109
    industries cover, 109

quantity theory of money, 58
Qwest, 99

raw-materials prices, 242–243
Raytheon, 39
real (constant dollars), 22–25
reference week, 73
rental income, 29
residential construction. *See New
        Residential Construction*
residential investment, 21, 36–37
Retail Trade and Food Services
        report, 149
    collection of data, 195–200
    e-commerce and superstores,
        198–200
    evolution of, 194
    GAFO (general merchandise,
        apparel, furniture, and other),
        195, 202–203
    holiday sales, role of, 207–208
    how to use, 204–208
    impact of, 193–194
    meaning of, 200–203
    same-store sales, 205–206

seasonality issues, 206
Robert Half, 85
Ryland Group, 171

sales, ratio of manufacturing and
        trade inventories to, 62,
        154–155
Sam's Club, 198
seasonal unemployment, 72–73
Security Analysis (Graham and
        Dodd), 1
service payrolls, 75–76
services, 20–21
shipments, 135
single-family housing starts 169–171
smoothing techniques, 140–141
Sports Authority, 205
Standard Industrial Classification
        (SIC), 91, 109, 133, 236
statistical discrepancy, 31
stock prices, 57–58
structural unemployment, 73
subsidies, 31
Summary of Commentary on Current
        Economic Conditions by
        Federal Reserve District, 129
Supplier Deliveries Index (ISM),
        121–123
Survey of Construction (SOC), 161
Surveys of Consumers, 176
    collection of data, 177–178
    evolution of, 177
    how to use, 185–191
    meaning of, 179–185
survey week, 73

Tanner's Council of America, 92
tape reading, 6
temporary workers, 84–85
Timken Co., 38

Toll Brothers, 171
transfer payments, 30–31
    personal income less, 54–55

underground economy, 17
unemployed, use of term, 72
unemployment
    claims, average number of
        weekly initial, 56
    duration, average, 62
    inflation indicators and, 80–81
    as a lagging indicator, 78, 80
    rate, calculation of, 74
    sentiment and, 81–82
    types of, 72–73
unfilled orders, 135
United Nations System of National
    Accounts, 18
U.S. Department of Commerce,
    Bureau of the Census, 53, 91
    *Manufacturers' Shipments,
        Inventories, and Orders* (M3),
        62, 131–146
    *Manufacturing and Trade
        Inventories and Sales*
        (MTIS), 55, 62, 147–157
    New Residential Construction,
        57, 159–171
    Retail Trade and Food Services
        report, 149, 193–208
    *Value of Construction Put in
        Place,* 162
    Wholesale Trade Survey, 62
U.S. Department of Housing and
    Urban Development, *New
    Residential Construction, 57,*
    159–171
U.S. Department of Labor, Bureau of
    Labor Statistics
    Consumer Price Index (CPI), 34,
        35, 64, 201, 229–244
    Employment Situation report, 54,
        69–87
    Producer Price Index (PPI), 34,
        119, 120, 229, 230–244
U.S. Geological Survey, 92
United Technologies, 114
University of Michigan, Survey
    Research Center, 61
    Survey of Consumers, 176–191

Value of Construction Put in Place,
    162
vendor performance diffusion index,
    57
vendor supplier index, 121–123

Wal-Mart, 204
warehouse clubs and superstores,
    198–200
wealth effect, 224–225
weekly manufacturing hours,
    average, 56
Whelan, Karl, 24
Wholesale Price Index (WPI), 230,
    231
    See also Producer Price Index
Wholesale Trade Survey, 62
Wilshire 5000, 224
Wolverine Tube Inc., 38
WorldCom, 99

yield curve plots, 59–61

About Bloomberg

Bloomberg L.P., founded in 1981, is a global information services, news, and media company. Headquartered in New York, the company has nine sales offices, two data centers, and 94 news bureaus worldwide.

Bloomberg, serving customers in 126 countries around the world, holds a unique position within the financial services industry by providing an unparalleled range of features in a single package known as the BLOOMBERG PROFESSIONAL® service. By addressing the demand for investment performance and efficiency through an exceptional combination of information, analytic, electronic trading, and Straight Through Processing tools, Bloomberg has built a worldwide customer base of corporations, issuers, financial intermediaries, and institutional investors.

BLOOMBERG NEWS®, founded in 1990, provides stories and columns on business, general news, politics, and sports to leading newspapers and magazines throughout the world. BLOOMBERG TELEVISION®, a 24-hour business and financial news network, is produced and distributed globally in seven different languages. BLOOMBERG RADIO℠ is an international radio network anchored by flagship station BLOOMBERG® 1130 (WBBR-AM) in New York.

In addition to the BLOOMBERG PRESS® line of books, Bloomberg publishes *BLOOMBERG MARKETS*™ and *BLOOMBERG WEALTH MANAGER®*. To learn more about Bloomberg, call a sales representative at:

Frankfurt:	49-69-92041-0	São Paulo:	55-11-3048-4500
Hong Kong:	852-2977-6000	Singapore:	65-6212-1000
London:	44-20-7330-7500	Sydney:	61-2-9777-8600
New York:	1-212-318-2000	Tokyo:	81-3-3201-8900
San Francisco:	1-415-318-2960		

About the Author

Richard Yamarone, vice president and director of economic research at Argus Research Corp., has more than fifteen years of experience on Wall Street analyzing and researching domestic and international economic trends, monitoring monetary and fiscal policy developments, and forecasting the U.S. macroeconomy. He has worked for several international banks and domestic money centers and investment banks in a variety of senior positions. In addition, he has taught numerous courses on macroeconomics and economic indicators at several colleges and institutions. He has served as president of the prestigious Downtown Economists Club of New York City and is a member of the National Association of Business Economists, the American Economic Association, the New York State Economic Association, and the NYU Money-marketeers. At Argus Research, Yamarone is responsible for establishing the firm's top-down economic and interest rate forecasts as well as its estimates for monthly economic indicators. He makes frequent appearances on business television and radio shows, including CNBC, CNNfn, Bloomberg TV and Bloomberg Radio, and National Public Radio.

FOR IN-DEPTH MARKET INFORMATION and news, visit the Bloomberg website at **www.bloomberg.com**, which draws from the news and power of the BLOOMBERG PROFESSIONAL® service and Bloomberg's host of media products to provide high-quality news and information in multiple languages on stocks, bonds, currencies, and commodities.